RESPONSIVE SECURITY

SECURITY

Be Ready to Be Secure

RESPONSIVE SECURITY

Be Ready to Be Secure

Meng-Chow Kang

CRC Press
Taylor & Francis Group
Boca Raton   London   New York

CRC Press is an imprint of the
Taylor & Francis Group, an **informa** business

CRC Press
Taylor & Francis Group
6000 Broken Sound Parkway NW, Suite 300
Boca Raton, FL 33487-2742

© 2014 by Taylor & Francis Group, LLC
CRC Press is an imprint of Taylor & Francis Group, an Informa business

No claim to original U.S. Government works

Printed on acid-free paper
Version Date: 20130812

International Standard Book Number-13: 978-1-4665-8430-3 (Paperback)

Library of Congress Cataloging-in-Publication Data

Kang, Meng-Chow.
  Responsive security : be ready to be secure / Meng-Chow Kang.
    pages cm
  Includes bibliographical references and index.
  ISBN 978-1-4665-8430-3 (pbk. : alk. paper) 1. Business enterprises--Computer
  networks--Security measures. 2. Electronic data processing departments--Security
  measures. 3. Information technology--Security measures. 4. Data protection. 5. Risk
  management. I. Title.

  HF5548.37.K38 2014
  658.4'78--dc23   2013031816

Visit the Taylor & Francis Web site at
http://www.taylorandfrancis.com

and the CRC Press Web site at
http://www.crcpress.com

Contents

List of Figures

List of Tables

List of Abbreviations

ALE	Annual loss expectancy
ATM	Automated teller machine
BCM	Business continuity management
BIRM	Business-aligned information risk manager
BSI	British Standards Institute
CCO	Chief control officer
CCTA	Central Computer and Telecommunication Agency
CEO	Chief executive officer
CERT	Computer emergency response team
CIO	Chief information officer
CIRO	Chief information risk officer
CIRT	Computer incident response team
CISO	Chief information security officer
CISR	Center for Information Systems Security Studies and Research
CISSP	Certified Information Systems Security Professional
COO	Chief operating officer
CRA	Computer Research Association
CSA	Control self-assessment
CSO	Chief security officer
CTO	Chief technology officer
DA	Data analysis
DCRP	Disaster contingency and recovery plan
DMSI	Dialectic model of systems inquiry
DNS	Domain name system
DRP	Detect–react–protect
DRP	Disaster recovery planning
ECDR	Education, competency, due diligence, due care, and reward to behave well
ECO	Extranet Connectivity Organization
ER	Emergency response
FIPS	Federal Information Processing Standard
FIRM	Framework for information risk management
FLAM	Five-level action map
FMEA	Failure mode effects analysis
HAS	Human activities systems

IA	Information assurance
IDS	Intrusion detection system
IRM	Information risk management (or manager)
ISAC	Information Sharing and Analysis Center
ISMS	Information security management system
ISP	Internet service provider
ISRA	Information security risk assessment
ISRM	Information security risk management (or manager)
IT	Information technology
KRI	Key risk indicator
LD	Losses and damage
LEP	Law and regulations, enforcements, and policies
LOB	Line of business (business division)
LOC	Location Operating Committee
LSASS	Local Security Authority Services Server
MAS	Monetary Authority of Singapore
MRTC	Mass Rapid Transit Corporation
ORC	Operational risk capital
ORM	Operational risk management
OSP	Outsource service provider
PDCA	Plan–do–check–act (ISO standardized management process)
PDR	Protect–detect–react
PFIRES	Policies Framework for Information Security
PKI	Public key infrastructure
R&C	Risks-and-controls
RA	Risk acceptance
RAISE	Regional Asia Information Security Exchange
RCA	Requirements for criticality alignment
RIRO	Regional information risk officer
ROSI	Return on security investment
RPC	Remote procedure call
SARS	Severe acute respiratory syndrome
SBU	Strategic business unit
SECD4	A collection of social science inquiry techniques, which includes stakeholder analysis (S), entry and contracting (E), convergent interviewing (C), dialectic data analysis (D), and Flood's Four Windows Systemic View (4)
SME	Subject matter expert
SNMP	Simple Network Management Protocol
SPSTC	Security and Privacy Standards Technical Committee
SQL	Structured query language
SSM	Soft systems methodology
TCC	Technology Control Council

TCSEC	Trusted computer system evaluation criteria (*Orange Book*)
TRC	Technology Risk Council
TVE	Threats, Vulnerabilities and Exploits
UA	Undesirable activities
UB	Undesirable behavior
UDP	User datagram packet
VPN	Virtual private network
WS	Weak systems

Preface

Managing information security risk is an important activity of business enterprises and government organizations to address related information security threats and vulnerabilities, ensure compliance with regulations and best practice standards, demonstrate due diligence to shareholders and customers, and achieve business objectives with minimum cost.

While many researchers and practitioners have contributed to the development and progress of information risk management, existing approaches have achieved only limited success and the practice remains problematic. This is frequently observed in recurring incidents of information security issues and needs, in particular, when businesses, operations, and/or technological environments are subjected to changes.

The nature of the challenges in managing information risk is complex. Its complexity emerges as the domain encounters increasing numbers of issues and dilemmas arising from often conflicting requirements, demands, perceptions, and influences, including but not limited to people (individual and groups), processes, and technology, fueled by the economics of business, political desires of authorities, and cultural constraints of people in the problem environment. Existing approaches that only partially manage the complexities have not been able to address those needs satisfactorily.

To address these issues and dilemmas, information security practitioners must be reflective in practice, be able to learn on the go, evolve their practice in a responsive and reliable manner, and handle changes in the risk environment in which they operate. Similarly, an organization must be ready and responsive. It must take a responsive or *piezoelectric* approach based on its *response readiness* needs to address its information security risk management requirements and incorporate the changing nature of the risk environment in which it operates.

The responsive approach is based on a substantive concept for information risk management known as the *piezoelectric theory*. The theory was developed over the course of an empirical study, using action research that involved multiple case studies, interviews of practitioners, and testing of devised methodologies in actual practice environments for more than six years.

The piezoelectric theory states that *if the design of information security practices of organization systems that enables a prompt realignment of the systems satisfies the systemic requirements for the changing risk condition of the systems environment, the potential negative effects of the new risk condition of the systems environment will be balanced or counteracted by the re-alignment activities.*

As a result of responsive behavior in organizational systems, the consequences of an emerging or new risk condition of the environment will likely cause less (negative) impact to organization systems. The significance of the impacts relates inversely to security readiness and thus the responsiveness of the organization. Readiness is an organization's preparedness to realign its activities and take the appropriate actions to balance against the negative effects of a changing risk environment in a timely and systemic manner.

Through implementation and practices, the responsive approach using the piezoelectric theory has shown effectiveness in addressing information security needs arising from changing risk situations that cannot be addressed effectively by traditional compliance- and controls-oriented approaches.

This book reviews the issues and dilemmas in current knowledge and practices, introduces the principles and methods of the responsive approach and the notion of security readiness, demonstrates viability and practicality of the approach in today's information security risk environment, and encourages adoption and practice. By involving more practitioners and researchers in the practice and discourse, I hope to also further develop and align the approach to address the changing problems faced by practitioners.

Acknowledgments

Many friends and colleagues in the field of information security and action research have been generous in sharing their thoughts and giving their support and encouragement through the various stages of this endeavor, in particular, Chuan-Wei Hoo, Professor Pauline Reich, Dr. Boon-Hou Tay, and Professor Bob Dick. I am also grateful to the editorial team at CRC Press, in particular, the guidance and assistance rendered by Ruijun He, Iris Fahrer, and Stephanie Morkert throughout the publication process.

This book would not be possible without the unwavering support, understanding, and endurance of my beloved family. Thank you all.

Meng-Chow Kang

Author

Meng-Chow Kang, PhD, has been a practicing information security professional for more than 20 years with field experience spanning from the technical to managerial in various information security and risk management roles for the Singapore government, major multinational financial institutions, and security and technology providers.

Dr. Kang has contributed to the development and adoption of international standards relating to information security since 1998 and his work has been recognized with numerous industry awards. He was the chairperson for Singapore's Security and Privacy Standards Technical Committee (SPSTC) from 1998 to 2007, and the first convener for the Security Controls and Services Standards Working Group (WG 4) at ISO/IEC JTC 1/SC 27.

In 2004, Dr. Kang cofounded the Regional Asia Information Security Exchange (RAISE) Forum (http://raiseforum.org) that serves as a platform for regional information sharing and contributes to international standards development in ISO and ITU-T. In May 2012, he was appointed the chairperson for a new ITSC Cloud Security Working Group focusing on the development of cloud computing–related security standards.

Dr. Kang earned an MSc in information security from the Royal Holloway and Bedford New College, University of London, and completed his PhD program in information security risk management at the Southern Cross University in Australia. He has been a Certified Information Systems Security Professional (CISSP) since 1998.

Introduction

1

1.1 Background and Motivations

A common objective of information risk[1] management is to ensure adequate protection of the confidentiality, integrity, and availability of information and information systems that are critical or essential to the success of a business.[2] Through my experience as an information security practitioner for more than 20 years, and ongoing discourse with fellow practitioners and researchers in this field, a common observation is that the knowledge and practice of information risk management lag behind other management disciplines and are often inadequate for supporting the needs of practitioners in the field.

To a large extent, rather than taking strategic approaches, practitioners' methods have been based mostly on individual experience, trial and error, and in some instances, adaptation of methods from other knowledge sources and disciplines. Most practitioners have focused on policy compliance, primarily addressing known risk issues and reacting to security incidents as they occur while recognizing the constantly changing nature of each organization's risk environment.

My interest in improving my practice in the field drove me to undertaking a study to identify or develop a suitable approach for managing information risk in the changing environments of business organizations. The study considers the knowledge gaps in the existing literature and the issues and dilemmas observed in practice. My experience in this field also shaped my thinking and analysis of the subject, steps in formulating the research problem, and developing the outcome. The study yielded an approach for managing information security risk known as the *responsive approach* that focuses on the response readiness of an organization to contend with the changing nature of its information risk environment.

This chapter introduces the thematic issues and dilemmas identified in information risk management that fueled the need for a research study. It contains a summary of the questions critical to the practice and a brief description of the study and research methodology that led to the development of the responsive security approach, and closes with an outline of the chapters that follow.

1.1.1   Business, Technology, and Risk Development

My research for a new or enhanced approach to information risk management began in January 2002 at ALPHA,[3] a multinational financial institution operating in more than 50 countries. I was a member of the information risk management (IRM)[4] team responsible for managing the organization's information risks for 11 cities[5] across the Asia Pacific region.

During that period, as the aftermath of the tragic September 11, 2001 incident[6] in the United States and subsequent war in Afghanistan negatively affected the economy worldwide (Madrick 2002, Moniz 2003), many business organizations began a series of rapid changes to reduce costs in view of a projected zero or negative growth in business revenue and reduced budgets (Yourdon 2002). ALPHA was not excluded from this development. The economic cycle seems to have repeated itself every few years since then. In late 2008, at the completion of my research study, economic recession again loomed in the United States and many other countries as a result of the credit crisis starting in 2007. At the time of this writing in 2012, the European economic crisis, declining growth in China, albeit moderate, and in many countries in the Asia region, and the slow economic recovery in the US all exhibit a return to cycles of economic uncertainties and constant changes.

In view of the economic downturns, many organizations (including ALPHA) accelerated their efforts to outsource and offshore[7] to reduce operating expenses related to information technology (IT) and other areas of business operations. The evolution toward an extended enterprise requires organizations to increase their reliance on external providers for services and operations and creates an extended trust environment that the business units increasingly depend upon to meet their goals. Such a change was common in the industry then (McDougall 2002a and b), and continues.

Regulators were mostly supportive and devised new policies to enable such an approach to globalization (Matsushima 2001, Yakcop 2000, Bank of Thailand 2003). Although these changes were planned, many organizations were not ready to address and manage the related changes in their information security risks. Knowledge and practices supporting the management of information risks focused on devising internal controls within a single organizational setting, relying mostly on contractual and service level agreements to manage external risk that could not be controlled adequately by internal policies.

In 2012, the concept of an extended enterprise was taken to a new level with the proliferation of cloud computing, virtualization technology, and mobility technology as new tools for chief information officers (CIOs) to enable them to keep operating costs down and improve efficiency. Businesses small and large are moving their infrastructures, operating platform systems, applications, and/or data to cloud data centers that may be provided by third parties (cloud services providers), built in-house, or combine in-house and outsourced services. Third party arrangements are normally preferred to minimize capital expenditures while relying on new technologies to improve efficiencies.

Further cost savings may also be achieved through a shared architecture (known as multitenancy), instead of a single client arrangement with a provider. We see similar dilemmas in the latest cycle of technology adoption. Information security and data privacy risk and uncertainties continue to exist, but new security measures are again being devised using mainly collections of controls from various sources based on past standards and regulatory requirements.[8] Combining the bliss of ignorance of the new risks, most unregulated organizations[9] are charging ahead with new technologies in view of expected economic gains.

To gain an economic advantage and better competiveness, ALPHA, like many other organizations in 2001, also undertook an expansion approach to its business and merged with two other major financial institutions with different specializations and risk cultures (one in the risk-taking investment banking and equities business and one in the more risk-averse investment and asset management business).

The merger required ALPHA to integrate organizations and business units of various cultures, sizes, practices, skills and expertise levels, risk tolerance philosophies, and risk management principles into a new enterprise. This also brought new challenges to the IRM function, with questions about how to close the gaps while maintaining compliance with regulatory restrictions and requirements that applied to the various entities as well as the combined new enterprise. Mergers and acquisitions and joint ventures across various industries are sprouting up even more today to obtain market and technology access as organizations attempt to increase competitiveness and reduce the time to move from innovation to new products. The IRM function must adapt and change with these business changes on an ongoing basis in order to remain relevant and help his or her organization manage its information security risk.

While these organizational changes took place globally, the Internet continued to grow and proliferate as a communication and collaboration vehicle for businesses and individuals (Furnell 2002, Hall 2001). The expansion was accompanied by an escalation of security incidents relating to software vulnerability exploitations (AusCERT 2002). Since then, the sophistication of attack techniques and motivations for financial fraud have also increased (Furnell 2002, Skoudis and Zeltser 2004, Lynley 2011, Whittaker 2013, Kelley 2013, Mello 2013). In September 2001, shortly after the 9/11 incident, a computer worm by the name of NIMDA (CERT/CC 2001b) caused a massive disruption of e-mail, web, and IT services in many organizations (Pethia 2001). This was followed by the SQL Slammer worm (Krebs 2003, Microsoft 2003a) incident in January 2003 and the Blaster worm (CERT/CC 2003b) incident

in August 2003. During the same period, incidents of unsolicited (SPAM[10])
e-mails also escalated exponentially (*Economist* 2003).

All this resulted in significant losses[11] and impacted ALPHA's information security risk status. However, the information risk managers'[12] roles and
responsibilities were unclear when the security incidents occurred, and many
organizations and individuals did not know how to respond when their systems were disrupted. A quick scan of the major information security-related
incidents on the Internet in 2012 showed that the cybercrime world has not
improved in the last decade (Whittaker 2012).

A peek into organizations' information security management today
reveals slow progress in changing practices, but there is a light at the end of the
tunnel. Technology providers are devising new capabilities aimed at providing better early warnings and detecting new attacks. Many organizations are
starting to deploy more capabilities to aid detection and response rather than
merely focusing on the earlier preventive measures. The progress is, however,
being further challenged by more intelligent mobile technology and personal computing devices in the forms of smartphones and tablet devices that
enable employees and contractors to quickly access and move data anywhere
inside and outside the enterprise network—a revolutionary change known
in the industry as the consumerization of IT (PricewaterhouseCoopers 2011,
Griffey 2012). As one technology company announced in 2009, organizations' networks are now "borderless" (Kerravala 2011).

Such changes once again impose new security and privacy risk issues
on organizations and individuals, and the dilemma is that simply adding
more security rules or controls cannot stop them. Information security
incidents are forms of unplanned changes that result from security events
that are often beyond the control of an organization. The effects of technology evolution and use by individuals and in organizations often introduce
risk issues that cannot be anticipated up front. How should information
risk managers learn and respond in order to manage such changing information risk situations?

1.1.2 Common Knowledge, Standards, and Practices

Managing information security risk is seen commonly as a task of identifying and assessing risks, applying mitigating controls,[13] and monitoring
the use of those controls to address recognized risks in a coordinated manner throughout the life cycle of a business system. In the security standards
arena, the former British Standards BS 7799 Part 2 (1999b) covering information security management systems (ISMS), which has been revised as ISO/
IEC (2005e) IS 27001, codifies management as a plan-do-check-act (PDCA)
process. This standard uses baseline controls such as the ISO/IEC (2000) IS
27002 standard for implementation.

The controls, also known as common practices or best practices, are security measures commonly applied by organizations to address risk-related concerns. The controls in these standards are, however, symptomatic and are categorized broadly, so that they may be selected and refined based on the results of a risk assessment process. Their use is subject to individual interpretations of risk, relying primarily on a risk manager's knowledge and experience.

Despite their status as international standards, revisions and updates are slow.[14] However, in a changing business and IT landscape faced with tight budgetary constraints, reduced development time, and rapid implementation needs, these security controls focusing on known issues cannot be updated quickly enough to keep up with changes. As a result, they are becoming internal obstacles when businesses plan to provide new services to customers. When the perceived benefits of not implementing security controls are higher than the uncertain or subjective value of having them in place, the implementation of controls may be ignored, rejected, or given low priority.

There has also been the lack of a standard lexicon or taxonomy for information security terminology and practices.[15] As noted in Jones (2005), this resulted in many unfavorable implications for the information security profession, with frequent ramifications ranging from "marginalization in the organization, difficulty in convincing organizational leadership to take recommendations seriously, to inefficient use of resources."

In the area of new IT systems and network communications technology, businesses strive to increase productivity, reduce the costs of operations and other overheads, and reach out to more potential and existing customers. Security standards and best practices are often not readily available in time to support the management of risks for the fulfillment of such needs, even if a business is willing to invest in protective measures up front. A primary reason is the lack of available best practices because of insufficient relevant security know-how and experience related to the new technology and related systems.

This created a need for business management and IT practitioners to take risks if they wished to capitalize on new approaches to solve business problems or improve business efficacy. In most cases, security measures that were previously devised for other business contexts and requirements were redeployed to secure the new systems and protect information involved. Discrepancies between the new and the old quickly become security gaps that businesses must manage separately.

Organizations did not want to dismiss new technologies or opportunities because doing so might disadvantage their competitiveness or profitability. We have seen this scene replayed in the adoption of cloud computing technology and services in recent years. Relying on a best practices approach produced the undesirable effect of keeping business IT operations lagging behind newer developments. How should information risk managers help an organization to respond to the needs of such a changing IT and business environment?

In addition to addressing the above challenges, information risk managers must demonstrate to management that the information risks[16] of the organization have been managed. In other words, he or she must be able to measure the effectiveness or performance of IRM-related activities and investment in a security program. Devising suitable metrics for such measurements has been essential for gaining support and resource investment in the IRM function. This includes investing in security processes, training people to be aware of risks and pitfalls to avoid and secure steps to take, conducting regular reviews and monitoring to identify security gaps, and addressing new security issues. Whether these actions have been accomplished, however, does not necessarily translate into zero security incidents in the organization, but the security practices are nevertheless auditable.

The primary approach adopted to measure the effectiveness of IRM at ALPHA and many other organizations, including those that participated in this research study, was to use audit and compliance ratings of the presence and integrity of the security controls as basic measurements, and also counting and aggregation of the numbers and types of security incidents. Such an approach provides limited benefits and only a partial view of the information risk status of an organization and the effectiveness of its information risk managers.[17]

Besides the use of compliance and stability metrics to determine internal performance, some organizations adopt a benchmarking approach to determine their relative positions compared to other organizations within their industries. This approach, however, also presents limitations due to cultural, business priorities, and other influencing factors, as will be discussed in Chapter 2.

These issues lead to the question of how to measure and assess the effectiveness of information risk managers, including their strategies and plans, and determine the risk status of an organization to gain a meaningful indicator of its risk exposure compared with the current approach of relying on the number of issues identified and their audit ratings.

1.1.3   Profession, Organizational Role, and Function

On a personal level, my interest in information security risk management research relates directly to my practice in a global financial institution (ALPHA) and in a technology-providing organization (BETA).[18]

At ALPHA, I was responsible for devising approaches and steps to help the organization manage its information security risk with the objective of reducing security-related exposures and uncertainties from the organization's use of IT (including the Internet). At BETA, I was responsible for providing professional advice to help IRMs and those with related roles in enterprises develop their security strategy and plans and execute those plans to achieve similar objectives such as those that I had in my role at ALPHA. Without a practice-oriented approach supported by research, the validity of a suggested information security strategy and plan was vulnerable to challenge. It was also hard to ascertain whether an observable reduction[19] of security exposures and uncertainties was an outcome of security actions.

The field of information risk management has continued to emerge. It has evolved from a focus on data security to information security protection to management to one that involves an integrated risk management discipline. Since the initiation of the research that led to the writing of this book, differences of opinions and understanding among practitioners and researchers and within various communities have surrounded the definition and scope of information risk management.

For example, a practicing regional chief information security officer (CISO) asserted that IRM is a discipline that evolved from the field of IT security and information security (Mahtani 2004). Maiwald and Sieglein (2002) suggest that the role is contingent on the purpose of the information security department, whether the latter has resulted from government regulation requirements, audit report recommendations, senior management or board decisions, or IT department decisions. In Chapter 2, based on a review of existing literature, I identified five different approaches to the definition of information security and differences in the definitions and scopes of risk management and risk assessment.

At the same time, organizations like ALPHA that maintain IRM functions regularly redefine the scope of the function.[20] Such frequent changes further support the view that the field needs more examination and evaluation to define what it entails and what needs to change in order for practitioners to achieve IRM objectives. I believe many practitioners face similar challenges and have a desire to improve their understanding of the field.

1.2   Purpose

This book is an adaptation from a research study conducted between 2001 and 2007 and is updated with subsequent insights from my continued practice. My purpose is to share the learning and understanding and take readers through a discovery journey of the responsive approach. This book discusses the key findings of the research study and practical methods for organizations to improve their management of information security risks. The approach proposed in this book is informed by personal learning and understanding derived from the research and is shared as a catalyst for further discourse and practices.

1.3 Questions

John Dewey once said, "A problem well put is half-solved." Summarizing the issues and dilemmas discussed above, three principal questions are critical for individual practitioners and for organizations managing information risk[21]:

1. What should an information risk manager do differently or change in a strategy for managing information security risk so that the result will not be a compliance-driven and/or control-oriented security culture?
2. How should information risk managers deal with information risks in a constantly changing business and IT risk environment, for example: (1) managing security risk development in an IT arena that could disrupt the business and/or IT operations, and (2) implementing changes in the business and/or IT strategy that could significantly change an organization's risk posture?
3. How should organizations resolve the conflict between measurement of the performance of an information risk manager and the outcome of a security incident? Should the manager's performance reflect the security risk status of the organization? In other words, what should the relationship be between the manager's performance and the security status of the organization?

A security implementation requires a business to incur a cost. A security risk management plan must enable the business to balance this cost with the potential gains from its objectives. These issues were therefore studied in the context of a business environment to ensure that the business objectives were adequately balanced with the information security risk management practices.

These questions about information security risk management have not been answered adequately by current literature in the field of information security. More importantly, inconsistencies in the use of terminologies and the basic principles for defining and addressing information security risk management requirements created much confusion for newcomers to the field. These areas require more studies and understanding in an effort to refine existing practices, develop new knowledge, and work toward an acceptable framework, model, and/or approach to improve the practice.

1.4 Research Methodology

The social–technical nature of information security risk management challenges and the exploratory nature of the research questions suggested the use of a qualitative approach for the study. Furthermore, the research questions arise from the workplace, which is an appropriate environment for seeking a desired outcome. Action research has been applied successfully by other researchers and practitioners in workplace-related research. For example, the work of Goh (1999), Kwok (2001), and Tay (2003) was used as the meta-methodology for the conduct of the study, to derive a theoretical approach to information security risk management and test its implementation.

The initial phase entailed identification of the issues and dilemmas of managing information risk based on the understanding gained at the ALPHA organization. The results were triangulated with those derived from a survey and a series of interviews with practitioners in the industry. After the initial phase of learning and understanding organization practices, an evolving model and associated change programs were developed and implemented to address those issues and dilemmas over the subsequent five action research cycles and the research was extended to two other organizations designated BETA and GAMMA.[22]

The initial research cycle adopted the Kemmis and McTaggart (1988) action research planner approach. Subsequent cycles were also influenced by the works of Avison et al. (1999), Dick et al. (2001), Dick (1993, 2001), and Costello (2003).

Data collection was achieved through interviews, questionnaires, and journaling. Analysis and interpretation of the data throughout the study included evaluation and reflection on the data collected using both dialectic and systemic analyses of the findings, leading to the derivation of a substantive theory and a management approach. The derived approach, supporting methodology, and tools were subsequently validated through case studies and test implementation in practice environments.

Appendix A provides a more detailed description of the action research cycles involved in the study.

1.5   Organization of Subsequent Chapters

Chapter 2 titled "Knowledge, Issues, and Dilemmas" reviews the current literature and approaches, and highlights the discrepancies and inadequacies of today's practice model and underlying assumptions. It seeks to address the question of why current approaches are not serving their purpose. The chapter further asserts the relevance and importance of addressing the research questions identified in Section 1.3 above and the potential application of a social–technical approach.

Chapter 3, "Practices, Issues, and Dilemmas," moves the focus from the knowledge domain to the practice environment. It begins with a discussion of the challenges experienced in an organization context and an explanation of the understanding gained from introducing two models of practices in an organization. The chapter also examines uncertainties in risk analysis and management and the causality of information security systems, further illustrating the inadequacies of current practice. The two models include principles and tools adapted from the field of social science study and provide two alternative social–technical approaches to address risk management requirements in a problem environment. At each juncture, we discuss the limitations, issues, and dilemmas discovered during the implementations of the models, and reflect on a series of incidents that emerged during that phase of the study.

Chapter 4 covers "Responsive Security" and continues the research and discourse from the findings of the previous chapters. It directs the study toward the notion of responsiveness that led to the derivation of the responsive approach. The approach assimilates the concept of piezoelectric behavior—the theoretical principle of responsive security—and creates a structural sequence (change event, situation awareness, and criticality alignment) that mirrors the characteristics of piezoelectric behavior. The chapter discusses three cases studies that validate and refine the concept and principles of piezoelectric behavior in information risk management, creating a framework suitable for general application in organizations. We also examine why an increasing focus on responsiveness is critical for addressing the changing nature of today's risk environment.

Chapter 5 titled "Conclusions and Implications" discusses the results of the research study and addresses the question of how an organization should respond to the challenges and complex nature of information security risk management. It provides resolutions to the questions listed in Section 1.3. It also discusses the implications of the responsive security approach for theory, policy, and practice, and finally closes with suggestions for future research topics and further improvements of this field.

Endnotes

1. In the late 1990s to early 2000s, a slight distinction emerged between the information security term (but not information security risk) and information risk. Some organizations (including ALPHA) began to separate information security and information risk into two functions, with the former focusing on technical aspects of threats, vulnerabilities, and security solutions, and the latter focusing on devising and implementing a holistic framework to manage threats, vulnerabilities, and solutions involving the people, processes, and technology used in an organization's information systems and network. Information risk management was regarded as a "new" risk management paradigm that required the same focus as managing market risk, settlement risk, and credit risk in a financial institution. The research for this book concentrated on information risk management—also called information security risk management in the industry.

2. The objectives of information security risk management may vary depending on an organization's business and the regulatory requirements that require compliance. This concept was noted in the information security literature reviewed in Section 2.2.

3. The ALPHA generic name is used to provide anonymity to the organization where this research was conducted. Anonymity of the research subject was also preserved so that readers and researchers will not have preconceived perceptions or biases based on knowing the identity of the organization.

4. The IRM function at ALPHA was established to identify and assess information security risks and to provide recommendations in the forms of mitigation, avoidance, transfer, or acceptance. The IRM function was also involved in tracking the progress of implementation of the risk treatment measures accepted and to managing issues arising from implementation.

5. Bangkok, Hong Kong, Jakarta, Kuala Lumpur, Manila, Mumbai, Seoul, Singapore, Sydney, Taipei, and Tokyo were the cities. Most information risk management activities, however, focused on Hong Kong, Mumbai, Singapore, Sydney, and Tokyo.

6. For a thorough account of the 9/11 incident, see the published report of the 9/11 Commission (Kean et al. 2004).

7. The offshoring term is used commonly by businesses to describe the transfer of business operations from a relatively mature site to a new site by leveraging the low infrastructure and human resources costs of the new site, normally located in a developing country such as India, the Philippines, and China. Unlike outsourcing that involves contracting an operation to a third party provider, an offshoring operation continues to be owned and operated by staff of the parent business.

8. The Cloud Control Matrix (CCM; CSA 2012) created by the Cloud Security Alliance (CSA) constitutes 99 high-level controls (dated September 2012) from a collection found in the security compliance arena and designated as recommended best practices for cloud services providers. The mapping indirectly provides assurance to the mapped compliance domains that implementation of the CCM will achieve necessary compliance with the related standards. The mapped compliance domains include ISO/IEC 27002, Payment Card Industry (PCI), HIPAA, ISACA COBIT 4.1, NIST SP800-53 R3, Jericho Forum, and NERC CIP published standards.

9. Regulated organizations such as the financial institutions in several countries (for example, in Singapore and Hong Kong) were stopped from leveraging such technology and services in view of the regulators' uncertainties and discomfort about risks that could negatively impact the stability of the industry.

10. SPAM has no universally agreed-upon definition. In general, the term refers to unsolicited electronic messages that are sent in bulk by unknown senders or senders with whom the recipients have no prior personal or business relationships.

11. According to Clark (2003), the Code Red virus cost the business community $2.6 billion; the Nimda worm infected close to 2.5 million servers and users worldwide in less than 24 hours; and the Melissa virus unleashed by a New Jersey programmer in March 1999 caused at least $80 million in damages. ALPHA was not spared from these attacks.

12. The information risk manager or IRM was part of the IRM function, whose job was to perform management tasks such as risk identification and assessment and provide suitable recommendations for risk treatments with justifications to business management. At a regional level, the regional information risk officer (RIRO) managed the plans and activities of the IRM. At a global level (across the entire ALPHA organization), the chief information risk officer (CIRO) managed the global policies, strategic directions, and plans from the headquarters office.

13. Such as those specified in ISO/IEC 17799 (ISO/IEC 2000, 2005f).

14. In 2005, the two standards were successfully revised (ISO/IEC 2005e, f) to address participating countries' concerns about the adequacies and applications of the standards and controls in their respective jurisdictions. More than 2,000 comments were reviewed in a process that started in 2002. Multiple projects in ISO/IEC JTC 1/SC 27 were again initiated in 2006 to revise these standards to address new risk issues arising after 2005. As of this writing in March 2013, the revision is still in progress.

15. This issue was only looked into in ISO/IEC JTC 1/SC 27 in 2006, with the development of the 2700x series of information security management systems-related standards, including a new standard, ISO/IEC 27000, to capture all related vocabulary and terminologies (ISO/IEC 2009a).

16. "Information risk" is used in this book to denote "information security risk." The terms have been used interchangeably in the industry.

17. In 2005, the ISO standards committee (ISO/IEC JTC 1/SC 27) responsible for developing information security-related standards began to look into developing international standards for measuring the effectiveness of information security management in organizations. Many disagreements arose among standards experts from different national bodies on the terminology for measurements and metrics. They were unable to agree on a specific method of measurement. A formal international standard was finally published in 2009 (ISO/IEC 2009b). This observation was gained from my personal participation in the ISO/IEC JTC 1/SC 27 meetings that were held every six months in various locations, between 2003 and 2012.

18. BETA is used for the name of the second company, a technology product provider, to maintain its anonymity. The anonymity of the research subject was also preserved so that readers and researchers will not have preconceived perceptions or biases due to prior knowledge of the identity of the organization.

19. Information security risk is "dynamic" in that it changes constantly as a result of technology use, human behaviors, and risk management activities. The complete elimination of risk or security exposure is impossible.

20. In 2004, ALPHA designated the function "information technology risk management" in order to ensure that the group focused only on information technology-related risks and not information in general. In 2005, ALPHA underwent another change of leadership in the risk management function, and the group was called "information technology control management" to emphasize the focus on control issues.

21. These are the research questions that served as the basis for the selection of the methodology and structuring of the research process, facilitated theoretical inquiries about the data, and guided the exploration and development of an approach suitable for use in managing information security risk in an enterprise.
22. The GAMMA name was selected to provide anonymity to the organization that implemented an information security risk management approach derived from this research study. Anonymity of the research subject was also preserved so that readers and researchers will not have preconceived perceptions or biases based on knowing the identity of the organization.

Knowledge, Issues, and Dilemmas

2

2.1 Introduction

This chapter presents a review[1] of existing literature to synthesize current knowledge, support the needs for, and highlight the significance of the responsive approach. The focus of the chapter is on literature that informs the field of information risk management and is commonly adopted by practitioners in organizations that recognize the need for managing information risk or are mandated by laws or regulations to do so. The review relates to practices covered in subsequent chapters in which we discuss the application of such knowledge to the practice environment.

The chapter begins with an overview of the concepts including definitions and principles of information security, risk, risk management, and information security risk management, then moves to strategies and programs commonly used to achieve information security in organizations. It examines the theories and knowledge expounded in current literature in the context of the concepts, strategy, and programs for managing information security risk against the key characteristics—changes and potential security failures—of the information security environment. These are the key themes underlying the research questions discussed in Chapter 1.

2.2 Information Security

It is often said that information security is not new (Piper 2006, Hoo 2000) but several definitions of the term have developed over time and are used in both the academic and business worlds. In many ways, the variety of definitions shaped the scope and approach toward achieving information security. To meet the objective of this chapter, we present reviews and explanations of the definitions.

The historical development of information security can be traced back to the ancient development of cryptography (Kahn 1996, Singh 1999) that was devised to protect the confidentiality of information. Data and information confidentiality have also been the primary concerns of national defense and intelligence, as shown by the early security models such as the then widely used Bell and La Padula (1976) model. As understanding of information communications developed and evolved, particularly via the business use of information technology, progress in information technology demonstrated that protecting the integrity of information is critical to ensure its authenticity, correctness and accuracy of content, and the authenticity of senders and recipients. New models for information integrity protection began to emerge, for example, the Biba Integrity Model (Pfleeger 1997) and the work of Clark and Wilson (1987) and Abrams et al. (1993).

Access control is used commonly to achieve integrity and confidentiality protection by ensuring the authorization of a user against the criteria in the access matrix of a protected resource or information (Denning 1982). Denning also introduced the notion of information flow controls and inference control to protect confidentiality of information in transit and stored in database systems, respectively. When an information system enforces these security mechanisms to protect information confidentiality and/or integrity, unauthorized users are blocked from accessing that information. However, if the security mechanisms are forcibly disabled or damaged, a perpetrator can tamper with the availability of the information by authorized users, thus preventing its use when needed. Clearly, availability is another important requirement in information security protection. Clark and Wilson (1987) were among the early researchers who highlighted the need for availability, particularly in business systems.

A common definition of information security is the protection of information to ensure its confidentiality, integrity, and/or availability; see Shain (1994), Hoo (2000), and Blakley et al. (2001). Over the years, practitioners and researchers invested much time in clarifying the meanings of information security terms. Their efforts led to expansion of the basic definition to include authenticity, accountability, and usability properties. One of the most elaborate expansions of this definition was by Parker (1998), who added authenticity, possession, and utility as extensions to the list of properties desired. Confusion nonetheless continues to prevail.

Clark (2003) defines security differently in various parts of his book and includes trust, privacy, nonrepudiation, and integration (without elaboration) within the definition in one instance.

Maiwald and Sieglein (2002) suggest that the role of information security is contingent on how the function originated in an organization that dictated its mission and objectives. In this case, the definition of information security relies on an individual's or organization's views and beliefs. Maiwald (2004) also defines information security as "measures adopted to prevent the unauthorized use, misuse, modification, or denial of use of knowledge, facts, data, or capabilities." While this definition added capabilities, knowledge, and facts to the meaning of information security, it excluded the confidentiality or privacy requirement.

In view of the lack of agreement about and consistency of the list of information properties in the definition of information security, members of the ISO/IEC 17799 (renumbered 27002 in 2006) revision working group adopted a different approach when the "Specification for the Code of Practice for Information Security" (ISO/IEC 2000) was revised in 2005. The group redefined information security as "the protection of information from a wide range of threats in order to ensure business continuity, minimize business risk, and maximize return on investments and business opportunities" (ISO/IEC 2005f). This approach emphasizes the relationship of information security to business and highlights the need to align information security to business objectives.

In Alberts and Dorofee's (2002) description of the OCTAVE[SM] approach,[2] "information security is determining what needs to be protected and why, what it needs to be protected from, and how to protect it for as long as it exists." In essence, this definition frames information security as a process used to identify information assets, prioritize the importance of each asset, understand the threats to the assets, and devise suitable measures to protect the assets against threats. In other literature, this process is known as risk analysis and risk management. For example, see Pfleeger (1997), Moses (1994), and Summers (1997).

Another approach, as Alberts and Dorofee noted, is to determine "how to assure your organization an adequate level of security over time." Volonino and Robinson (2004) emphasize the importance of gaining assurance, but take a law-oriented approach including issues related to the parties involved in the conduct of an electronic business transaction. They define information security as:

> ...the policies, practices, and technology that must be in place for an organization to transact business electronically via networks with a reasonable assurance of safety. This assurance applies to all online activities, transmissions, and storage. It also applies to business partners, customers, regulators, insurers, or others who might be at risk in the event of a breach of that company's security (Volonino and Robinson 2004).

The various ways in which information security has been defined show that the scope of what is now a knowledge field encompasses many aspects of information and information systems. Synthesizing the existing literature, we found at least five distinct areas to consider to address this topic comprehensively:

1. Information security properties or attributes such as confidentiality, integrity, and availability
2. Policies, processes, and functions, from information creation to destruction

3. Priorities or criticalities as functions of the threat and regulatory environment, their potential impacts on a business, and available resources of the business
4. Techniques or measures applicable to address security requirements or issues
5. Assurance to verify and validate the completeness and effectiveness of the measures taken to provide security properties, secure or support the processes and functions, and address the priority threats and regulatory requirements

The relationships between these areas and the context of their identification, assessment, implementation, operations, and maintenance must be relevant to the business. Another need is to evaluate and relate how information security in an organization will address changes in the business environment, particularly when adverse conditions emerge due to changes and failures in the environment.

With the exception of a few studies such as the one by Dhillon and Backhouse (2000),[3] most literature focuses on specific methods for responding to changes and issues that have already occurred or are known. The methods do not anticipate or prepare organizations to respond to emerging changes as they unfold. In other words, most studies are concerned with understanding the past and present and devising solutions that would have helped to manage and address those issues. They do not advocate approaches and plans for dealing with ongoing changes and future events.

2.3 Principles and Approaches

To achieve the objectives of information security covering the five areas highlighted in the previous section, different approaches have been devised and implemented. To help determine the appropriate approach, researchers and practitioners have over the years used a number of basic principles in the design and development of information security systems.

Swanson and Guttman (1996) referred to those principles as a "certain intrinsic expectation [that] must be met whether the system is small or large or owned by a government agency or a private corporation." As part of this review, we discuss and analyze four fundamental principles that are used widely in information security management and the approaches that have been largely influenced by or based on these principles, namely: (1) the weakest link; (2) defense in depth; (3) no perfect security; and (4) risk management. For discussions of additional security principles, see Swanson and Guttman (1996), Schneier (2003), and Summers (1997).

2.3.1   Security: As Strong as the Weakest Link

"A chain is no stronger than the weakest link." ... No matter how strong the strongest links of a chain are, no matter how many strong links there are in it, a chain will break at its weakest link. Improve the strength of the weakest link and you improve the strength of the chain (Schneier 2003).

This metaphoric principle has been widely cited in information security literature and suggests consideration of all aspects—people, processes, and technology— and not concentrating on one or a few areas as a reaction to a recent adverse incident or legal, regulatory, or audit requirement.

When identifying the weak links in a system, Schneier (2003) emphasizes that different threats often have different weak links. The design of a specific security measure to counter a weak link therefore will not work for all threats to a system. For a more detailed discussion and examples of the use of the weakest link principle, see Browne (1976), Denning and Denning (1979), Schneier (2003), and Viega (2005).

As noted in Browne (1976), "it is important to be systematic and come up with interlocking measures that prevent or recover from nearly all types of contingencies"— proposing the need for a "fortress" of security supported by the "defense in depth" principle.

2.3.2   Defense in Depth

Defense in depth is about "protecting assets with not one countermeasure, but multiple countermeasures" (Schneier 2003). By overlaying or complementing each countermeasure, we cover a security weakness at a lower layer by protection rendered at higher layers and vice versa. When devising layered security solutions by using the defense in depth principle, information risk practitioners commonly suggest a review of the people, process, and technology requirements.

Howard and LeBlanc (2003) and Schneier (2001, 2003) also cite the weakest link principle as the basis for implementing defense in depth to reduce the surface areas of attacks on software products and application systems. From a detection perspective, such a principle helps increase the probability that an attack will be discovered earlier if a system has monitoring mechanisms at each layer. Practitioners also consider the provision of redundant and backup security mechanisms as implementation of defense in depth (Pfleeger 1997). For an example of this principle in practice, see Microsoft Corporation (2006b).

While weakest link and defense in depth are sound principles for reducing vulnerabilities and providing layers of defense to overcome unexpected problems, the cost increases with each layer of security added to a system. As reported by Venables (2004), the increased layers of security also add complexity to the environment. The complexity produces emergent behaviors that create new, unanticipated weak links and make security more difficult to manage.

2.3.2.1 Use of Security Technology

Historically, a common research approach in computer security, usually considered a subcategory of information security, is to identify weaknesses and possible attacks and devise techniques and mechanisms to protect against them. When addressing information security risks, especially when applying the defense in depth principle, some practitioners and researchers regard information security as a technology problem. One assertion is that, "Given better access control policy models, formal proofs of cryptographic protocols, approved firewalls, better ways of detecting intrusions and malicious code, and better tools for system evaluation and assurance, the problems can be solved" (Anderson 2001b).[4] As noted in Blakley et al.:

> Information security is important in proportion to an organization's dependence on information technology. When an organization's information is exposed to risk, the use of information technology is obviously appropriate (Blakley et al. 2001).

Even when considering social requirements, the tendency has been to translate them into technical measures for implementation. For example, Kohl (1995) states, "The problem of security is drifting from technological security, whose main interest lies in the sound calculation and possible certainty about the nonhuman world, toward an area of human relationships which are technologically induced, so that the aim of security is becoming once again a state between humans." To address these needs, Kohl (1995) proposes a set of technical security mechanisms providing information self-determination, nonrepudiation, reproducibility, and design potential for end users.

Technology vendors have favored this for several reasons besides the obvious business motivation. They often suggest that building and using security technology will provide better integration of security with technology, eliminate the need to deal with error-prone human procedures, and lower the cost of security (Kluepfel 1994, O'Kelley 2013). Similar thinking also appears to prevail among end user organizations (Allen 2002). While such an approach to information security led to many technological innovations (antivirus measures, firewalls, intrusion detection, and intrusion prevention), the innovations can hardly claim victory over the changing risk environment, particularly on the Internet.

Security features designed to meet specific requirements become difficult to change when business needs or policies change. For example, mechanisms such as security labeling, mandatory access control, object reuse, and other measures designed to meet early Trusted Computer System Evaluation Criteria (US DoD 1983, 1985) specifications fixated on the various levels of security in the military policies defined according to the Bell and LaPadula model (1976). These security mechanisms, when implemented in computer systems, cannot be used in commercial operations unless the operations align their security policies to those of military and defense organizations—which is quite impractical. Similarly, while a firewall system can block undesirable network traffic on predetermined network ports, it is ineffective for application-level attacks that use legitimate network services by tunneling through authorized network ports that the firewall rules permit.

An application-level security mechanism must work as an addition to a firewall to deal with newly identified risks. Security features designed to cater to a wide range of requirements often become too complex to manage or configure (requiring additional tools and skills) or cannot fulfill specific needs comprehensively and still perform with reasonable efficacy.

Volonino and Robinson (2004) also note that such an approach has been problematic as "it often gets defeated by faulty configuration of the tools, neglected maintenance, or a process failure, such as the failure to close out the network IDs [access identifiers] of terminated employees." Also, the approach "shows little senior management commitment; has no specific economic justification; [and] requires little to no active participation from employees." Similar issues in relation to various aspects of information systems and network implementations were discussed by Kang (1996), Schneier (1997, 2001), and others who emphasize the potential human errors in the information system life cycle and highlight the need to focus on people, policies, and processes for implementing and managing information security. As noted by Blakley et al. (2001):

> Current information security technology, however, deals with only a small fraction of the problem of information risk. In fact, the evidence increasingly suggests that information security technology does not reduce information risk very effectively.

Blakley and coworkers argue "that we must reconsider our approach [of using security technology singularly] to information security from the ground up if we are to deal effectively with the problem of information risk." Nonetheless, reporting on the PricewaterhouseCoopers and UK Department of Trade and Industry (DTI) April 2002 survey results, J. H. Allen emphasizes that "people still look at security as a technology issue, when it should be a business matter." In 2004, after a follow-up survey, the DTI reported that "some progress had been made in putting security controls in place." But most focused on technology-related solutions. As PricewaterhouseCooper and DTI (2004) summarized:

> Businesses tend to rely solely on their firewall to defend their Internet gateway and website against attack.
>
> Fewer than one in ten businesses (and only a quarter of large ones) have tested their disaster recovery plans to see if they would work in practice.
>
> Neither overall awareness of BS 77996 nor the number of UK businesses that have implemented it, has increased over the last two years.
>
> Spend[ing] on information security, while increasing, is still relatively low and is seen as a cost rather than an investment.
>
> Companies now spend on average 3 percent of their IT budget on security compared with 2 percent two years ago. Large businesses spend roughly 4 percent. Overall levels of investment in security are still considerably below the 5 percent-10 percent benchmark level.
>
> Under half of all businesses evaluate return on investment on security spend[ing].

As shown by these reports and studies, security technology has the potential to provide defense in depth through deployment across the infrastructure layers, but defense in depth is normally not achievable. Due to cost and other resource constraints, organizations tend to rely on a single security technology to address multiple needs. Even if they maintain adequate secure practices and measures for people and processes, potential weak links still exist at the technology layer for nontechnology reasons, for example, software vulnerabilities resulting from coding errors or misuse of software features. Relying on security technology has not fulfilled the objective of the weakest link principle.

2.3.2.2   Baseline Security

By building on the strengths of available security technology, addressing vendor-driven solutions, and focusing on softer issues such as people, processes, and policies, the baseline approach has become more comprehensive by setting up a minimum level of security with less attention to cost[7] and implementing it across all information technology systems and infrastructures of an organization (Summers 1997).

The use of baseline security was common from the 1980s through the early 1990s, when businesses began to increase their dependency on this approach. Baseline security involved the establishment of best practice standards that were acceptable to all organizations in similar industries. Ferris (1994) noted that an organization could establish "a framework of tools for deciding acceptable risks, and acceptable social behavior." The baseline approach was also formalized and published as an international standard. ISO/IEC Technical Report 13335 (1999) promulgated it as a method suitable for managing IT security in organizations.

To deal with specific security requirements, a number of standards have also been developed by industry and international organizations. Examples are the BSI BS 7799-1 (1999a) and ISO/IEC 27002 (2000, 2005f) standards.[5] The "Trusted Computer System Evaluation Criteria" (TCSEC) of the US Department of Defense (US DoD 1985) served as a set of baseline standards. The US government used TCSEC to establish a standard-based policy to achieve better assurance and a measurable level of security (Ferris 1994) to address various levels of needs with a set of predefined classes of security (Summers 1997). Although the policy was based on a set of security principles, it used technical security measures as the main approach for addressing policy requirements. TCSEC evolved into the Common Criteria and became an international standard designated ISO/IEC 15408 (2005b, c, d). The standard articulates security features and their measurable assurances in computer systems. It also defines the processes by which various industries with computer security needs can craft their own variations of security standards (protection profiles) intended to provide more flexibility for all types of industries.

The baseline security (or checklist) approach (Dhillon and Backhouse 2001) involves certain high-level steps for managing information security:

- Use of checklists (as risk assessment tools) to identify security requirements and issues
- Defining acceptable policies and standards
- Implementing standards-based solutions across all systems
- Using a combination of technology and procedural measures
- Use of compensating controls to address new issues until technical controls are available to close the gaps (identified from a checklist review)
- Security reviews and audits as assurances of compliance and implementation (based on checklists)

The main criticisms of the baseline approach are the lack of continuous risk analysis and assessment process as part of information security management and the increased cost of security across an organization when noncritical business and information assets are accorded the same set of baseline measures. The spread of costs leads to undue administrative overheads when noncompliance with baseline measures by noncritical business or information assets is revealed in audit reviews. From an audit perspective, if a common baseline is part of a company's policy, a failure to implement a baseline security control even by noncritical assets would be considered a noncompliance issue. This approach therefore has the side effect of driving compliance instead of ensuring adequate management of information security risk.

Compliance has in fact been a strong driver of information security in most companies. According to Sullivan (2006), in a survey conducted by Merrill Lynch in 2006 that involved responses from 50 chief information security officers (CISOs), regulatory compliance topped the list of reasons driving demand for security software. Ferris (1994) commented that

> One shortcoming of the policy [of using a baseline standard across his orga-
> nization] was its lack of emphasis on the importance of establishing an infor-
> mation security policy, which is critical to the successful implementation of
> discretionary access control. This is a critical management issue, but not a
> technical one (pp. 75-76).

To reduce the cost of security controls, Venables (2004) proposes establishment of a "high universal baseline" focusing on solutions and component
integrations to "make it easier to do security than not to." A reduction of
the cost of security, however, has not been proven possible when adopting
a high universal baseline. This baseline adds the costs of additional security administration and monitoring to noncritical assets (assets that do not
handle or store critical or sensitive information). Nevertheless, this approach
can potentially minimize the exposure of critical assets by weak links from
noncritical assets. According to Dhillon and Backhouse (2001):

> The [baseline] checklist approaches, although still widely used, carry less
> conviction when searching for theoretical foundations in security. They indi-
> cate where exclusive attention has been given just to the observable events
> without considering the social nature of the problems. Checklists inevitably
> draw concern onto the detail of procedure without addressing the key task of
> understanding what the substantive questions are. Procedures are constantly
> changing and for this reason offer little in the way of analytical stability.

From a legal perspective (Hoo 2000), "the basic premise [of a baseline best
practice approach] is that conformance to a set of best practices will ensure
protection against negligence-based liability lawsuits in the event of a security breach." However, Volonino and Robinson (2004) comment that baseline

> best practices are not necessarily recognized by the courts as the standard
> providing a sufficient defense. That is, best computer security practices for an
> industry may not be an effective defense for a company if those practices can
> be shown to be substandard or outdated.

The *best practices* term has been a common source of disagreement among
practitioners and researchers. At the 2003 Computer Research Association
(CRA) workshop on research related to national security, McKeown et al.
(2003) reported that "the security subgroup had the least agreement on
what constitutes best practices, opting for the term 'plausible practices'
instead." At the launch of the first "BS 7799 Goes Global" conference in
Singapore, Humphrey (2002) emphasized that "best practices, in reality,
are common practices."

Standards such as BS 7799 (now ISO/IEC 27002) eased the selection of
security measures and provided a common language for information security

practitioners when discussing security risks and safeguards. Practitioners use standards to improve information security, but standards must be included in an organization's risk management system to support its security policies and requirements.

Updating standards (such as ISO/IEC 27002) to keep abreast of evolving risk issues creates another set of challenges. Revision of a standardization process commonly requires more than two years, assuming all participating members agree to the updates at the onset—which is unusual. Even if an organization manages to implement all the relevant security controls based on a set of standards, the risk relevance of those controls lags the present state of risk by at least two years.

The changing IT environment led to exponential increases in digital communications and connectivity due to wide access to IT systems. Ferris (1994) notes that "IT security standards have to evolve along with the technical environments that they serve," and

> This new environment requires flexibility in adjusting to, or adding on, new technical applications and assessing the risk impacts. Reliance on technology for new control functions in terms of integrity (e.g., electronic signatures) and access control (e.g., privacy) has increased dramatically (pp. 75–76).

To meet the changing requirements, Ferris (1994) suggests a "security services orientation, with services requiring a tool box of standard IT security products to support the services." He also advocates alternative techniques for satisfying IT security requirements to give system planners better choices and empower decision makers to determine the balance between cost and risk acceptable to their organizations. In other words, instead of a common set of baseline standards and security measures, a wider set of alternative standards is necessary to support different needs. The questions of how to determine needs and decide what standards to use are paramount in a multiple baseline standards approach.

These shortcomings in the baseline approach imply the continued existence of weak links in the system. Multiple baselines mean additional cost and complexity in implementation. These issues were also cited in the discussion of the defense in depth approach.

2.3.3 No Perfect Security

The generally accepted principle of "no perfect security" is based on the notion that information systems involve human actions and humans are not perfect. The field of cryptography is based on the concept of "no perfect secrecy." The "one-time pad" (Denning 1982, Singh 1999) data encryption technique was a classic cryptosystem designed to achieve perfect secrecy but it was too expensive to implement for practical use. Variations of the one-time pad were developed but used only in highly sensitive systems such as those involving national security. The system involved trade-offs such as difficulty of use, increased cost of implementation and use, slowed communications, and acceptance of the risk that the system might be breakable under certain conditions. In other words, the attempt to achieve perfect security required the acceptance of certain weak links in the system.

McKeown et al. (2003) report about the 2003 CRA workshop on research related to national security that:

> Best practice is often limited ..., [it is] often decades behind the techniques put forth by the research community. This dichotomy between research and practice in security means that different recommendations must be developed for different situations. Given that all of our systems have vulnerabilities, it is unrealistic to expect that any system can ever be entirely secure.

In essence, the "no perfect security" principle is contrary to the principles of weakest link and defense in depth. It requires a risk manager to take a more pragmatic approach when implementing defense in depth by accepting the idea that weak links will be present regardless of the number of defense layers used. The risk manager must accept trade-offs between risk and available resources and this is the basis of risk management (Schneier 2002, 2003).

2.3.4   Information Security Is Information Risk Management

Recognizing the wisdom of the "no perfect security" principle and the need to prioritize and decide resource allocations within a limited security budget, a risk management approach seems logical and has been widely proposed for managing information security. Summers (1997) designates risk management as a cost–benefit approach. Denning and Denning (1979) suggest that "the goal is cost-effective internal safeguards, sufficiently strong that computer hardware and software are not the weakest links in the security chain." Swanson and Guttman (1996) state the requirements for risk management in two principles: (1) computer security supports the mission of the organization and (2) computer security should be cost effective.

Blakley et al. (2001) rationalize that since information security concerns the protection of business-critical or sensitive information and related IT systems and infrastructure, failures of information security will trigger adverse events, resulting in losses or damages that will exert negative impacts on a business. Information security must be a risk management discipline that manages risks by considering their costs and/or impacts on a business. In other words, "information security is information risk management" (Blakley et al. 2001).

While adopting a risk-based principle for information security appears sound and may be recommended—see Alberts and Dorofee (2002), Clark (2003), Schneier (2003), PricewaterhouseCoopers (2003), and the Electronic Banking Group of the Basel Committee on Banking Supervision (2003)—challenges must be faced when adopting all the principles concurrently to address the needs of information security.

2.3.4.1 Risk, Risk Assessment, and Risk Management

Risk has been defined as the "possibility of incurring loss, injury, or harm" (Manser and Turton 1987), the "possibility of suffering harm or loss" (Alberts and Dorofee 2002), a "combination of the probability of an [adverse] event and its [negative] consequence" (ISO 2001), or simply exposure "to the possibility of a bad outcome" (Borge 2001). *Possibility* implies an element or chance or probability. *Loss* is associated with the value of a tangible or intangible asset, for example, an organization's reputation. Risk is often associated with hazards that threaten valuable assets.

The combined processes of identification, analysis, and evaluation of asset values, threats, vulnerabilities, attacks, exploits, and impacts is known commonly as risk assessment.[7] According to Borge (2001), "risk management means taking deliberate actions to shift the odds in your favor—increasing the odds of good outcomes and reducing the odds of bad outcomes." Risk management has been described as "the ongoing process of identifying risks and implementing plans to address them" (Alberts and Dorofee 2002). ISO Guide 73 (2001) on risk management vocabulary defines risk management as "a set of coordinated activities to direct and control an organization with regard to risk." Risk management encompasses risk assessment, risk treatment,[8] risk acceptance, and risk communication.[9]

2.3.4.1.1 Assessing Risk
ISO Guide 73 (2001) defines risk analysis as the "systematic use of information to identify sources and to estimate the risk," and further states that, "Risk analysis provides a basis for risk evaluation, risk treatment, and risk acceptance. Information can include historical data, theoretical analysis, informed opinions, and the concerns of stakeholders." Risk analysis commonly involves use of qualitative methods such as measuring risks as low, medium, or high. Business management often prefers quantitative risk measurements to allow numerical comparisons with other financial data for decision-making purposes.

Qualitative risk assessment methods range from the simple low, medium, and high characterizations of the probabilities and consequences of risks to complex formulae that utilize expert systems, but have achieved very limited success. CRAMM[10] and RISKPAC,[11] for example, were commercial risk assessment tools commonly used in the 1990s for qualitative assessments (Moses 1994). In the late 1990s and early 2000s, the proliferation of Internet use and its inherent risks led to development of more technical methods such as penetration testing[13] (Maiwald and Sieglein 2002, Klevinsky et al. 2002, Tiller 2003), threat modeling (Schneier 2001, Howard and LeBlanc 2003), and scenario analysis (Hoo 2000) for conducting qualitative risk analysis and assessments.

Qualitative risk assessment is commonly used in business enterprises, due mainly to dissatisfaction with quantitative methods. As noted by Moses (1994):

> There was a need to be able to properly identify values of data assets in rela-
> tion to the potential effects of impacts that were really impossible and illogical
> to present purely in financial terms, for example, endangerment of personal
> safety, and to assess the level or likelihood of threat source manifestation and
> level of seriousness of vulnerabilities without subjective specification of fre-
> quency of occurrence and other figures.

The validity and reliability of qualitative risk assessment methods are, how-ever, subjective, and often rely heavily on the experience, knowledge, and rigor of the risk analysts. Quantitative measurements provide a sense of "authoritative, confident-sounding expressions of uncertainty" (Adams 1999). In information risk literature, quantitative risk analysis often mea-sures potential losses using annual loss expectancy (ALE) computed as a function of the annual probability of loss (p) and the value of the asset (v) as $ALE = pv$. For examples of ALE computations, see Blakley et al. (2001), Moses (1994), Schneier (2001), and Summers (1997).

The US National Bureau of Standards (1975) proposed ALE as Federal Information Processing Standard (FIPS) 65. Although the standard was withdrawn in August 1995, it continues to be cited as an approach to quan-titative risk assessment. Hoo (2000) attributes the appeal of the ALE metric to "its combination of both risk components [probability of loss and value of asset] into a single number." The combination, however, is also a major dis-advantage because distinguishing high-frequency, low-impact events from low frequency, high-impact events based on a single number is no longer possible. Making a decision based on ALE alone may be risky. A high ALE number due to high-frequency, low-impact events may be tolerable but a high value based on low-frequency, high-impact events may be catastrophic (Perrow 1999).

To simplify risk computation, some quantitative methods eliminate the probabilities of losses. Hoo (2000) calls them valuation-driven methodolo-gies. These methods and other second generation approaches utilize only the valuations of assets and potential impacts in risk computations, allowing risk managers to "focus on issues of managerial acceptance, institutional inertia, and other deployment issues." Hoo, however, adds that:

Although attractive for their simplified approach and avoidance of controversy, these valuation-driven methods suffer significant theoretical flaws by virtue of that same simplification. Their exclusive focus on asset value and ignorance of safeguard costs, efficacy measures, and frequency of security breaches could result in either over-securing assets or under-securing them. Both possibilities are economically inefficient and could cause competitiveness to suffer. Without the capacity for performing cost–benefit analysis or the requirement of basic statistics collection, these methods provide no mechanism to motivate refinement of their security specifications. Although convenient in the short term, valuation-driven approaches are not viable long-term solutions.

After learning from the ALE approach, researchers started promoting a more expanded view of risk assessment that Hoo (2000) describes as a common framework approach. This view considers the security requirements (R), assets (A), security concerns (C), threats[13] (T), safeguards (S), and vulnerabilities[14] (V) when deriving a risk assessment outcome (O). This framework is used to promote an iterative assessment process that includes threat analysis, safeguard selection, and cost–benefit analysis. The method can be used for both qualitative and quantitative risk analyses.

Several commercial software implementations such as @Risk and CRAMM have been made available and achieved varying degrees of popularity. According to Hoo (2000), "Throughout the 1990s, sporadic research efforts in computer security risk models can be found, and despite the best efforts of those involved, the framework and other ALE-based approaches failed to gain widespread acceptance." Hoo based his judgment on three main flaws:

1. A mismatch between the scenario-based method and the task of mathematical or computer modeling that affects its accuracy when it aims for simplicity, but becomes overly complicated and impractical if the users consider all possibilities.
2. The model requirement for a deterministic problem space, "assuming that all quantities [are] precisely known," but not on a probabilistic scale, and "the inability to recognize and capture uncertainty-handicapped risk modelers."
3. The requirement for and assumption of the availability of all information—frequency, valuation, and efficacy data; such data remain largely unavailable.

Hoo's categorization of second generation approaches (2000) includes integrated business risk management frameworks,[15] valuation-driven methodologies, scenario analyses[16] and best practices approaches.

Barton et al. (2002) report that scenario analysis and self-assessment employing checklists are commonly used in risk management systems for risk identification purposes. A best practices approach has been in use by the US government and several multinational companies since the 1980s, before risk management became common practice, and into the twenty-first century. In line with the literature, Hoo notes that "the challenges of complexity and uncertainty [remain] unaddressed." Hoo also states that:

> The four new approaches to managing risks are, in general, short-term solutions to the problem. Although they have been relatively successful in addressing organizational acceptance and deployment issues, they have left largely untouched the technological and informational challenges of the previous-generation methodologies. Their lack of cost justification, inability to forecast future trends, and disregard for safeguard efficacy measurement will impel organizations to seek a more satisfactory, quantitative framework for managing computer security risks.

Notwithstanding the limitations of the ALE approach, Blakley et al. (2001) comment that:

> Security technology development and selection should be based on quantitative observational studies of effectiveness, not on synthetic *a priori* assurance of vulnerability avoidance. Probabilities of exploitation must be balanced with consequences. ALEs (that is, observed outcomes) must rule, not the emotion of a good story and the fear, uncertainty and doubt that continues to be the selling proposition for most security technology.

Denning (1999) also reports concerns about the validity of quantitative risk assessment methods, and many information security experts believed that it was impractical to attempt to achieve a degree of exactness about risk:

> Risk assessment is not an exact science. It is impossible to estimate precisely the likelihood of an attack or the losses that would be incurred. There are many potential adversaries—hackers, competitors, criminals, foreign governments, terrorists, and so forth—each with different motivations and skills and each having a different impact on the target. Vulnerabilities are not always known until they have been exploited, and security mechanisms can have costs that are too hard to quantify or predict in advance (p. 386).

Even though the weaknesses and limitation of a quantitative risk assessment approach are profound and the methods have not been well accepted or used in practice, Hoo (2000) assesses the methods of risk management utilized in the insurance and liability risk industries and concluded that:

Insurance, liability, and competition are underlying forces that will push computer security risk management away from the nonquantitative, second-generation approaches and back toward a quantitative framework of risk assessment and management similar to the first-generation ALE-based methodologies.

Based on this assumption, "a new approach is needed, tempered by the lessons of the past and capable of adapting to the future demands that these forces will soon thrust upon it" (Hoo 2000).

At the 2003 CRA conference on "Grand Challenges in Information Security and Assurance," a risk management approach to security was identified by the participants as one of the important challenges. Like Hoo, the conference participants emphasized the need for quantitative risk measurement rather than leaving the approach open, even though they clearly noted the lack of understanding of the full nature of the causes of IT risks, the emergent behaviors of some vulnerabilities and systems, and dependencies in the failures of networked systems. One specific goal to be met within 10 years was to "develop quantitative information-systems risk management that is at least as good as quantitative financial risk management (CRA 2003).

At the time of writing this chapter at the end of 2012, this goal has not been reported as accomplished. The bias toward a quantitative measurement of risk (noted at the CRA conference and in general) has been fueled by the notion that "we cannot manage if we cannot measure." The CRA conference participants also noted that "what you measure is what you get" and "measuring the wrong thing is as bad, or [is] worse than not measuring anything at all." The group cited a need for the measures to be consistent, unbiased, and unambiguous and the conference report (CRA 2003) raised the following questions:

How much risk am I carrying? Am I better off now than I was this time last year? Am I spending the right amount of money on the right things? How do I compare to my peers? What risk transfer options do I have? For that matter, they have no corresponding ability to match their efforts to warning levels such as yellow, orange, or red.

The last point is in fact the most crucial, as it relates to emerging or changing risk situations that organizations face constantly. Even if the five questions can be answered accurately and fully substantiated with charts and graphics of quantitative measures, the inability of an organization to deal with escalating risks will result in damages and losses, making all earlier efforts and measurements irrelevant.

From a risk communication perspective, Gigerenzer (2002) reports that the use of probabilities does not help to facilitate risk communication and suggests that "when thinking and talking about risks, use frequencies rather than probabilities." Gigerenzer asserts that frequencies provide more clarity of a risk through the use of a reference class. Such an approach, however, has not been adopted in information security risk analysis.

While quantitative methodologies continue to gain the interest of researchers, studies of qualitative approaches remain limited. This can be attributed to the technical focus of the field of information security. To better understand and develop qualitative methodologies in risk analysis and assessment, qualitative, empirical studies of information risk management, like the work of Bjorck (2005), are important and should be encouraged.

2.3.4.1.2 Managing Risk   While risk analysis seeks to identify and evaluate the significance of risk to information assets in organizations, risk treatment determines appropriate actions (or nonactions) for dealing with risks that have been identified and evaluated. Blakley et al. (2001) suggest that "risks can be managed using a variety of mechanisms, including liability transfer, indemnification, mitigation, and retention." In accordance with the definition of risk management,[17] for example, in ISO Guide 73 (2001), these risk management steps are commonly known as risk treatment mechanisms.

Organizations involved in risk treatment have been overly biased toward mitigation rather than other approaches even though the number of insurance companies offering the options of using liability transfer[18] and indemnification[19] has increased (Hoo 2000, Blakley et al. 2001, Gordon et al. 2003). Blakley et al. note that the lack of risk data covering vulnerabilities, incidents, and losses is one of the main issues arising when using liability transfer or indemnification approaches for risk treatment. Hoo (2000) also notes that "practical implementation issues aside, no consensus yet exists on the specific quantities to be monitored, as evidenced by the distinct lack of consonance among computer security surveys."

The concept that insurance provides a means for liability or risk transference is flawed. As noted by Boyne (2003), insurance risk is determined from the perspective of loss potential of an insurance business—not the perspective of the business or individual customer insured. To manage such risks, insurance companies review the histories of risk events relating to the profile of the customer to be insured. A premium is established based on the probability of the occurrence of a similar incident experienced by the insured. In this way, the insurance company can collect substantial premiums and face minimum exposure to payouts. Aggregation is common practice so that the collective exposure will be much larger than the potential payout of an individual company in case of a mishap or simultaneous mishaps within a short time.

From the perspective of an insured, subscribing to an insurance scheme does not actually transfer his or her risk. It provides only limited *recoverability* when the insured individual is exposed to a condition or event that produces substantial loss including loss of life. The same principle applies when a company uses an insurance policy as a component of information security risk management. Recoverability is possible but the risk remains.

Gordon et al. (2003) report that using insurance to address information risk is still in its infancy. When facing challenges surrounding issues such as adverse selection[20] and moral hazard,[21] insurance companies have been uncertain about economically sound pricing of their products. Relying on insurance alone to manage risk presents its own risk. Gordon et al. (2003) maintain that risk assessment remains important[22] and understanding a company's risk tolerance is a key determinant of the appropriateness of an insurance policy.

Risk mitigation involves the use of security measures including technology and processes, with or without the addition of new human resources, to protect a system, information, or environment against identified risks. This usually takes the form of controls, for example, by removing or disabling "risky" features and functions. The result may cripple the usability of information systems in an effort to mitigate or eliminate risks considered significant.

Mitigation measures are seldom welcomed by end users and are often seen as impediments to productivity. Risk mitigation typically involves the use of best practices baseline security standards such as ISO/IEC 17799 (2000, 2005f) to address known risk issues and implement technical security measures to ensure secure use of specific technology and/or integrate the mitigation into work flows and processes. A vast number of online and printed publications detail mitigation measures. For examples of both technical and procedure mitigation techniques, see Pfleeger (1997), Garfinkel and Spafford (1997), Summers (1997), Potter and Fleck (2003), Meier et al. (2003), Egan and Mather (2005), Hellen and Goetz (2004), and Maiwald (2004). To address issues that have no technical solutions, additional procedural measures are normally devised as temporary controls.

In risk acceptance or risk retention, the evaluated risk is tolerated or accepted by management, often based on a perception that the probability or impact of the downside is so insignificant that ignoring the risk is acceptable. If an organization tolerates a risk, it must be financially prepared to sustain the impact of its occurrence (Degraeve 2004). The financial industry in which ALPHA participated is highly regulated but has a very low appetite for risks and uncertainties that cannot be quantified or estimated and assigned probability values. Risk acceptance is seldom a viable option, even if an organization utilizes a documented procedure for accepting risks.

2.3.4.2 Problems of Risk-Based Approach

A risk-based approach, despite its benefits, presents numerous challenges and issues as described below.

2.3.4.2.1 Common Terms Risk-related terms such as threat, vulnerability, attack, adverse event, impact, crisis, and danger are often used loosely,

sometimes in confusing ways that do not differentiate type of occurrence from one another. For example, in describing the changing risk environment as a result of new technology and security attacks on the Internet, Egan and Mather (2005) cite "blended threats" and "rapid spreads of these threats" and comment that "the threats are expected to continue to grow." In reality, the probability of occurrence and not the threats can be expected to grow. When an information risk manager conducts a risk assessment, he or she may not understand whether the issues assessed are threats, attacks, vulnerabilities, or risks per se. Confusion of the two terms, *risk assessment* and *risk management*, is also noted in Hoo (2000), and discussed earlier in Section 2.3.4.1.

2.3.4.2.2 Probabilities In analyzing driving safety and seat belt policies in the United Kingdom, John Adams (1999) notes that the probability of loss in the context of a risk assessment is different from the probabilities related to throwing a pair of dice. Unlike dice, information risk events are not necessarily deterministic, and the outcome of information risk is not independent of previous or other risks (or throws).

If we are to apply statistical measurement of risk, we must collect and analyze information about similar earlier events, and project the past statistical trend into the future to make a predictive judgment. As noted by Blakley (2001) and Hoo (2000), we lack data and consensus in data formats (and schemas) that would permit accurate statistical measurements of risk. Even if these constraints were resolved, we still face issues related to the use of statistical data. As highlighted in Levinson, data quality, sample size, population, and expertise of the risk assessor impact the conclusions of a risk assessment in various ways:

> Reaching conclusions about an entire population from the statistics of a sample is like enlarging a photograph. Small defects are magnified into serious blemishes. If a sample does not take proper account of the classes that make up the population it is supposed to represent, it is called a biased sample.
>
> But the failure of a sample to take account of all possible distinctions by no means proves that it is a biased sample. It is only the omission of essential distinctions that renders a sample inadequate, and it is not always evident in advance which characteristics will turn out to be essential. This indicates a fundamental difficulty against which the statistician (and the critic of statistics) must be continually on guard. In a sense he cannot know with certainty how to collect the data for his sample until his investigation is in an advanced stage. He may find, for instance, after exercising every precaution that his data contain some unknown disturbing factor, and this may be due to the failure to separate in his sample two classes that should have been separated.
>
> When the statistician is himself in control of the collection of the data for his investigation, the difficulty is not insuperable, although it may mean a large added amount of labor. But when he is forced to use data collected by

others, perhaps for entirely different purposes, and possibly years ago, he is in danger of finding himself with a hopeless statistical problem on his hands. All this requires the soundest sort of judgment, for which no amount of technical mathematical skill is an adequate substitute.

On the other hand, the statistician with a defective knowledge of higher mathematics will find that the technical aspects of the subject absorb an undue proportion of his attention and energies, to the detriment of his handling of the investigation as a whole. If he has no knowledge of higher mathematics, he is incompetent and has no business to conduct a statistical investigation.

In addition to the danger of reaching false conclusions due to a biased sample, there is the danger of reaching equally false conclusions because the sample is too small (Levinson 1963).

Boyne (2003) adds that "if neither a priori nor statistical measurement of risk is possible, we are forced to resort to 'estimates.'" When a risk issue is estimated to have a profound impact, it is likely to receive a higher rating. Adams (1999) remarks that "when risks become perceptible, when the odds are publicly quoted, the information is acted upon in ways that alter the odds." The accuracy of quantitative risk analysis therefore becomes subjective and this subjective nature is likely to produce an incorrect assessment, leaving weaknesses (or weak links) in a system with a false sense of security.

2.3.4.2.3 Risks of Risk Analysis Charette (1991) comments that "the premier risk in doing any risk analysis is that the recommendations for the management of the risks reached are inaccurate." An overestimation of risk would require an excessive amount of mitigation effort—beyond what is truly required—to overcome the perceived risk. Conversely, underestimation would probably create a false sense of security and undesirable surprises, often coupled with management panic about how to react to the unplanned consequences. In both cases, confidence in a risk assessment and recommendations would be affected in subsequent analysis.

Ironically, the true value of a highly accurate risk analysis would also be subverted because the risk would be considered effectively managed and no adverse events or losses would be expected. Justifying more resources or continuation of the risk management activities would probably not receive appropriate management attention.

Risk analysis has also been misused in organizational politics to resist change and maintain the status quo. It is also used as a form of blame analysis leading to intimidation instead of improvement of a situation (Charette 1991). Adams (1999) argues that

Risk is a continuously reflexive phenomenon; we all, routinely, monitor our environments for signs of safety or danger and modify our behavior in response to our observations—thereby modifying our environment and

provoking further rounds of responses ad infinitum. [As such,] the act of measurement alters that which is being measured (p. 23).

As potential events instead of certainties are assessed, the assessment cannot
be subjected to quality control, and the value of an analysis therefore cannot
be ascertained (Charette 1991).

2.3.4.2.4   Costs   Charette (1991) and Summers (1997) note that "risk analysis has its own costs" that include software tools and the time and expenses
incurred by the analyst in completing the analysis. Despite finding that "the
results are imprecise and lack empirical validation," Summers (1997), citing
Perry (1985) and Baskerville (1991), comments that:

> Risk analysis is worth doing, even when not mandated. It provides insight into
> security and improves security awareness, and sometimes it is the only way to
> justify expenditures on security. Risk analysis gives managers a familiar kind
> of information— measures of costs and potential gains and losses (p. 616).

2.3.4.2.5   Risk Identification and Perception   In many ways, the media,
both press and broadcasting, also play a significant role in providing risk
information by influencing the perceptions of stakeholders and other opin-
ion providers including risk analysts. According to Boyne (2003), "When the
media tell the public about risks, they will do so in relatively simple terms,
based on official and attributable sources, reducing access damage to their
channels of support as far as reasonably possible; and they will do all this
in such a way as to maximize sales." The proliferation of online and print
media has introduced additional risk and uncertainty factors into the analysis process.

2.3.4.2.6   Management   According to Magretta (2002), management as a
business discipline has been regarded as the most important innovation of
the past century:

> Management makes organizations possible; good management makes them
> work well.... Management's business is building organizations that work....
> Underneath all the theory and the tools, underneath all the specialized
> knowledge, lies a commitment to performance.... Organizations are chang-
> ing dramatically, and they are taking new forms but, without organization of
> some sort, nothing would get done.

Drucker (1973) cautions that "bureaucracy, a management that has come to
misconceive itself as an end and the institution as a means, is the degenera-
tive disease to which managements are prone and especially those managements that do not stand under the discipline of the market test."

In the context of information security risk management, few studies focus on the management and organizational aspects of information security risk, particularly from Drucker's perspective of minimizing bureaucracy. Many articles and standards [Alberts and Dorofee (2002), Stoneburner et al. (2002), ISO/IEC 13335-1 (2004), and ISO/IEC CD 13335-2 (2005)] focused on the techniques and mechanics of conducting risk assessments. More recent and relevant work on the management aspects of information security risk management revolved around what is now known as ISMSs. For example, BS7799-2 (BSI 1999b), Bjorck (2005), and ISO/IEC IS 27001 (2005e) mainly address the mechanics of implementing and operating risk management processes in organizations.

The underlying motivation for risk management remains as an approach to prioritize and allocate limited resources to gain the highest return, putting aside issues and problems that are seemingly insignificant. While it is critical to focus on efficient utilization of resources in significant risk areas, the overall performance of information risk management should not be limited to resource allocation. Blakley et al. (2001) report the lack of studies and discourse relating to the issues and challenges of managing people, organization, structure, financial and other resource allocations, and performance in the course of managing information security:

> We also know very little about the effectiveness of the measures we take to prevent adverse events or alleviate their consequences. The people to whom these events happen have few incentives to report them; conversely, they have many incentives to suppress information about them. Finally, the system we are attempting to protect (roughly composed of the global Internet and everything attached to it) is far too complex to be understood in detail (p. 100).

Essentially, the existing approach of risk management leaves certain issues and risks as they are, based on the results of risk assessments and business priorities. These issues and related risks may also be assessed inaccurately and therefore run the risk of becoming the weakest links in the system. Anderson (2001a) summarizes the issues from the perspective of security engineering[23] relevant to business organizations:

> Risk management may be one of the world's largest industries. It includes not just security engineers but also fire and casualty services, insurers, the road safety industry and much of the legal profession. Yet it is startling how little is really known about the subject. Engineers, economists, actuaries and lawyers all come at the problem from different directions, use different language and arrive at quite incompatible conclusions.
>
> There are also strong cultural factors at work. For example, if we distinguish risk as being where the odds are known but the outcome isn't, from uncertainty where even the odds are unknown, then most people appear to

be more uncertainty-averse than risk-averse. Where the odds are directly perceptible, a risk is often dealt with intuitively; but where the science is unknown or inconclusive, people are liberated to project all sorts of fears and prejudices. So perhaps the best medicine is education. Nonetheless, there are some specific things that the security engineer should either do, or avoid (p. 492).

Anderson concludes that the issues relating to information security risk management "are amongst the most important—and most difficult—of any in our field, but receive little attention, because they lie at the boundaries with software engineering, applied psychology, economics, and management." This further supports the need to identify or develop suitable approaches to address the questions of information security risk management from a social–technical perspective in an organizational context.

2.3.5 A Circular Problem

The above analysis of the four common security principles shows a circular connection by returning to the original problem of the weakest link, which is where the analysis started (Figure 2.1). Approaches based on these four principles without considering their circular nature are inadequate for addressing the needs of information security and the fundamental issues of the weakest link that unfortunately prevail in today's business environments and information systems.

To achieve progress, new approaches should not add to the circularity of current principles. The need to consider the circularity problem should be one of the criteria for assessing the quality of newly proposed principles for addressing the information risk management challenges.

Figure 2.1 Circular problem of information security principles.

2.3.6   IT Security Governance

Based on events such as the collapses of Barings Bank (Leeson 1996, BBC Online 1999, Degraeve 2004, Colombo 2005, Holton 2006a) and Enron (Bazerman and Watkins 2004, Holton 2006b, Greenspan 2007), "legislatures, statutory authorities, and regulators have created a complex array of new laws and regulations designed to force improvement in organizational governance, security, controls and transparency" (Brotby et al. 2006).

Through the adoption of new regulations such as the Sarbanes–Oxley Act of 2002 (Moeller 2004), noncompliance impacted business organizations and imposed personal liabilities on the executive officers responsible for such financial catastrophes. As noted by Byrum (2003), "a strong IT security control structure is crucial to Sarbanes [-Oxley] compliance."

> Without it, management will have to either disclose a significant deficiency in the corporate internal control structure or expose the organization's executive officers to personal liability in the case that they certify inaccurate financial statements. While the legislation may not have been specifically written to address IT security controls, as compliance efforts progress, the impact of the Sarbanes–Oxley Act on IT security will be substantial.

Based on growing threats of information system disruption and security breaches from hackers and terrorists, the need for a governance approach to information management has been recognized widely. For example, the Basel Committee of Banking Supervision stated in a 2003 report:

> Because the board of directors and senior management are responsible for developing the institution's business strategy and establishing an effective management oversight over risks, they are expected to take an explicit, informed and documented strategic decision as to whether and how the bank is to provide e-banking services. ... Effective management oversight is expected to encompass the review and approval of the key aspects of the bank's security control process, such as the development and maintenance of a security control infrastructure that properly safeguards e-banking systems and data from both internal and external threats. It also should include a comprehensive process for managing risks associated with increased complexity of and increasing reliance on outsourcing relationships and third-party dependencies to perform critical e-banking functions.

The IT Governance Institute (Brotby et al. 2006) further states that:

> Whilst senior executives have the responsibility to consider and respond to the concerns and sensitivities raised by information security, boards of directors will increasingly be expected to make information security an intrinsic

part of governance, integrated with processes they already have in place to govern other critical organizational resources.

The institute proposed five basic outcomes of information security governance that include risk management as a key outcome. The governance approach places information security emphasis at the senior executive level of an organization and gives an information security manager an appropriate mandate to drive his or her programs and initiatives. Understanding information risk management and having a suitable strategy for devising and implementing appropriate programs for execution are key success factors for delivering the objectives of the governance model.

My review of the motivation for risk management principles and current knowledge in the field reveals inadequacies in the current information risk management discipline. They result in weak links that may be subjectively assessed as low risk issues, potentially jeopardizing the governance of information security. The governance approach brought security to the top management level, giving it the highest level of attention required, but it also created another challenge for risk managers.

Most senior managers have limited time to discuss risk management issues and therefore require all details to be summarized to short paragraphs on one or two pages along with graphics and charts in quantitative formats where possible. Risk managers are therefore driven to eliminate uncertainties and improve performance based on the quantitative figures and tend to focus on showing returns on investments, improvement in security-related scorecards (or dashboards) and related measures such as the number of audit issues and security incidents, and the status of mitigation. Compliance and controls are again keys to improving the values captured in quantitative matrices.

As reported in a survey conducted by Ernst & Young, 81 percent of the respondents[24] rated "complying with corporate policies" as one of the most important information security functions" (Ernst & Young 2005). The question of whether such an improvement in quantitative measures will translate into improved information security in organizations, however, has not been answered in the current literature. Vijayan (2005) also reports that corporate security executives expressed similar concerns about this development.

The above review of risk assessment indicates that quantitative and qualitative measures are not ready to provide accurate measurements of risk. Based on the studies conducted by Adams (1995, 1999), Boyne (2003), and Lupton (1999) discussed in earlier sections, quantitative measures will always have limitations, and risk measurement will continue to be subjective due to the effects of risk perception and risk compensation. The field therefore needs more studies to devise better approaches for addressing the issues and dilemmas of information security and managing the related risk. Specifically, the following thematic questions should be addressed:

1. What should an information risk manager do differently? How should his or her strategy and plan for managing information security risk be changed so that it will not result in a compliance-driven and/or control-oriented security culture?
2. How should an information risk manager control information security risk in a constantly changing business and IT risk environment? How should he or she manage (a) security risk development in the information technology arena that could disrupt the business and/ or IT operations, and (b) changes in the business and/or IT strategy and implementation that could significantly change the organization's risk posture?

2.4   Information Security Risk Management Strategy

Risk management is used to identify significant risk areas and prioritize and allocate resources for resolution. Baseline controls and security technology are designed to address specific concerns. However, they are tactical and task-oriented, but not strategic. According to Vincent LeVegue (2006):

> The basic design of a strategy involves a situation, a target, and a path. ... The situation for an information security strategy is the organization's current environment, consisting of the current technology and management environment. ... The target for an information security strategy is the desired management system (organization structure, staffing, reporting relationships, policies, and procedures) and the desired technical system (computing devices and networks).... The path for an information security strategic plan is the set of project plans designed to advance from the current state to the proposed future state (pp. 1–2).

"Strategy enables us to quickly make the right decisions so that we do not simply react" (Gagliardi 2004). In information security risk management, a management strategy is necessary for developing an information security program (as discussed in Section 2.5) and helps management decide on suitable actions when faced with contentious risk issues.

In the current literature, the concept of information security risk management strategy[25] has not been widely discoursed. The strategy topic is applied casually when describing specific action plans or programs; see APEC-TEL (2004a) and PricewaterhouseCoopers (2003). Strategies may be defensive or offensive. Consideration of the use of offensive strategy in achieving information security in business organizations has been very limited, except for example, in relation to information warfare[26] (Denning 1999, Kittler 1998) and bounty programs[27] (La Monica 2003). The focus of this book is on defensive strategies. Two fundamental strategies are: (1) protect–detect–react and (2) detect–react–protect.

2.4.1 Protect–Detect–React (PDR)

In practice, a common *de facto* strategy that shapes the thinking of information risk managers in devising plans is the PDR model composed of the following high-level steps:

1. Attempt to *protect* information resources against identified risks, mainly through prevention or avoidance of attacks, and/or reduction if not elimination of vulnerabilities, by controlling the behavior of the system and/or people involved.
2. Attempt to *detect* unauthorized behavior or activities in and around the system, mainly through monitoring, regular security, and log or audit trail reviews, penetration and vulnerability testing, and/or observations to identify human or system-identifiable unacceptable behavior or patterns. Detection may serve as an additional layer of security (as in defense in depth), or as a compensating measure when no other deployable protective measure can be used against an identified vulnerability.
3. Prepare to *react* or respond when an undesirable event is detected or has occurred. In practice, this includes two main tasks in the information security plan, i.e., incident handling and management, and business continuity planning and disaster recovery.

The PDR strategy has been widely accepted, with a few variations used in practice environments. For example, Microsoft (2006a) defines plan–protect–detect–respond as strategic categories. Doll et al. (2003) cite the three Rs of digital security (restrict–run–recover) to regroup after PDR.

2.4.2 Detect–React–Protect (DRP)

From a timeliness perspective, Schwartau (2001) discovers that the PDR model, if executed in the protect–detect–react sequence would provide adequate security for an organization only when the time required for the protective measures to be overcome exceeds the total time for detection of a security breach and the time before the security team reacts to the problem. In other words, the following equation must hold true to secure the organization:

$$Pt > (Dt + Rt)$$

Pt denotes the protection time; Dt is the detection time; and Rt indicates the reaction time. If Pt is less than $(Dt + Rt)$, the difference would provide a perpetrator a time gap to compromise a system or information asset without detection and reaction on the part of the organization. The result could be damage or losses to the organization.

Based on this concept, Schwartau suggests reordering of the PDR model as a time-based security strategy utilizing a detect–react–protect (DRP) sequence. DRP emphasizes detection and reaction over protection. If an organization has the ability to detect and react to security events promptly, even without protection, many incidents may be prevented or avoided. This strategy can result in significant savings since the costs of protection may be reduced or eliminated. However, the additional cost for devising and implementing a timely detection and reaction security system may be significant.

Cohen (1998) comments in a review of an early edition of Schwartau's book titled *Time-Based Security* (1981) that using time as a metric to measure security was not a new idea but was nevertheless an important element for evaluating security.[28] Cohen also expresses reservations about the assumptions Schwartau used relating to greater emphasis on detection:

> Detection has its own problems, the chief one being that detection can never be done perfectly in practice. There are always false positives and false negatives and detection takes time. Even if we had perfect and instantaneous detection, our ability to effectively respond is limited by the fact that we don't know how to do appropriate response based on the situation and response itself takes time.

On equating the cost of security to time:

> It seems clear that if we are to measure time in terms of money, we need financial models of situations. This in turn requires a system of modeling in which the model changes as dynamically as the environment it models. The model must be fed financial and security information on an ongoing basis and the set of prevention, detection, and response capabilities must be adapted with time to meet the changing business environment (Cohen 1998).

Citing *The Art of War*, a military classic by the renowned Chinese General Sun Tzu, Gagliardi (2004) notes that it is not possible to have a perfect strategy since new challenges will always appear:

> We must also understand that no position is perfect for meeting every challenge, and there is no position that does not degrade over time. There is no ultimate victory that ends the strategic struggle. There is no final resting place

where everything is perfect. No matter how far we advance, we will always be confronted with new challenges (p. 19).

Similarly, although the four elements—protection, detection, reaction, and time—identified in current literature are not perfect, they are nevertheless important issues to be assessed in devising a security plan. At a minimum, they provide a useful starting point for developing a successful security strategy.

2.4.3   Need for Strategic Thinking

In addition to the PDR and DRP strategy models, practitioners like Venables (2004) and Wang (2005) have developed enterprise-specific strategies for managing information risks in their respective organizations. Venables observes that "security is an emergent property of a complex system," and suggests that we rethink and change the strategy and approaches based on the theory of complexity. Wang attributes the constant failure of organizational security programs to the lack of strategic thinking and the formulation of business organization-specific security strategies that often do not align with business strategies. These enterprise-specific initiatives that evolve from practice signal the lack of strategic thinking in the information security risk management literature. In the aftermath of the 9/11 tragedy, Yourdon (2002) notes that the increased proliferation and convergence of IT, rapid changes in IT and related risks, and globalization created a need to reevaluate existing approaches to risk management from multiple strategic perspectives and effect a necessary paradigm shift to continue to achieve the objectives of business.

2.5   Information Security Program

In line with LeVegue's (2006) concept of a "path" as part of a strategy, an information risk manager must develop an information security program to implement the selected approaches[29] to achieve the objectives for the business. Also known as an information security plan (Bhagyavati and Hicks 2003) or a corporate information assets protection program (Kovacich 2003), an information security program is an integral part of an information security strategy. It provides the blueprint for achieving an organization's information security objectives.

Summarizing current literature, seven major areas are considered in an information security program: (1) organization and people; (2) risk assessment and management; (3) policies; (4) communication (to ensure awareness), education, and training; (5) development, including designs of applications, systems, and products; (6) operational security, including administration, monitoring, response, and recovery; and (7) performance measurements.

2.5.1 Organization and People

The mission and vision of an organization determine the design of the organizational structure and roles and responsibilities within the information security risk management (ISRM) function. The line of reporting and hierarchical layers between ISRM and senior executive management also influence the amount of authority and range of influence of the ISRM function on the rest of the organization.

The organizational structure of the ISRM function may be centralized or decentralized. The former requires the establishment of a core corporate-wide ISRM function as a service to support various businesses and divisions. In this structure, the ISRM function may report to the CIO, chief operating officer (COO), chief technology officer (CTO), or an equivalent senior executive. In a decentralized structure, the ISRM function operates within a specific division, with only a small strategic group at corporate level providing coordination and standardization support to ensure consistent policies and practices among business groups. For more detailed discussion of the various information security organizational models along with samples of mission statements, see Dorey (1994), Kovacich (2003), Kowalski (1995), Maiwald and Sieglein (2002), and Summers (1997).

Both organizational models and combinations of centralized and decentralized controls present benefits and challenges. However, few accounts in the literature explain how these models influence the practices of information security risk managers, strategies for managing information security risk in organizations, or the state of security operations in practice. More importantly, discussions about security organization models in the literature reviewed seldom consider the implications of the rapidly changing risk environment or current issues such as mergers and acquisitions, outsourcing, and the changing IT landscape that were characteristic of organizational changes when research was conducted for this book.

People are often regarded as weak links in a security chain. This concept applies to users, operators, developers, and managers of IT systems and information assets and people working in the information risk management function. In addition to the need to improve security awareness and competence of people in organizations in general, Blakley et al. (2001) note that lack of formal education and professionalism are key issues challenging the information risk management profession. While professional certification schemes (e.g., the Certified Information Systems Security Professional or CISSP certification[30]) have existed since the late 1980s, no requirements cover licensing requirements for information risk managers or obligate information risk managers to report important risk incidents or information to proper authorities.

Blakley et al. (2001) suggest the inclusion of a "broader and integrated view" for risk treatment to improve the competence of information risk managers. This suggestion leads to questions about how information risk managers should learn and keep their knowledge current and relevant, particularly in a rapidly changing risk environment. These issues have not been addressed adequately in the literature.

2.5.2   Risk Assessment and Management

As discussed in Section 2.3.4.1, risk assessment and management are key topics attracting numerous studies, but they also raise more questions, given the issues and dilemmas highlighted in Section 2.3.4.2. As a result these topics serve as the focus of the research reported in this book.

2.5.3   Policies

Information security policy is considered a critical element for achieving information security in an organization (Shain 1994, Whitman 2003). A security policy is a fundamental need of every information security program. For example, the US government measures the security maturity of government departments by their use of security policies (NIST 2000). Most security surveys ask about the existence of a security policy. AusCERT (2002, 2003, 2004, 2005), PricewaterhouseCoopers and DTI (2002, 2004), Bogolea and Wijekumar (2004), Whitman (2003), and others consider a security policy as a key indicator of the security posture of an organization:

> Although the term "policy" is widely used, it did not have a clear and unambiguous definition. "Policy" may be used to mean a broad orientation, an indication of normal practice, a specific commitment, or a statement of values.... That the term is so widely used suggests that the idea of "policy" has a wide appeal, which leads to its being mobilized in a range of social settings (Colebatch 2002).

"Security policies define the security philosophy and posture the organization takes, and are the basis for all subsequent security decisions and implementations" (Whitman 2003).[31] Dorey (1994) further states that in a commercial organization, policies "provide a mechanism where the directors and senior management can lay down a clear statement of direction and 'rules' for the successful operation of the company." Effective security policies help to "define security requirements, allocate responsibilities" and contribute to the development of security measures and the control environment.

Guidelines and templates for writing information security policies are widely available. Dorey (1994) clarifies the differences among policies, procedures, guidelines, and standards. Wood (1995) provides policy templates that can be used to ensure consistency of policy statements.

In practice, however, frequent policy failures have become critical issues. Control Data Systems (1999) cites organizations' failures to recognize the four key factors of security (1) if not designed and managed appropriately, security is a barrier to progress; (2) security is a learned behavior; (3) an organization should expect the unexpected; and (4) "there is no perfect mousetrap."

Many ready-to-copy policy templates are available (Wood 1995) for quick adoption. It has become easy for risk managers to take a shortcut approach to policy development and bypass the necessary risk assessment step that ensures that appropriate policies are developed to address specific risks. Also, many managers are reluctant to change policies that have been published because the revision process is often long and tedious. Rees et al. (2003) cite the problem of "keeping up with the increasing rate of change in technology or applications."

Colebatch (2002) proposes a life-cycle approach that "sees policy as a logical succession of steps" for addressing policy failures. Control Data Systems suggests a three-stage life-cycle (formulation and maintenance, enforcement, and assurance). Rees et al. (2003) propose a Policies Framework for Information Security (PFIRES) incorporating distinct stages: assess, plan, deliver, operate.

Rees et al. (2003) suggest using the PFIRES life-cycle approach to facilitate communications between senior management and technical security management for an organization to be "better positioned to successfully achieve its objectives." However, they recognize that "much work remains to be done in this area" relating to "international and regional concerns, organizational behavior, legal issues, supply chain factors, and industry-specific concerns." These are "a few areas that would benefit from an in-depth exploration of related information security policy." They also recommend more research to determine "how well the life cycle meets the policy management needs of today's organizations and what improvements need to be made to ensure future success."

A social construction perspective on policy, which differs from the life-cycle approach, sees policy as "something that has to be constructed and sustained by the participants in circumstances where they are likely to have choices about which interpretive map to use, which cues to follow."

> It draws on work in a range of the social sciences—sociology, social psychology, organizational analysis and the 'governmentality' approach deriving from the work of Michel Foucault—all of which ask 'what makes for collective action?', and see this as the question to be answered (Colebatch 2002, p. 4).

In a rapidly changing information risk environment in which behavior and actions exert significant influence on the outcome of addressing security issues, such an approach toward policy construction and evaluation justifies further examination. The attributes of policies include order, authority, and expertise, but policies also limit choices. They form the basis for "interrogating organized activities" (for example, in auditing and enforcement of policies). The outcomes and processes are both important factors (Colebatch 2002) to be considered in an information security program.

Traditionally, the need for performance measurement in information security has been de-emphasized by the inclusion of information security requirements in corporate policies. For example, Shain (1994) reports that:

> In practice, resources are invested in safeguards only when there is a net return when measured against organizational goals—whether such goals are chosen or imposed (the latter usually by law or regulation). The need to allocate resources for security controls implies that each organization should understand what it is that should be protected, and why. The answers will determine the choice of protection strategy and this thinking should be captured in security policies generated by management.

When senior management mandates policies, they become parts of business requirements and are seldom challenged, even though they may be ineffective (Colebatch 2002). Relying solely on policies to drive information security objectives is both inefficient and inadequate.

Policies and regulations are static measures and procedures established to address known security risks. A perpetrator who attacks a system looks for the weakest link in the information security chain, often exploiting new weaknesses that policies, regulations, and other protective measures failed to address.[32] At the same time, the weakest link would not necessarily be known to or addressable by risk managers or auditors. Even if they have techniques to keep current about changing vulnerabilities, they have no way to know whether perpetrators may have devised more recent methods since finders may not report incidents for financial, political, or other reasons (Arora et al. 2004).[33]

The time and effort required to effect policy changes to match new or evolving security needs in a changing business and risk environment must be considered. When the efforts and resources required for information security expand beyond basic policy mandates, senior managers begin to question the cost of security. If business systems or information assets are subjected to new attacks that are not addressed by existing policies, information security risk managers will be caught off guard and management will also penalize them for security breaches. The changing threat environment requires information security risk managers to find new ways to justify an investment in information security that exceeds the scope specified in policies.

2.5.4 Communication

The need for communicating information security is motivated by the common belief that "many instances of data loss/corruption or computer service unavailability can be avoided if personnel are properly trained" (Dorey 1994). Several studies have focused on the training aspects of information security programs. Kovacich (2003), Siponen (2000a), and Yngstrom (1995) studied the planning and delivery of security awareness and education programs. Hinson (2005) provides an informative summary on the value of information security awareness. Research institutions such as the Center for Information Systems Security Studies and Research (CISR)[34] have undertaken studies relating to security competency, particularly related to education and curricula for information security students.

The need for a security program to incorporate training to build psychological awareness and resistance to social engineering attacks (requiring employees to challenge strangers and improve understanding of their security responsibilities[35]) was recognized early in the development of the information security field—see Dorey (1994), Mitnick et al. (2002), and Siponen (2000a, b). While studies and suggestions for improving security awareness and practices from a social–psychological view are available (Kabay 1993, 2002), social engineering presents one of the major risks of the Internet.

In a study of the interrelationships and effects of culture and risk communications on setting Internet security goals, Koskosas and Paul (2004) conclude that "these perspectives have an ultimate effect on the level of security goal setting." Studies of the social–technical aspects of information security risk management in organizations are needed to clearly demonstrate the issues and dilemmas in practice and find new strategies and models for improving communications.

2.5.5 Developments

Identifying security requirements and incorporating them into IT systems, applications, and products as part of a systems development life cycle are critical factors leading to the success of an information security operation. IT security measures affect both security outcomes involving information systems, applications, and products and the follow-on operational security and supports. As discussed in Section 2.5.6, poorly designed applications and systems create problems in administration, monitoring, and enforcement of security policies.

Baskerville (1993) utilized a social perspective in studying the security considerations for designing and developing information systems products and applications. Howard and Lipner (2005), Howard and LeBlanc (2003), and others extensively studied the engineering aspects of designing and developing software information security requirements, and implementing them into security development life-cycle practices. The US National Institute of Standards and Technology (NIST) published a formal standard covering this aspect of information security in June 2004. The standard provides security guidance to federal agencies concerning information system development life cycles (Grance et al. 2004).

Howard and Lipner (2005) included a response element in their security development life cycle covering changes and updates that differentiates it from other approaches. The question of how a security development life cycle should support a rapidly changing risk environment remains relatively unexplored.

2.5.6 Operational Security

Operational security is used in two different contexts. In the military, it refers to securing the environment and systems in an operational environment, for example, in a training area or on a battlefield. In business organizations, operational security means operation of security functions as an aspect of IT operation management and encompasses security administration, monitoring, incident response and handling, and business continuity and recovery planning.

In most organizations, using the PDR strategy that is biased toward the use of controls for risk mitigation, the major emphasis is on administration:

Selecting appropriate controls as protective safeguards
Installing and configuring the controls
Maintaining configurations
Administering users' use of systems and related controls (user identifier and password maintenance, user recertification, and maintenance of access control listings)

On the problems of security administration, Dorey (1994) notes that a large amount of "mal-administration" (malfunction administration) including installation, configuration, maintenance, and monitoring relate to the design of applications, products, and systems serving business needs and security requirements. Security requirement considerations, including operational aspects, are critical to operational security. In addition, the technical expertise of the security staff is also crucial. Staff should understand security policies and requirements and be able to combine policies and requirements to determine suitable configurations and parameters for monitoring and enforcement in different use scenarios (Dorey 1994).

While more automation and integration of security management requirements into technical systems and solutions (suggested by Dorey and others) would reduce malfunction administration issues, it is also important to understand the social behaviors arising from a changing risk environment, particularly when an organization undertakes a strategy other than PDR. Understanding social practices and related issues in the operational security areas of an information security program and potential impacts (positive and negative) on security administration and management (related to people, in particular) arising from changes in security strategy is of particular interest in this book.

Besides administration and management, operational security involves planning and executing incident responses, management, business continuity, and disaster recovery planning. Although these areas are considered critical in information security risk management, most of the literature is vertically (silo) oriented and focuses on damage control and recovery; see Greenberg (2003).

Organizations often implement business continuity and disaster recovery planning as separate functions from information security (Dorey 1994) even though they are increasingly regarded as essential elements of information security management systems (ISMS; ISO/IEC 2000, 2005f). Consequently, different groups in an organization often undertake planning and execution of business continuity and disaster recovery.

2.5.7 Performance Measurements

In the United States, a number of new regulations require IT security performance measurements. NIST also issued guidance on "how an organization, through the use of metrics, [can identify] the adequacy of in-place security controls, policies, and procedures" (Swanson et al. 2003). The purpose of the NIST standard (SP 800-55) is to:

> provide an approach to help management decide where to invest in additional security protection resources or identify and evaluate nonproductive controls. It explains the metric development and implementation process and how it can also be used to adequately justify security control investments (Swanson et al. 2003)

Such metrics, however, focus on measuring the effectiveness of security controls implemented and fail to measure how well an information risk manager performed in the areas of risk assessment, security control design and selection, and implementation.

Updated security standards such as ISO/IEC 27001 (2005e) also emphasize the need for and importance of performance and effectiveness of the information security management system requirements they promulgated. New standards for measuring the performance of information security management systems in relation to the implementation of ISO/IEC 27001 have also been developed (ISO/IEC 2009b). They complement the earlier NIST (Chew et al. 2006) guidance on performance metrics for information security (SP 800-80).

The various standards and guidance propose a programmatic approach for aligning performance measurements to the objectives of information security. One of the common measurements of the effectiveness of information security is the state of security delivered by an information security program. Maiwald and Sieglein (2002) discuss two methods of reporting: metrics and risk. Metric reporting considers measurable security attributes such as the numbers of system vulnerabilities, policy configuration violations, detected attacks, employees reached by security awareness programs, failed access attempts, and security incidents. These parameters reflect the stability of the risk environment. Risk level is affected by the effectiveness of risk reduction activities in an information security risk management program. The successful completion of risk reduction activities helps reduce or even eliminate information-related risks.

The utility of the proposed metrics of Maiwald and Sieglein (2002) is limited. Organizations that implement preventive security controls may enjoy periods of stability (few or no security incidents) until a security exposure is discovered or an incident occurs. The length of a stability period is always uncertain. No incident may have occurred because a perpetrator has not yet identified an organization as a viable target or has not yet found a profitable use for the known vulnerabilities of an organization at a given point in time. Similarly, a perpetrator may be conducting subtle reconnaissance of identified exposures while planning a major attack that will surprise the victim organization. Using stability (counting incidents, vulnerabilities, and violations) is an inadequate measurement of the security status of an organization.

A detrimental side effect of using stability as a measurement is the false sense of comfort of senior management when no incidents are reported. As a result management may see no need for further investments in security protection. Nonetheless, when a newly discovered vulnerability results in a security incident, losses or damages will be incurred. Management will question the effectiveness of the risk manager, the cost of security, and the organization's return on investment even though the seriousness of the incident may be insignificant. An incident involving significant damage may also cost the information risk manager his or her job.

Clearly, if known risks and attacks continue to result in negative impacts, the risk manager's approaches and measures will be questionable. He or she must reevaluate and change the security strategy and tactics to address the impacts. Experiencing a large number of security incidents involving known risks[36] is unacceptable even though the numbers are not adequate indicators of performance. Few or no incidents do not indicate that an organization is well protected. Security incidents and the security status of an organization have a nonlinear relationship. It is necessary to also consider other aspects of associated events when incorporating them in performance measurement.

In addition to the use of metrics and risk, Maiwald and Sieglein (2002) suggest tracking the return on security investment (ROSI) to determine how security facilitates business opportunities and/or produces cost savings, for example, reduced insurance premiums due to better security. The use of economic models such as ROSI to evaluate security investments recently garnered substantial interest in the research arena and numerous models and approaches have been published, for example, Gordon and Loeb (2002), Mercuri (2003), and Rodewald (2005). For a comprehensive list, see Anderson (2006). Cavusoglu et al. (2004) observe that:

> The lack of a comprehensive model that incorporates the specific features of IT security technologies has prevented firms from applying rigorous quantitative techniques to make security investment decisions. The current set of tools such as risk analysis and cost effectiveness analysis work with very high-level aggregate data, so these tools are of limited value in an IT security setting.

Cavusoglu et al. (2004) propose a probability model to evaluate IT security investment based on the potential damage from a materialized risk. A risk assessment is a prerequisite to the use of this model. The value of alternative IT security investments, for example, setting up a perimeter network infrastructure against the risk of potential hacking attacks on the company network versus acquiring such a network infrastructure from a third party network provider is analyzed against the potential damages to determine the optimal approach based on the maximum cost savings among the alternatives.

One challenge in such an approach (and in other cost-based analyses of security investments) is its heavy reliance on past incident data and predictions of similar incidents in the future. The assumption of a similar incident covers only a limited scope of potential risk for an organization and does not adequately consider uncertainties. As noted in Section 2.3.4.2, probability and statistical measurements present certain limitations that make such techniques subjective.

Cost savings figures are misleading. It is not always possible to establish a clear relationship between past incidents that have not recurred and the financial outcome of a security investment.[37] More importantly, future incidents will likely be different. Hackers may use another method of attack or select another target. It is difficult to predict the vulnerabilities that they might exploit, the scale of an attack, and potential impacts. The ability of a security investment to protect against new types of attacks would be an obvious benefit. However, if a security investment focuses only on past issues, it may be unable to withstand future attacks that employ different tactics, exploit new vulnerabilities, or combine known techniques in a well orchestrated manner as described in Richmond (2011).

If an investment is to address new attacks, it faces the challenge of predicting the types and tactics of attacks including their possible impacts since no data about future attacks would be available. The use of such an approach is thus limited to justifying spending (or investing) against known (identifiable) risks, in particular, pervasive risks that recur easily in the absence of specific protection.

Citing Marin (1992), Bjorck (2005) asserts that "the optimum level of security, from a strict financial perspective, will be found in the situation in which the cost of *additional* security countermeasures *exactly equals* the *resulting* reduction in damages arising from security breaches." Optimum security means profit maximization for an organization (Bjorck 2005). Citing Adams (1995), Bjorck also reports that:

> In many cases, the total cost of current security countermeasures and the damages arising from current security breaches are not known. And, looking into the future, the potential costs-and-benefits of new countermeasures are even more challenging to estimate.

From a regulatory perspective emphasizing management accountability, members of senior management could potentially face risks of incarceration if they focus too much of their effort on return on investment (Berghel 2005).

One approach adopted by some organizations to determine their security status is benchmarking security practices, incident counts, financial and/or reputation impacts from incidents, audit ratings, and a series of other measures and compare their results with those of other organizations in the same industry. This approach presents several limitations. The timeliness of information and responses, the organizational and risk culture, and the operations practices often differ even among companies in the same industry. An alternative approach suggested by Bjorck (2005) is to perform an "evaluation benchmark" against specific standards such as the ISO/IEC 27002 (2005f) and ISO/IEC 27001 (2005e). While standards provide comprehensive scope of coverage, their use should be based on an assessment of an organization's information risks and requirements.

Benchmarking provides only an indication of the maturity of an organization's information security practices compared with information about peers or from selected standards. It does not reflect the risks and uncertainties of information risk management. The usefulness of benchmarking is also limited from a budgetary view (Jones 2006). The challenges of current approaches to performance measurement confirm the need to address other questions relating to the thematic concerns of the study:

> How should organizations resolve the conflict between the performance measurements of the information risk manager and the outcome of a security incident? Should the information risk manager's performance reflect the security risk status of the organization, or, in other words, what should the relationship be between his/her performance and the security status of the organization?

While measuring performance and effectiveness of security (in terms of investment or resources used) is critical from a management perspective, the measurable items are past events that indicate only the likelihood of the organization to survive in a *known* risk environment. To understand the true status of security, organizations must move from understanding the past to dealing with the present. The existing literature lacks information about what should be monitored and measured to determine present risk status and how to translate the measurements to assess an organization's ability to deal with changes in the risk environment. This is another issue requiring further studies, and supports another research question:

> How should information risk managers manage the information security risk in a constantly changing business and IT risk environment, such as (a) security risk development in the information technology arena that could disrupt the business and/or IT operations, and (b) changes in the business and/or IT strategy and implementation that could significantly change the organization's risk posture?

2.6   Responding to Change

As observed from the literature review covering the scope of information security risk management discussed earlier, one recurring theme in current studies is dealing with changes in the risk environment. The review shows that responding to change has become a key factor in ensuring effective information security risk management. Anderson (2001b), Yourdon (2002), and Gupta et al. (2002) study the problems of information security management from different perspectives and also reflect this view.

From a macroeconomic perspective, Anderson observes that "information insecurity is at least as much due to perverse incentives." Network externalities may cause commercial systems to delay introducing new features (including security features) until the next version for reasons of economics. Nevertheless, changes in technology systems are ongoing. Also for competitive reasons, "constant struggles to entrench or undermine monopolies and to segment and control markets" continue and affect many of the environmental conditions that security systems must monitor and address. Over time and due to market pressures, security technology and IT systems will improve in resiliency and reliability. However, they will not reach a point of 100 percent or almost 100 percent security (Anderson 2001b). The "no perfect security" principle in Section 2.3.3 verifies this fact.

From an information warfare view, the technical bias favors the attackers rather than the defenders because defenders have large surface areas to protect. An attacker needs to find only a single weak link to strike. This one-sided advantage is aggravated by the theory of asymmetrical information that encourages potential attackers to keep secret the vulnerabilities they find so they can use them for later attacks or simply sell them for profit (Grow et al. 2005). Reporting vulnerabilities to vendors would help them protect their customers (defenders) and make the attacks harder to accomplish.

Macroeconomic analysis shows that "the management of information security is a very much deeper and more political problem than is usually realized; solutions are likely to be subtle and partial, while many simplistic technical approaches are bound to fail" (Anderson 2001b). In analyzing the security implications after the September 11, 2001 attacks (Kean et al. 2004), Yourdon (2002) asserts the need for a paradigm shift in risk management:

> [T]oday's risks can occur and then change so quickly, and because they may involve completely unfamiliar situations, the "official" information about risk-status and risk-mitigation may be obsolete, misleading, ambiguous, or downright wrong. When given information about potentially serious risks, it's extremely important to look for alternate, independent sources of information—e.g., from news media in other countries—before reaching a conclusion about what to do (p. 154).

An experimental analysis of the implications of security policies and risk management approaches in online banking systems by Gupta et al. (2002) showed that being "proactive in recognizing the threats and devising policies to counter them generated greater revenue and [they] were able to focus on the core activities." From a management strategy perspective, Gagliardi (2004) commented:

> We must also understand that no position is perfect for meeting every challenge, and there is no position that does not degrade over time. There is no ultimate victory that ends the strategic struggle. There is no final resting place where everything is perfect. No matter how far we advance, we will always be confronted with new challenges (p. 19).

In numerous studies that call for paradigm changes or new strategies to address information security risk management [Hoo (2000), Dhillon and Backhouse (2000, 2001), Blakley et al. (2001), Yourdon (2002), and Bjorck

(2005)] none has been specific about how to respond to change when managing information risks in organizations. The current literature focuses on changes arising from Internet proliferation and how to address the information security issues resulting from the changes. Dealing with or managing change is a major aspect of current paradigms, strategies, and approaches. In the practice environment, change has also been recognized as a significant contributor to IT failures (Mayengbam 2006).

2.7 Current Research and Social Perspectives

In recent years, researchers have undertaken more studies on the combined topics of information security and risk management and focused on (1) the economics of information security (Anderson 2001b, Gordon and Loeb 2002, Anderson and Moore 2006, 2007) that contribute to quantitative measurements of information risks and related investments; and (2) social aspects of information security management for gaining better understanding of information security risk management practices including the design and implementation of security management programs, awareness, education, and training (Dhillon and Backhouse 2001, Clarke and Drake 2003).

The interest in the economics of information security risks should foster better understanding of information security in relation to business risk and the cost focus of management when deciding on security spending. The understanding that people are often the weakest links in a security chain further motivates studies on the social aspects of information security. In studying the technical aspects, including the economics, researchers should consider the social implications and leverage the psychological and social characteristics of individual and group behaviors to advance the practice of information security.

Studies by Clarke and Drake (2003) and Dhillon and Backhouse (2001) that adopt the sociological paradigms of Burrell and Morgan (1979) indicate that most research and literature about information security contain predominantly technical and functionalist preconceptions. The materials are largely rule-based and control-oriented when suggesting strategies for and solutions to information security problems.

Dhillon and Backhouse (2001) attribute this to the methods that are mostly "grounded in a particular well-defined reality, i.e., that of the military." Attribution, however, is not the only issue. As discussed in Section 2.2, researchers tend to take a reductionist approach to information security problems. Most studies focus on the data instead of the information and technology instead of systems.

Clarke and Drake (2003) observe a "poor theoretical grounding for information security as a discipline, and literature which is available casts the field as one focusing on secrecy and restriction, in which a rule-based approach is seen to be relevant." In a previous review, I found that their claim that current research focused mainly on secrecy (or confidentiality) was not accurate (Kang 2004). For example, the sequence of information flow and information integrity and availability were studied and emphasized as early as the 1980s, in Clark and Wilson (1987). As highlighted in Section 2.2, Parker (1998) suggests several limitations relating to the use of the confidentiality, integrity, and availability model and proposed the additions of usability, authenticity, and possession.

> These are also generally recognized as implicit characteristics to availability, integrity, and confidentiality. It may be worth considering these other views from the critical theory perspective and participants' views before concluding that current emphasis has been on confidentiality (Kang 2004).

In addition, when applying the sociological paradigms to analyze information security studies and literature:

> ...the context of use and security requirements should be considered. If a different security requirement is desirable or inherent in a specific view, then perhaps we should consider taking a different view when the context differs (Kang 2004).

The review in this chapter discusses the various approaches and methods that are not profound, especially from a sociological perspective. Clarke and Drake (2003) report that a trend toward the interpretive paradigm has become obvious. However, "social theory suggests problems with interpretivism, in that the kind of open debate necessary for human viewpoints to be recognized and acted upon may be suppressed or distorted by power structures within a social, and particularly organizational, context." Such a phenomenon may also be attributed to the lack of professional recognition of the information security risk management profession—a topic that has attracted concern and attention in recent years (Piper 2006). According to Dhillon and Backhouse (2001), a "literature search found few examples of a social–organizational perspective for evaluating information systems security, pointing to a greater need for more empirical research to develop key principles for the prevention of negative events and therefore to help in the management of security." Similarly, Bjorck (2005) reports that "empirical research on the management of information security is [still] lacking." With direct participation in the social context, the research upon which this book is based is therefore an important undertaking that also contributes to the social–organizational perspective of information security risk management.

2.8 Conclusion

While the weakest link principle promotes the adoption of a defense in depth strategy for information security, defense in depth creates complexity and adds cost. Complexity leads to emergent behaviors that may be adverse and create new weak links in a system. Increasing cost drives the reduction of security measures, thus removing layers of protection and promoting weak links. Focusing on removing the weakest links and applying defense in depth is like attempting to achieve perfect security, which is known to be an overly costly and impossible outcome.

Risk management appears to be a solution that strikes a balance between defense in depth and the drive for security perfection. By applying risk management, however, issues that are assessed as low risks normally are accepted without mitigation or pushed to the low priority bucket where they are forgotten over time. Retaining or accepting risk leaves gaps in a system and may create weak links available for perpetrators to exploit.

The outcomes of risk analysis and assessment are affected by the knowledge and experience of the analyst. When an analyst assigns a low risk to an issue because he or she lacks historical data and does not know the risk relates to the future, the assessment is subjective. A subjective assessment may allow a low risk item to escalate to a high risk level if the systems environment changes.

The concept of risk compensation (Adams 1995) demonstrates that risk cannot be managed completely. The moment we attempt to deal with a risk, the risk will change. Risk is always accompanied by uncertainty. In current information security practices of several organizations, the elements of risk compensation and uncertainty are ignored or insufficiently considered. Suggestions for dealing with these elements are also lacking. To be effective, information risk managers have to consider such risk phenomena and address them as components of their risk management strategies and plans. Most organizations rely on incident management and recovery plans that deal with the aftermaths of incidents instead of managing the point at which changes in the risk environment are detected.

In summary, while the underlying principles of information security are individually sound, they do not necessarily complement each other and resolve the primary issue of weak links. They cause conflicts that lead to the circular problem (Figure 2.1). How should information risk managers respond? Based on our review of the existing literature, we must ask whether current approaches using traditional risk management strategies and techniques to achieve information security are indeed adequate or practical. An adequate answer requires more studies and research on the practice of information security risk management.

It is also clear that current literature and research on information security risk management continue to emphasize technical engineering aspects to improve or renew the tasks, technology, and processes involved in managing information risk resulting from the convergence and proliferation of information technology and systems in the new millennium. Recognizing the critical role that people play in organizational systems, studies since the late 1980s and early 1990s that focus on managing information security have shifted toward understanding the relevant social phenomena. The focus has, however, remained on specific subdomains such as system design and development and security awareness and education rather than strategic management.

Since early 2000, researchers have studied the economics of information security to better understand the issues and dilemmas of managing information risks. In their attempts to quantify risks and security investments to better justify the need for, technology, and processes of information security risk management, the difficulty arises from the constantly changing nature of the problem space. Changes are inherent because of business fluctuations and technology development and proliferation, but more subtle changes result from economic conditions, the political and competitive advantages to be gained by stakeholders, and the supply–demand nature of business.

These factors demonstrate the need to focus on responding to change when managing information risk. Methods for responding to change are largely missing from the literature. Analyzing and interpreting the thrust of the literature review, I propose that:

1. Information security risk management should be responsive to change or be capable of dealing with constant changes in the information risk environment.
2. Information security risk management problems are considered "hard" (difficult and complex) as suggested by Anderson (2001b) but are not "hard" from a research perspective. Instead, information security risk management systems are essentially parts of human activities systems (HAS)[38] and therefore classified as "soft" problems.
3. To understand information security risk management, and improve practices in the field, studies should evaluate the social (soft) human behavioral aspects of managing information risks, in particular in the practice environment where the technology, processes, and people interact and managers deal with information risks.
4. Besides focusing on the social aspects of information security risk management, we must consider two other critical aspects of information risk that fall into the technical research paradigm: (a) the close relationship of information risks and information technology; and (b) the constantly changing nature of the technology, business systems, and environment.

5. The social and technical aspects are coproducers of the intended outcomes of information security risk management. Their individual characteristics must be respected or contradictions will intrude and their complementary natures will not be utilized effectively.

These propositions suggest the need for a paradigm shift by using a social–technical approach to information security risk management that encompasses both the social (soft) and technical (hard) aspects of managing information risks while meeting the need to deal with or respond to constant change in the information risk environment. Such a social–technical approach is critical for bringing improvement to the practice.

Endnotes

1. The review conducted for this chapter included published work found in academic research journals, books, conference proceedings, and related articles and discussions from the trade press, journals, magazines, security forums, conferences, and seminars including online versions. Keyword searches for specific terms such as *security, information security, information risk, risk assessment, risk analysis, risk management, information security management, security management, information risk management,* and *information security risk management* were performed on ACM digital library, Southern Cross University's online databases, IEEE online digital library, and the National Library of Singapore. Relevant publications were reviewed as part of the study. This chapter does not include a review of literature relating to the data or findings from the practice environment; they are covered in the research cycles and reported in the chapters that follow.

2. OCTAVE[SM] is the acronym for operationally critical threat, asset, and vulnerability evaluation. This risk evaluation methodology was conceived at Carnegie Mellon University to define a systematic, organization-wide approach to evaluate information security risks. During the initial phase of this study, ALPHA evaluated OCTAVE for adoption and use as its primary tool for information risk management. It was, however, not selected due to the complexity of the methodology and cost of implementation.

3. Dhillon and Backhouse suggest responsibility, integrity (personal reputation), trust, and ethicality as additional principles that information security management should consider when addressing the challenges of new technology development and convergence and the way business has evolved in the new millennium. These principles relate closely to the individuals acting in a business environment. Dhillon and Backhouse focus their research on the social and organizational aspects of information security management.

4. A common belief among some practitioners is that if we can fix the security issues at the technology layer, the issues will be resolved.

5. BS 7799 was a two-part standard published by the British Standards Institute (BSI) that provides a "Code of Practice for Information Security Management" (BSI 1999a), and guidance for "Information Security Management Systems"

(BSI 1999b). As of 2006, BSI withdrew both documents and replaced them with ISO/IEC 17799 (2000, 2005f) and ISO/IEC 27001 (2005e), respectively. ISO/IEC 17799 was subsequently renumbered as ISO/IEC 27002.

6. The cost of security is usually considered much later in the baseline approach, during the product or solution selection process, and involves the use of purchasing volume to negotiate with product or solution providers or utilizing a lowest-cost bidding approach to select providers.

7. Risk identification involves identifying an asset and its associated value as the first step. If an organization has no assets to protect, it has no risks to assess and manage. In an information system, information is regarded as an asset. To protect information, the physical system (network, hardware, storage media, and application software) is also regarded as an asset because system security affects the security of information processed, transmitted, or stored in the system. The value of these information and physical assets varies from organization to organization. Over and above the monetary value, other intangible assets such as an organization's reputation or goodwill will be affected by the loss or unavailability of its information or physical assets. For each asset identified, the possibility of loss is assessed. The possibility of loss may arise through deviation from an expected outcome or event or the characteristics of the assets involved. Risk analysis is the process used to assess risk potential.

8. Risk treatment is the process of selection and implementation of measures to modify risk, including avoiding (or preventing), optimizing, transferring, and/or retaining risk. Risk acceptance is the result of a decision to accept or retain a risk.

9. Risk communication is defined as "the exchange or sharing of information about risk between the decision-maker and other stakeholders" (ISO 2001).

10. CRAMM was developed by the United Kingdom Government's Central Computer and Telecommunication Agency (CCTA) and BIS Information Systems Ltd. (BIS) and released in 1988. CRAMM is an acronym for CCTA risk analysis and management method.

11. RISKPAC was a commercial product of Chemical Bank Information Systems and Profile Analysis Corporation in the US. The software product provided a framework that can be loaded with a set of questionnaires. Assessment was made using a scoring system to measure risks and calculate the result of the analysis.

12. The *penetration testing* term is commonly used in the building industry to test the strength and reliability of core structures. In the IT industry, it refers to the use of hacking techniques to try to overcome the security protection of an IT infrastructure or systems and determine security vulnerabilities as part of the risk assessment process.

13. The potential to cause harm or exploit a weakness is a *threat* to a system. If no one has an interest in harming a system, its owner faces no threat and no attack (or exploitation) will be expected. In the context of an information system, common threats include unauthorized reading or disclosure, unauthorized writing or updating (forgery or corruption), and denial of service or access that makes a system unavailable when needed. Similarly, no attack can occur if a system allows no means to exploit its vulnerability. Although software and systems engineering have advanced, many inherent properties of information

systems cannot be predicted completely. The complexity of information systems may lead to unexpected behaviors that have at times produced unintended vulnerabilities. It is impossible to ensure that information systems are free from every vulnerability. At best, we can only eliminate weaknesses revealed by past experiences with similar systems.

14. Vulnerability is commonly considered a flaw or weakness in a system (hardware, software, or procedure) that allows security breaches. Unlike other functional features of a system, vulnerabilities are often hidden even to designers, or can be parts of system features. This therefore makes vulnerability identification and assessment at odds with the objective of risk assessment.

15. The integrated business risk management framework was essentially justified based on the premise in Blakley et al. (2001). The approach regards information security and technology-related risks as one of a number of business risks and focuses on bottom-line business impact or value added instead of risk modeling.

16. Scenario analysis approaches involve the construction of various scenarios by which computer security may be compromised to illustrate the vulnerability of an organization to information attacks. The technique is also used to encourage brainstorming about computer-related risks to demonstrate their variety and severity. The scenarios deemed most likely and severe serve as bases for developing a risk-mitigation strategy (Hoo 2000).

17. In practice, risk management coordinates the activities of risk assessment, risk treatment, risk acceptance (or retention), and risk communications. It is important to evaluate risk management at the appropriate level; effective risk treatment alone does not guarantee effective risk management. For example, failure in risk communication can result in negative perception of an organization and other undesirable consequences, even though the organization may have taken the most appropriate measures to treat risks that were identified and evaluated accurately.

18. In commercial operations, liability may be transferred by the use of a disclaimer or agreement. A disclaimer involves undertaking an activity with the explicit understanding that the organization will not be held responsible for the consequences of certain adverse events without specifying who will be responsible for those consequences. An agreement imposes an obligation on another party to take responsibility for the consequences of certain adverse actions.

19. Indemnification is commonly carried out by pooling or hedging risks. Pooling is the sharing of the costs of certain risks by several businesses on the assumption that adverse events are unlikely to happen simultaneously to a meaningful number of the organizations in the pool. Insurance policies are the most common risk-pooling schemes; they increase the predictability of the cost of risk while decreasing the costs of risks for all members of the pool. Hedging involves betting on the odds that a risk will not occur. It essentially capitalizes on risks to make money.

20. Adverse selection is an insured's knowledge of certain risks that are not reported to its insurer.

21. Moral hazard is a lack of incentives by an insured to take actions that reduce the probability of a loss subsequent to purchasing insurance.

22. Insurance companies will typically be concerned about adverse selection when offering a policy. Organizations that do not understand their own risk profiles will be assessed as higher risks than those that do. Conversely, organizations that understand their own risk profiles may know of certain risks and keep them from the insurance company to prevent payment of higher premiums.

23. According to Anderson (2001a), "Security engineering is about building systems to remain dependable in the face of malice, error, or mischance. As a discipline, it focuses on the tools, processes, and methods needed to design, implement, and test complete systems, and to adapt existing systems as their environment evolves." http://www.cl.cam.ac.uk/~rja14/Papers/SE-01.pdf.

24. According to an Ernst & Young report (2005), the survey covered 1,300 respondents from 55 countries.

25. LeVegue's (2006) contribution to the information security strategy literature was fairly recent and focused mainly on the methodology and processes for developing a strategy rather than specific strategic approaches to information security issues and dilemmas relating to this and similar research studies.

26. Information warfare involves identifying the information needs of potential attackers or competitors and taking measures to control information flow to the potential attackers or competitors. The controls may range from the creation of false information to the sanitization of information. The objective is to confuse, mislead, or simply prevent the attacker or competitor from acting positively to gain an advantage.

27. A bounty program is establishment of a reward system to promote "whistle blowing" about known perpetrators so that the victim organization and/or law enforcement can take legal action to stop future attacks.

28. Timeliness was one of the nine principles recommended in OECD's "Guidelines for the Security of Information Systems" (1992). In 2002, it was replaced by the response principle.

29. The approaches may be information risk management, baseline security, use of security technology, or a combination of these principle-based approaches. In practice, organizations are likely to use a combination of approaches to address various needs and compensate for the shortcomings in each approach. All three approaches are used in most organizations.

30. The CISSP certification scheme is managed and promoted by the International Institute of Systems Security Certification Consortium (ISC²). For more information, access http://www.isc2.org/.

31. In the context of information security risk management, an example of a broadly applied policy may be "use of all network access points will be logged and monitored." An indication of normal practice may be "company policy is to use local security consultants for risk assessment." A specific commitment may be "there has been a policy decision to phase out the use of passwords for all business applications in two years."

32. These weaknesses are often unintentionally omitted or ignored by risk managers or IT auditors due to differing opinions about their significance or knowledge of their existence at the point of assessment.

33. In the IT industry, reporting vulnerability publicly without first addressing it with a technology provider is highly discouraged because it exposes end-user systems to greater possibilities of attack. Most vendors promote the concept of

responsible disclosure based on published *Guidelines for Security Vulnerability Reporting and Response Process – V2.0* of the Organization for Internet Safety (http://www.oisafety.org/). Both the vulnerability finder and the vendor should follow the guidelines to ensure end-user systems security without aiding potential perpetrators.

34. The CISR is one of the centers for military research and education in information assurance (IA), defensive information warfare, and computer and network security. http://cisr.nps.navy.mil/index.htm

35. Security responsibilities include ownership, custodianship, control, system users, and accounting. For more details on these concepts, see Dorey (1994).

36. Known risk issues are information risks known within an organization.

37. For example, an exploit that worked in the past may not work at present due to technology changes that eliminate the targeted vulnerability or earlier techniques may have become incompatible.

38. See Checkland (1981), Checkland and Scholes (1990), and Checkland and Holwell (1998) for more insights on human activities systems (HASs) and the notion of the "soft problem."

Practice, Issues, and Dilemmas

3

The issues and dilemmas in the knowledge domain that we discussed in the previous chapter certainly do not help practitioners address organizational information security requirements and the ongoing security challenges from organizational, technology, social, and other environmental changes. Understanding the issues and dilemmas, however, is important to reduce or eliminate potential pitfalls in strategy development. Similarly, we must identify and understand the issues and dilemmas in a practice environment to determine any discernible patterns of similarity to those we found in the knowledge domain, and discover other problems that require additional considerations in our search for resolutions to the research questions.

We wanted to test whether a social–technical approach, as suggested from the literature review, could address the challenges in a practice environment and provide suitable answers to the information security risk management questions (2 and 3) cited in Section 1.3.

We begin this chapter with a discussion of the practices and related issues and dilemmas experienced at ALPHA during the initial phases of the study and describe two models of practices introduced subsequently. ALPHA is unique as a business organization and its approach is atypical of many global firms, particularly financial institutions with regional or global presences. The issues and dilemmas faced by ALPHA mirror to a large extent those of other organizations. These studies and other sources of data provide comprehensive guidance for identifying and developing suitable strategies and addressing the research questions. The structure of this chapter follows the phases of the research study through the first four action research cycles described in Appendix A.

3.1 Information Risk Management (IRM) Practices

As a huge institution operating in more than 50 countries, ALPHA maintained a global IRM structure as did many other multinational corporations. The global IRM function focused on global policy, strategy, and plans that could impact the entire organization. Several regional IRM groups provided local support to regional businesses and ensured global policy and strategy alignment.

The Asia IRM group was one of the regional teams established to focus on the Asia Pacific subsidiaries' requirements. The team had full time members based in Singapore, Japan, Sydney, India, and Hong Kong (the five main business hubs in the region). While the team was considered regional, most members had functional roles that required them to have direct reporting lines to the relevant function within the global risk and control group. For example, two regional team members were on the global computer incident response team (CIRT) and rotated to provide incident response and handling services when required. Another member was part of the Extranet Connectivity Organization (ECO) group and participated regularly in ECO meetings to review and assess the security of external network connections requested by business units.

ALPHA just completed a number of mergers and acquisitions in early 2000 and its near-term focus was to remediate the information security control gaps resulting from the newly integrated organization. More than a hundred gaps were prioritized and reprioritized in an ongoing effort by global and regional teams as regulators and auditors (external and internal) continued to discover new issues in various audit programs.

Since ALPHA was a financial institution, its global operational risk function adopted the Basel II operational risk management approach and implemented the recommended operational risk capital[1] (ORC) provision practice under which business functions that did not meet operational risk control standards were required to allocate parts of their operating budgets to handle any unplanned risk that materialized. If a business function received a poor or below average audit rating, a surcharge was applied to increase its ORC—and further reduce its operating budget.

3.1.1   Organization and Management Commitments

Although industry practitioners made anecdotal comments from time to time about the lack of management commitment as the biggest inhibitor of effective information security, the lack of commitment did not surface as a significant issue in our study. The presence of issues and dilemmas does not signify a lack of understanding by senior management of the importance of information risk management. On the contrary, management's demands for addressing information risk issues were always high, at least during the period of the research study.

At ALPHA, the inhibition of effective information security was attributed to the ORC approach to risk management. At BETA, the inhibition resulted from a negative organization-wide impact on the company from a series of security incidents related to the company's products in the early 2000s. In the mini-survey conducted through questionnaires and follow-up interviews of 30 practicing industry professionals, the following observations were made:

1. Information security has become a recognized function in most enterprises, including government organizations, with significant senior management visibility at a level that is not more than four degrees from the chief executive officer (CEO). This was unchanged according to a follow-up survey (with the same set of questions) conducted in early 2013.
2. The prevalence of information security considerations was supported by 87 percent of respondents who reported having security plans in their organizations, and 93 percent of these respondents based their plans on risk management decisions. In the follow-up survey conducted in early 2013, the results were close at 80 and 95 percent, respectively.

These observations caused us to ask why managing information risk continued to be problematic in organizations. That question led to the need to understand the underlying issues and dilemmas involved in the practice environment.

3.1.1.1   Stakeholder Support for IRM Program

In its role at ALPHA, IRM needed to coordinate activities and influence program adoption and secure practices across various organizational functions and businesses. IRM also had to understand the stakeholders' goals, motivations, supports, and influences in their respective areas and cross functional areas. In the initial phase of the study, the stakeholder analysis identified ten categories of stakeholders: (1) Asia[2] IRM team members[3]; (2) global corporate IRM management[4]; (3) global IRM team members in lines of business outside Asia[5]; (4) global information security subject matter experts (SMEs); (5) technologists in the various business lines; (6) business managers in the various business lines; (7) operation managers in the various business lines or locations; (8) general staff members in technical support functions; (9) senior managers and technologists in technical support functions; and (10) members of the senior management team in the Asia Pacific region.

As shown in Figure 3.1, 14 percent of the stakeholders were opposed to IRM initiatives, 37 percent were indifferent, and 49 percent were favorable to IRM's function. In other words, more than half of the stakeholders were assessed initially as unconvinced of the benefits of the IRM initiatives in the organization because they had seen few positive outcomes from past IRM activities. On the other hand, more than two-thirds of the stakeholders were able to influence IRM's plans and activities (Figure 3.2). These two charts show that not all stakeholders were aligned to the objectives of IRM, but their overall influence could negatively affect the outcome of IRM programs

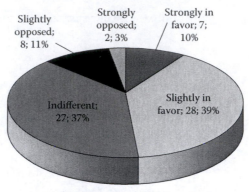

Attitudes toward IRM Function

Figure 3.1 Stakeholder analysis: attitudes of stakeholders toward IRM function.

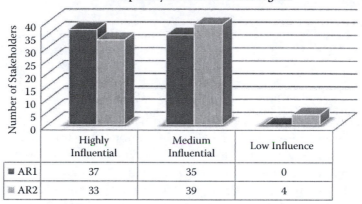

Figure 3.2 Stakeholder analysis: capability of stakeholders in influencing IRM program.

and activities. Engaging those stakeholders as part of the IRM program was therefore critical.

In the 30 organizations surveyed as part of the research study, risk decisions were found to be based on assessments made by different groups of stakeholders in the organization including IT auditors (12 percent), business managers (14 percent), IT project managers and teams (19 percent), IT operation risk (24 percent), and IT security staff (26 percent). External consultants (2 percent) played an insignificant role in risk assessment.

In devising and executing their plans and activities, information risk managers must involve the influencing stakeholders and resolve alignment issues. Finding common goals of IRM and stakeholders is an important step in achieving alignment. Although the objectives of information risk management should be common across the organization, individuals and functional groups' goals and agenda often have higher priority because they also act as performance measurements. Information risk managers therefore need to investigate the goals and agendas of these individuals and groups to identify possible opportunities for alignment.[6]

Actions of groups located in Asia usually had more direct impacts on short term plans and initiatives. The dilemma was that they were often not given adequate priority even by the global IRM function due to other priorities at the corporate level.

3.1.2   Culture of Compliance and Control-Oriented Risk Management

The ORC provision approach at ALPHA was designed to make everyone pay attention to operational risk issues and ensure that they were addressed. However, the approach had side effects. When a business function obtained a less than satisfactory audit rating, its ORC increased and its operating budget was reduced. This created a direct negative impact on individual annual bonus payments. As a result, individuals and groups were highly concerned about the outcomes of compliance audits of their departments.

In certain groups, managers who dealt with such issues frequently tended to devise shortcuts and find ways to ensure that their bonuses would not be affected instead of endeavoring to identify and address control issues effectively. As long as they were able to identify issues before the auditors did, they could devise plans to address auditors' questions. They postponed as many issues as possible and found an experienced individual (or audit-trained IRM) to act as the point of contact with the auditors and prepare their groups to be "audit-ready." Consequently, genuine risk issues were buried unless they could be resolved quickly. This achieved positive audit ratings but created a false sense of security.

In some business functions, the managers were more proactive and anticipated audits before they received notifications. To identify potential audit issues before the auditors did and cover them in remediation plans, IRMs were often called upon to conduct security reviews (in the form of pre-audits) before the auditors arrived. The focus was to pass the audit, so fundamental issues were often assigned lower priorities than specific policy compliance control issues. While this measure increased the chance of passing an audit, the underlying security systems remained weak.

These cat-and-mouse games with auditors were highly unproductive. They did not address the underlying security risk issues and continued to keep the organization exposed. The side effects were ignored because rewards and recognition were directly at stake.

The principle behind the ORC provision is logical. However, research determined that the main issue was in the metrics rather than the consequences of audit ratings. The status of compliance with predefined policies and controls was the baseline for the measurement. If a specific security issue did not map to an existing policy or control requirement, it had no direct effect on the metrics. Noncompliance was a clear violation that had a clear impact. Over time, a culture of compliance emerged and drove the behaviors of individuals and groups. Managing compliance equaled risk management. Selecting appropriate metrics became critical to the success of implementation of the principle. How was such a culture of compliance possible, given that the system had functional separation of the IRM from the business and independence of auditors who reported to the board rather than to business management?

The following subsections discuss the analysis and interpretation of the collected empirical data that revealed the issues and dilemmas affecting the compliance and control-oriented risk management culture. More importantly, the findings revealed the development and continuation of the culture and practices and the responses necessary to address the issues.

3.1.3   Theory of Action and Theory in Use

According to Borge (2001), "risk management means taking deliberate actions to shift the odds in your favor—increasing the odds of good outcomes and reducing the odds of bad outcomes." At ALPHA, however, because of the focus on audit-related metrics, shifting the odds of a poor audit rating became the unwritten objective of risk management. Managing risk was about managing compliance with audit requirements, i.e., with the IT control policy. Risk of noncompliance was clearer than any other risk. A compliance-focused culture focused on the IT control policy instead of dealing with genuine information risks faced by the business.

Evaluating these findings against the work of Argyris and Schon (1991) and Argyris (2004) revealed a "theory of action" at play on the part of information risk management. The stakeholders espoused a theory that managing information risk was essential for effective management of information in the organization. However, they demonstrated a different theory in that they were more concerned with good audit ratings and IRM was positioned to achieve good audit ratings. In most cases, this theory of action was expressed subtly, noticeable only by observing the differences in responses to IRM-raised risk issues versus auditor-raised control issues. When an issue raised by IRM did not get the auditors' attention, the stakeholders showed little interest in addressing them.

As defined in ISO Guide 73 (2001), risk management includes "a set of coordinated activities to direct and control an organization with regard to risk." As a result of the "theory of action" at ALPHA, the coordinated IRM activities were shaped by the compliance culture to focus in two areas (1) the conduct of pre-audit reviews (as noted earlier), and (2) the facilitation of CSA.[7] Both activities were intended to ensure compliance with ALPHA's IT control policy. As part of the ORC provision approach, the organization implemented CSA. The principle of CSA was to induce a risk mindset by requiring business function owners to utilize resources to regularly identify, assess, and remediate operational risks within their functions.

The CSA report formed the basis for the business to understand its risk status and also served as a component of ORC computation. The report was also used as an input document to the audit process. Auditors validated the findings of CSA reports to ensure their integrity and followed up on control issues that were not resolved after a certain period.[8] This drove the businesses to set up specialized risks-and-controls (R&C) functions within their departments or engage IRM to conduct and validate CSA assessments.

In some cases, an R&C manager undertook a coordinator role by sending questionnaires to business managers, collating the results, and updating scorecards showing organization status. Some R&C managers performed the assessments on behalf of the business managers. More proactive R&C managers conducted their own pre-audits with or without the help of their IRMs.

Information risk was considered a subset of operational risk and assessed by CSA questions. The questions were formulated by translating each requirement in the corporate policy manual. Any new or emerging issues not addressed by the existing policy were omitted from the CSA checklist, resulting in a gap between issues handled by R&C and business managers and issues investigated by auditors. Interestingly, IRMs were required to identify those gaps during their pre-audit reviews. Their success, however, was based on having better knowledge and experience than the auditors.

Because IRM and R&C functions conducted pre-audit reviews, the usefulness of CSA diminished because pre-audits duplicated the CSA process. The pre-audits also indirectly indicated to the business managers that they could take the CSA procedure less seriously since IRM or R&C would update and validate the issue database before any audit review.

Since most pre-audit reviews were reactive to the audit schedule, IRM and R&C staff had very limited time to dedicate to comprehensive reviews. They therefore focused on what they thought the auditors would look for and interpreted the scoping documents provided by the auditors as part of their entry process. When they guessed a focus area correctly, the auditors would not find major issues because the issues would have been resolved or rationalized before the audit. As a result, a business would most likely obtain a neutral or positive report. The value contributions of IRM and R&C would be clear and positive even though the organization would not know the information risks it faced or whether the risks were managed adequately.

The pre-audit approach imposed a risk. If the IRM or R&C staff prepared the business to address the issues in an area on which the auditor decided not to focus or failed to address an area that the auditor decided to evaluate, the outcome of the audit review would be detrimental. As a result, the business managers would question the capability and value of the IRM or R&C and those functions would be penalized for discrepancies in business practices. To manage such "risks," IRM and R&C staff often volunteered to act as coordinators for a business throughout the audit process. This put them in a position to ensure that the responses to questions and documentation requests from the auditors were handled appropriately.[9]

These approaches to information risk, controls, and audit issues that were still in practice by IRM during the initial action research cycles raised questions about the true value contributions, roles, and responsibilities of IRM and also its practices. Proponents of the existing approach including a number of IRMs claimed that it was the only way IRM could demonstrate a value contribution to the business—and touched on the IRM concerns about job security.[10]

Argyris (2004) noted that the theory of action perspective exhibited the defensive reasoning characteristic "to protect and defend the actors," revealing their practice of a theory in use that focused on audits and compliance. The theory in use "worked" when an audit rating was neutral or positive. When the audit rating was poor or negative, IRMs claimed a lack of awareness of the issues and accused auditors of looking for problems. They also blamed business users for not following the system or audit procedures. Over time, IRMs became "skilled in their incompetence" by not managing genuine information risks and very competent in managing compliance and audit risks.

As Argyris (2004) noted, "a consequence of generating skills is designed ignorance." From a knowledge perspective, it was clear that these practices were inappropriate. IRMs were either ignorant of or indifferent to consequences because their practices "worked" by justifying their continued existence.

> Another issue, according to Argyris' theory of action is that organizational defensive behavioral systems encourage cover-ups: "In order for a cover-up to be effective, the intention must also be covered up. It is unlikely that human beings will give or receive useful feedback to deal with their skilled incompetence and skilled unawareness" (p. 12).

This means that the competence of IRM in identifying and managing information security risk is questionable.[11] By dealing with audit issues and compliance requirements, IRM was not required to identify true information risks. As long as audit ratings remained at a neutral or positive level, the lack of IRM competency was not a concern, i.e., the lack was covered up. Since IRM was expected to understand risk issues, businesses felt the IRM group was in the best position to deal with the auditors and ensure that appropriate audit responses were generated. From an information risk objective perspective, such a practice is inappropriate and unprofessional. It avoids transparency, and is a form of self-deception or "cover-up" that constituted the characteristics of defensive reasoning. Such a mindset inhibits learning:

> The consequences of defensive reasoning include escalating misunderstanding, self-fulfilling prophecies, and self-sealing processes. All these escalate because the logic used is self-referential, which does not encourage the detection and correction of error. When these conditions are combined, a generic syndrome against learning is created (Argyris 2004).

The effects on organizational learning and long term consequences involving the integrity of the business practice from the use of pre-audit reviews were potentially detrimental. Auditors rightly expressed concerns about these practices during my interviews. The practices defeated the purpose of conducting audits and hindered the auditors from understanding the integrity of the business system. Ultimately, these practices blinded the business to the real risks in its environment.

Even if IRM or R&C succeeded in identifying all risk issues before every audit review, the approach was highly reactive and introduced a fundamental problem from a systems perspective. As shown in Figure 3.3, the system was at risk of interruption due to the external events depicted in items (6), (7), and (8). Because IRM, R&C, and CSA activities focused on reacting to audit and compliance needs, they had limited time to address control gaps before reviews and temporary measures were often adopted. Root cause information risk issues were not identified and thus remained unsolved.

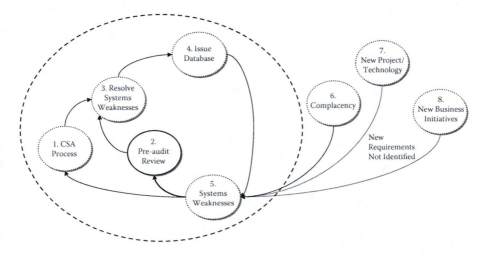

Figure 3.3 Causal view of audit and compliance-focused risk management practice at ALPHA at initial action research cycle of study.

Users and managers were not made aware of risk issues and had no understanding of appropriate security practices for preventing and managing them. This indirectly permitted complacency, as depicted in item (6) in the figure. When a business environment changed, new projects, technology, and business initiatives [items (7) and (8)] introduced new security and risk issues, adding to the system weaknesses shown in item (5). Clearly, changes were required in the IRM operating model and practices. Measures to address the thematic concerns of the stakeholders were also needed. The competency of IRMs also required examination.

The focus on compliance was not peculiar to ALPHA. According to a global information security survey conducted by Ernst & Young (2005), 81 percent of the respondents rated compliance with corporate policies as one of the most important information security functions. To validate this finding, relevant questions were included in a mini survey[12] of 30 respondents from the industry. The survey established that while the main driver for information security was business continuity, regulatory compliance remained a strong motivator and activities were biased toward a compliance-focused defensive approach. This trend continues, as shown in the results of a 2013 follow-up survey.

IRM needed to achieve its objective of helping the organization manage its information risk and all stakeholders had to understand this objective. IRM had to present this objective to the stakeholders to gain their support without producing a compliance- and/or control-oriented culture. The intent was to have stakeholders focus on information risk instead of compliance and control. The focus on compliance revealed the organization's control status, but not its risk status. Furthermore, a new approach had to accommodate constantly changing business environments including IT systems and related risks.

Hanford (2003) notes that "strategic and operational thinking represent very different, albeit complementary, orientations and skills." IRMs at ALPHA mainly performed short term operational activities involving resolution of existing performance problems and improving efficiency. Hanford states that an effective manager should be able to identify key issues and opportunities over the longer term, be reflective, and continue to learn. That was not the philosophy within ALPHA's IRM organization. The IRM practice had to change to address the true needs and challenges.

3.1.4　Risk of Habituation

At ALPHA, the business systems users in the various lines of business (LOBs) performed CSAs twice a year as part of the operational risk management (ORM) system. The ORM group believed that business users worked in the LOBs, were familiar with the businesses, and with sufficient awareness of the business and IT policies, they could find discrepancies in their areas or the systems they used. This assumption was certainly debatable.

Eric Raymond and Rob Landley (2004) wrote, "As humans repeat tasks, they form habits—a change that pushes the task from conscious cognition to unconscious cognition." Habituation, "the process of habituating" or "the state of being habituated" is defined in a Merriam-Webster dictionary (2006) as "a decrease in responsiveness upon repeated exposure to a stimulus." When habituation occurs, a person is accustomed to a stimulus, loses attention, or becomes indifferent to the stimulus.

Business users within business systems build expertise by acquiring familiarity with systems and related processes. In designing business systems, Raymond and Landley (2004) emphasize that good interfaces "encourage benevolent habituation." Over time, users understand interfaces and become proficient in using them with little or no conscious thought. Similarly, if a business application has a security problem or a vulnerability, habituation eventually sets in and users no longer react.

As a result of habituation related to the CSA process, users developed a tendency to assess security weaknesses as "normal" conditions rather than exceptions, unless they recently learned about specific weaknesses or discovered new weaknesses. Discovery is unlikely because users rarely read security policies documents unless they had recent exposure to a security issue.

Habituation becomes risk, particularly when users of a system use self-assessment as a process to detect risks. As a result of habituation, users can be blindsided about control issues within their spheres of knowledge and expertise. This served as a plausible explanation for the business area discrepancies discovered by IT auditors when CSA was conducted before audits. The discrepancies raised questions about the value of the CSA process in managing information risk. CSA was required for regulatory compliance and business governance purposes. Whether it was relevant or useful, however, was not important to the business. The IRM program needed to address the risks of habituation.

3.1.5 Information Risk Management Organization

In addition to the role of IRM, and its value contributions to the business, its organization and reporting structure were of interest to key stakeholders. Two approaches practiced in the heritage organizations were (1) business-aligned,[13] reporting to a business head or operation, and (2) IT-aligned,[14] reporting to the head of IT services. Stakeholders from the business side (including business IT operation and application development) preferred the business-aligned IRM approach, citing ownership and accountability of information risk issues.

Stakeholders from IT preferred a centralized IRM organization that would continue to report to the regional head of IT services for the Asia Pacific region. They cited (1) resource efficiency, better cost control, cross-training and learning opportunities for IRM; (2) ability to provide an independent view; (3) better integration and coordination of IRM activities with IT product managers and project managers since they all shared the same end customers; and (4) enabling IRM to disengage from day-to-day business security and risk mitigation operation activities.[15]

In addition to organizational alignment and reporting, questions arose about the geographical location of IRM activities—whether IRM should be centrally located or distributed across the region, and if distributed, a method to determine distribution had to be devised. The data analysis showed, while there were agreements for a distributed model, the focus of the stakeholders was on ensuring that regional centers had local IRM managers, since those centers were critical to the businesses and IT operations in the region.

A centralized model would involve higher costs since IRMs would have to travel frequently to regional centers and branches to execute tasks locally. Disagreements about a distributed location model were related to the cost and availability of competent IRM resources in all regional centers. The suitable resources issue was more prominent for the centralized model. The business stakeholders were also concerned about creating location "silos" that would prevent IRM resources from scaling up to meet increasing business and IT demands. This also presented cost implications.

The geographical location of the IRM team also raised a concern about offices for the team and responsibilities including participation in Location Operating Committee[17] (LOC) meetings. Some IRM team members occupied line-of business offices; others were centrally located in a separate area near the IT services function. Businesses preferred the former arrangement that allowed them to request IRM help easily but this arrangement affected communications among IRM team members, resulting in a lack of information sharing and poor understanding of work issues and challenges.

3.1.5.1   Systems of Knowledge Power

A systems of knowledge power analysis questions the fairness of designs with the aim of determining the beneficiaries of the efficiency of processes and effectiveness of structure of an IRM program. According to Flood (1999), "problematising knowledge power dynamics deepens appreciation of efficiency and effectiveness and further sensitizes people to the ethical nature of designs and decisions" (p. 118).

The question of IRM reporting from the perspective of the fairness of the function in its focus and recommendations versus the reality of the lack of support of IRM programs by IT services group was one dilemma. From a management view, parallel reporting appeared a reasonable solution, but this approach was found to be inadequate from a research perspective. In the business management domain, according to Peter Drucker (1973), "organization structure is the oldest and most thoroughly studied area in management." This, however, did not seem to be the case in relation to information security risk management.

As noted in Section 2.5.1, despite the salience of organizational issues, little literature covered the possible approaches or organizational models or indicated their importance in a practice environment. Available literature about information security risk management [Jackson et al. (1994), Pfleeger (1997), Berti et al. (2003), Kovacich (2003), and Alberts and Dorofee (2002)] does not cover or discusses only briefly the organization and reporting structures for IRM functions.

Dorey (1994) provides a brief tour of the topic and notes the pros and cons of reporting to a technology function, corporate security, and an internal audit department and highlights the trend toward reporting to technology functions. Parker (1998) emphasizes the importance of management commitment and the establishment and scope of a security oversight management committee. Parker's discussion focuses on the role and scope of responsibilities and the tasks (program contents of the function).

Drucker (1973) further states that an "organization does not start with structure but with building blocks; that there is no one right or universal design but that each enterprise needs to design around the key activities appropriate to its mission and its strategies." It is reasonable that most researchers and practitioners focus on the activities of information security risk management when discussing the organizational aspects of the discipline. Despite this, Drucker adds:

> The best structure will not guarantee results and performance, but the wrong structure is a guarantee of non-performance. All it produces are friction and frustration. The wrong organization puts the spotlight on the wrong issues, aggravates irrelevant disputes, and makes a mountain out of trivia. It accents weaknesses and defects instead of strengths. The right organization structure is thus a prerequisite of performance (p. 519).

According to research results, the requirement for IRM to report to IT services raised the question of fairness—whether IRM could remain objective in its work for the businesses while it needed the support of IT to ensure its welfare (and its performance would be measured by IT yardsticks rather than those of the businesses.

> Indeed, the purpose of the structure is to make it possible for each person to "do his thing." A hierarchy does not, as the critics allege, make the superior more powerful. On the contrary, the first effect of hierarchical organization

is the protection of the subordinate against arbitrary authority from above. A scalar or hierarchical organization does this by defining carefully the sphere within which the subordinate has the authority, the sphere within which the superior cannot interfere. It protects the subordinate by making it possible for him to say, "This is my assigned job." Protection of the subordinate underlies also the scalar principle's insistence that a man have only one superior. Otherwise the subordinate is likely to find himself caught between conflicting demands, conflicting commands, and conflicts of interest as well as of loyalty. "Better one bad master than two good ones," says an old peasant proverb (Drucker 1973, p. 525).

In discussing the strategy for improvement of systems of knowledge power, Flood (1999) writes:

There is no short-cut when it comes to knowledge power. There is no quick fix. There is no instant satisfaction. Yet, engaging in questions [relating to the systems of knowledge power] … may reveal that improvement simply cannot be reduced to and measured in terms of efficiency and effectiveness. It will not work from anyone's point of view, whether it is because of unrealized potential in efficiency and effectiveness, or unfair consequences of biased action (pp. 121–122).

The findings and assertions of Drucker and Flood and my analysis concluded that the parallel reporting line to COO Asia could not resolve the IRM dilemmas. The COO Asia reporting line risked the creation of conflicting commands from another authoritative individual and increased the complexity of managing the relationship with the regional heads of IT services and the businesses.[18] It also required a closer alignment of IRM activities with the COO's agenda and the agendas of IT services. Another fairness issue concerned the "responsibility axis" discussed in Drucker (1973):

The organizations of business enterprises and public-service institutions have a number of axes: decision-authority but also information; the logic of the task but also the dynamics of knowledge. The individual jobs have to be designed and positioned in contemplation of a number of axes—task and assignments; decision-responsibility; information and relation (p. 527).

While the authority axis of IRM was divided into three areas (including one to the global CIRO function), the responsibility axis remained tightly aligned to the global IRM group. IRM staff members were required to participate in weekly international conference calls with their respective global counterparts to provide updates of local progress and issues and receive information about recent developments in the global arena that might impact local activities. The calls were set at New York morning time (11 to 15 hours later in the

Asia Pacific region, depending on location). IRM members in the Asia Pacific region had to sacrifice one night a week to participate in the global conference call meetings. Fairness was not considered, and conference calls outside normal hours became accepted practice.

The analysis suggested that the organization and reporting structure of the IRM organization were as important as those of other groups. Besides directly affecting the effectiveness and efficiency of staff, an appropriate structure was needed to promote fairness of practice and eliminate any perceived biases arising from certain lines of reporting. In addition, the allocations of time and resources by staff members were influenced by their reporting axes.

While Drucker's principles for designing suitable structures were published in the early 1970s, their adoption and practice in IRM domains were inadequate at ALPHA and in most other organizations.

The principle of systems of knowledge power utilized in the analysis of this research cycle suggests the importance of considering this perspective in IRM design. Mapping the principles against the issues and dilemmas of IRM organization design will serve two basic needs of information security risk management by (1) creating awareness, and (2) providing useful principles for avoiding related issues and dilemmas in a practice environment.

3.1.6 Responding to Security Incidents

During the initial action research cycle, ALPHA encountered two significant but unexpected security incidents: (1) a Simple Network Management Protocol[19] (SNMP) vulnerability (CERT/CC 2002); and (2) an increase in SPAM[20] volume that impacted its e-mail services.

3.1.6.1 Incident 1: SNMP Vulnerability

In early 2002, ALPHA's global CIRT issued a security advisory after the discovery of a vulnerability on SNMP.[19] A similar advisory was also issued by an external computer emergency response team (CERT). It was rated critical and advised Internet users of the vulnerability and available countermeasures (CERT/CC 2002).

Since the security vulnerability was considered critical, the CIRT advisory required the business IT functions (e.g., application development) and IT services to respond to the discovery of the SNMP vulnerability by identifying the extent of IT and network systems that required updating (patching) so that IT services could apply the security updates to immunize the systems against security exploits[21] that might capitalize on the vulnerability.

The first step was to collect information about the numbers and types of networking devices and computer systems that potentially had SNMP vulnerabilities in their builds.[22]

Because I was at the global IRM group meeting the evening before the CIRT advisory was released, I was requested by global CIRT to assist in data collection in the region. The next day, I quickly learned that I was trapped in a system of miscommunication and confusion between IT services, CIRT, and business IT groups. The organization had no centralized or current databases of IT and network systems. Simultaneous requests for information issued by various global functions noted different timelines response and requested different information. This disconnect became a learning experience but the responsiveness problem that emerged was not recognized.

3.1.6.2 Incident 2: SPAM Mail

In early 2003, a security engineer on the regional IRM team advised that the CIRT observed an increase in SPAM[22] e-mail. SPAM was also a growing industry issue (*Economist* 2003). Business users complained about the mailbox space occupied by SPAM and noted the productive time lost in clearing the messages. The security team was unsure about suitable countermeasures that users could take. The team began working in New York to determine suitable technology solutions to the problem. The incident was another signal indicating the need for IRM to consider SPAM and related emerging issues and incorporate a measure in its program to prepare the organization to respond effectively. SPAM did not emerge as an issue that I needed to consider because the global CIRT had already attempted to look for a solution. These incidents illustrated a major weakness in the information security risk management program at ALPHA and elsewhere in the industry. In particular, they revealed that a focus on compliance and controls prevents an organization from responding effectively to new security issues and incidents.

First, the approach and principles adopted by regulators often focused on known security issues. Second, protection via controls and preventive measures was regarded as more effective for achieving compliance than preparing for unknown or unexpected events. Finally, questions about dealing with unknown or uncertain risks seldom arose within the organization or among IRM practitioners. Most discussions centered on technology solutions for known issues deemed most pressing by auditors and regulators or events that received significant media attention. The practice of risk management during the nonevent period did not entail any action that would improve responses to security events.

In the case of the SNMP vulnerability management incident, the immediate issues detected were the lack of coordination and need for an updated database of IT and network systems to allow prompt assessment of the state of security of the IT environment. The consequences were miscommunication, confusion, and uncertainty about responsibility for the required data collection. From a control perspective, such discrepancies were unacceptable.

These incidents reflected the lack of preparedness in the event of a security event. The incidents also signaled the need for IRM to also consider preparedness and perhaps initiate activities to prepare the organization to respond effectively. However, the first actions centered on correcting the surface defects relating to communication, coordination, and the lack of a central IT asset database system.

The incidents were not new to ALPHA. Like many other organizations, ALPHA was impacted by network worms but incidents such as the sadmind/IIS worms (CERT/CC 2001a) in 2001 (before research for this book started) were not translated into learning and follow-up actions. Repeated incidents under different names continued to appear and disrupt IT services and business operations. From an organizational behavioral perspective, the repetition indicated learning disabilities (Senge 1990, Argyris and Schon 1991) across multiple functions, as we shall discuss in Sections 3.2.1.2 and 3.2.2.3.

3.1.7 Uncertainties in Information Security Risk Analysis and Management

As reported in Chapter 2, knowledge domain faces various terminology interpretations, risk probabilities, and choices of methods of risk assessment and management. Collectively, these factors add costs to risk analysis, and more importantly create uncertainties in an organization. The uncertainties involved in risk analysis are key issues in risk management.

The common methods of risk analysis and management [Alberts and Dorofee (2002), Stoneburner et al. (2002),[23] and ISO/IEC 13335 standards (2004, 2005a)] may be grouped into four main steps (although some methods describe more than four steps.) The first is to identify threats, vulnerabilities, and exploits that may exert negative impacts on an organization's IT environment and information. Next, an assessment is made of all the identified threats, vulnerabilities, and exploits to determine the probability of occurrence. The third step is conduct an impact assessment for all the identified threats, vulnerabilities, and exploits identified to determine their potential impacts or damages. The impacts are usually classified as low, medium, or high.

The results of the first three steps of risk analysis can be plotted in a chart similar to Figure 3.4. The X axis represents the probability that a threat or vulnerability will be exploited. The Y axis denotes the potential impacts to the organization if a threat or exploit materializes.

The placements of items along both axes and the boundaries between them are often arbitrary (as observed at ALPHA) and subjective, depending on the experiences and knowledge levels of risk managers and the risk appetite of an organization from a policy perspective (based on interviews with the risk managers and personal experiences). Some organizations use

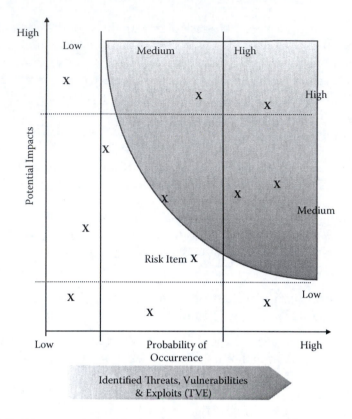

Figure 3.4 Common risk analysis and management approach.

additional risk categories (catastrophic, highly critical, and insignificant) to improve clarity. Knowles (2005) used the concept of "materiality"[24] to signify the criticality of risks. Figure 3.4 shows an example of a simple low, medium, and high categorization approach.

The fourth and final step is developing recommendations for managing all the risks categorized. The assessment and resulting chart should demonstrate to risk managers and senior management that the top right corner areas of the chart should be the focus for actions and resource allocations that will produce the best returns of investments in risk management.

When additional resources are available, the medium categories are the next in line for action. A risk manager will also consider acting on them if the cost of action is low or affordable. In most information risk management literature, this option is denoted as a curve in the shaded area in Figure 3.4. Low risk or impact categories are often justifiably left out of action plans and information security risk management programs because their occurrence is not highly probable or they present low impacts.

After assessment, a common IRM strategy is to drive the curve (as shown in Figure 3.4) toward the left as much as possible so that more risk issues are addressed. This strategy was adopted at BETA. The lower risk areas are usually regarded as "acceptable" risks to the organization.

However, this strategy alone may increase the cost of security. As noted by Knowles (2005), spending to implement security plans must be justified, since security is considered a cost. A security cost is optimal when it eliminates or reduces the level of risk and produces maximum potential savings. The cost of implementing security is estimated and compared with the potential business impact to derive the optimal focus of resources. A number of security solutions must be analyzed to determine their costs and potential business impacts.

This approach to risk management has several limitations in ensuring information security. A significant point is the ability of an organization to respond to new risks, errors in risk assessments, and other security events and catastrophes as discussed in Section 3.1.6. Peter Drucker (1973) commented on management's fear of risk:

> What is lacking in the management sciences as applied today is the emphasis throughout its literature and throughout its work on "minimizing risk" or even on "eliminating risk" as the goal and ultimate purpose of its work.
>
> To try to eliminate risk in business enterprise is futile. Risk is inherent in the commitment of present resources to future expectations. Indeed, economic progress can be defined as the ability to take greater risks. The attempt to eliminate risks, even the attempt to minimize them, can only make them irrational and unbearable. It can only result in that greatest risk of all: rigidity (pp. 511–512).

Analyzing security incidents (Section 3.1.6) from a systems perspective requires an organization to go beyond risk mitigation. The inability of ALPHA to respond was a key factor that prevented it from addressing emerging events appropriately. This suggests possible discrepancies between the action strategies in existing IRM practices and the processes used to address new or emerging risks. One of the discrepancies can be traced to the limitations of the common risk analysis and management approach adopted in organizations like ALPHA.

Risk identification and categorization measures are subjective and very dependent on the experiences of the individual risk manager. As noted in Section 2.3.4, no reliable method exists for quantifying information security risks. Risk assessments are therefore qualitative. When quantitative methods are used, the numeric assignment of risk level still becomes a qualitative assessment. The use of probability is common but it has issues (as discussed in Section 2.3.4). Two risk managers with different experiences may qualify and quantify the same risk issue differently.

Kabay (2002) states that the perceptions of security and risk vary among individuals. When a security weakness in a system is identified and an attack appears easy to execute, the probability of occurrence may be deemed high. If the attack is assessed to be difficult to execute, the probability of occurrence would normally be categorized as low. This assertion is only partially true. Not all difficult-to-exploit vulnerabilities will necessarily have low probabilities of occurrence. An exploit might be considered difficult to execute based on a risk manager's background and ability but a perpetrator may have already developed the tools required for an attack. The risk perception problem is highly asymmetric.[25] A risk manager has to know a lot about the systems under assessment, but still will not know what a perpetrator knows. The perpetrator only needs to find a security weakness to exploit.

Taking a risk assessment lesson from the insurance business, many risk managers base their assessments on probability as a primary indicator. Experience influences perception cognitively. As noted by Elizabeth Styles (2005), prior exposures contribute to experience:

> The processes involved in visual perception enable us to act and react to the visual environment safely and accurately. We need to know what things are and where things are, and where we are in relation to them.… Together with attentional and memory processes, perceptual processing gives rise to our experience of the visual objects and events around us (p. 49).

John Adams (1995) postulates that "perceptions of risk are influenced by experience of accidental losses—one's own and others'." Experience of past incidents therefore contributes significantly to a risk manager's assessment. However, many factors contribute to most accidents. Along with incorrect practices, Adams notes that accidents may also result from risk taking behaviors. A previous risk event provides data to show the possibility of another risk event. Actions of the risk managers and changes in an organization may bring closure to exposures from a risk event or make the organization more vulnerable. On the other hand, the nonoccurrence of a risk event does not signify a low probability for its occurrence in the future.

When a risk manager has no prior incident or precedent to rely on for assessment, his or her imagination and creativity based on past experience may play an important part in a risk assessment. Posner (2004) comments about the risk associated with the September 11, 2001 attacks and notes that, "It would be a mistake to dismiss a risk merely because it cannot be quantified and therefore *may* be small—for it may be great instead." In the aftermath of the Hurricane Katrina[26] (CBC 2005, CNN 2005b) disaster in New Orleans, Daniels et al. (2006) assert that:

> It is not easy to assess low-probability events and people often disregard them. There is ample evidence that people often do not want to consider data on the likelihood that an event might occur, even when the information is available

to them. Only after a disaster do most people pay attention to it, and then they overestimate its likelihood (pp. 6–7).

The final assessment of the risk manager is therefore subjective, highly dependent on her beliefs, shaped by her risk perception, and how she influences other stakeholders to her perspective. Low risk areas charted below the curve in Figure 3.4 may be assessed erroneously and present high risk in reality. It could turn out to be a Black Swan event (Taleb 2007). Similarly, a high risk item may be classified on the basis of a rare prior occurrence, as Taleb (2004) calls it, "fooled by randomness."

From a cost management perspective (Knowles 2005), optimal cost, low risk, budget-dependent medium risk issues are unlikely to get management attention. However, due to their asymmetric natures, they are likely to be targets of perpetrators. This creates a risk management paradox. In addition to errors and perceptions that lead to the subjectivity of a risk assessment, unknown factors (that may be known to potential perpetrators, but not to risk managers) may impact an organization's risk situation.

Consider undisclosed vulnerabilities that are known only to a perpetrator but kept secret for various reasons. A perpetrator may gain economic benefits from exploiting vulnerabilities. As reported in *Business Week*, skilled hackers are on the payrolls of businesses for competitive reasons (Blank 2001). According to Masnick (2006) at Techdirt.com, malware[27] writers "are more likely to be in the virus-writing business for profit rather than fame or for kicks."

> That also means that the type of malware being written is changing as well. Rather than go for the big hit, with a virus that spreads super fast and makes the headlines, virus writers know that they're better off being sneaky. The less well known their viruses are, the less likely they are to be stopped by security software... and the longer there is to profit from the malware (Masnick 2006).

Undisclosed vulnerabilities may remain unknown to risk managers, even though perpetrators may already know them. Some of those vulnerabilities may also be known to technology providers based on their internal research or reports received from other researchers and not disclosed publicly. BETA is a technology provider. It could not share publicly unknown vulnerability information with end user organizations because doing so may inadvertently disclose the information to potential perpetrators who could then use it to their advantage.

Furthermore, if a security weakness has not been fixed, releasing the vulnerability information without providing a fix could produce undue panic in end user organizations. Most technology providers therefore promote the principles of "responsible disclosure"[28] that limit sharing of vulnerability information only to responsible parties until a fix has been completed and published.

Even if a risk manager can identify and quantify all the risk dependencies, a risk assessment (as shown in Figure 3.4) provides only a snapshot of the challenges an organization faces. The operating environment inside and outside an organization changes constantly. Each change can exert neutral, negative, or positive influences on risk items individually and systems as a whole. Changes may be planned (e.g., implementing a new information system) or unplanned as in the case of the SNMP vulnerability, SPAM, SQL Slammer and Blaster worms attacks, the severe acute respiratory syndrome (SARS) epidemic, and the tsunami tragedy. Risk may be identified and managed as a planned change but often becomes visible only after an unplanned change. This means that risk related information that can be learned from personal experience and information sources are limited.

As Perrow (1999) observes, the characteristics of complex systems mean that the effects of failure in one component often result in unpredictable changes and subsequent failures of other components leading to eventual failure of the total system. Technology systems that are interactive and/or tightly coupled are most prone to such failures. Perrow calls them normal accidents or systems accidents and concludes, "No matter how effective conventional safety devices are, there is a form of accident that is inevitable."

As observed by other practitioners and researchers [Venables (2004), Mahtani (2004), and Blakley et al. (2001)], the information security risk environment is highly complex. Not all information security risks can be identified or predicted accurately. Uncertainty prevails in all complex systems. The potential for errors, perceptions, and uncertainties of risk assessment are the key limitations to the common methods for managing information security risks in organizations. Collectively and individually, they contribute to the losses and negative consequences from security incidents and natural disasters.

Most organizations like ALPHA address the uncertain risk issues as a segment of disaster recovery or business continuity management if an X–Y axis view denotes them as high-impact low-probability risks. This leaves significant gaps between risk management and incident recovery and implies a need to reconsider IRM and planning for business continuity and disaster recovery as discussed in Section 3.2.2.4. Risk managers are often surprised when seemingly low risk issues were exploited to cause massive business disruptions as in the cases of the SQL Slammer and Blaster worms incidents.

3.1.8 Causal Analysis of Information Security Systems

Causal analysis[29] provides another means to explore the systemic issues of an environment or system. Figure 3.5 depicts a causal view of information security systems (Kang 2005a). This empirical view may not be the most

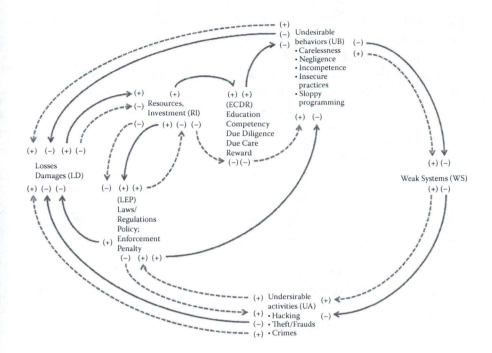

Figure 3.5 Causal view of information security system.[30]

complete, but it captures the essence of an information security system and the related attributes that are sufficient for this discussion.

The dotted lines show a negative influence along the direction of the arrowhead. The solid lines show a positive influence. The plus (+) and minus (−) signs at the beginning and end points of each arrow show the respective increases and decreases of the activities depicted at each point in the system. For example, an increase (+) in undesirable behaviors would lead to an increase (+) in the number of weak systems and vice versa. An increase (+) in education activities would lead to a decrease (−) in undesirable behaviors and consequently a decrease in the number of weak systems.

When we examine the history of information systems security, and criminal exploitation of vulnerabilities, undesirable activities (UAs) caused harms to organizations and individuals. One plausible cause of UAs like hacking, theft, and fraud is the presence of weak systems[31] (WS), without which perpetrators would have no targets to exploit. Keeping information systems secure is fundamental to reducing UAs.

What produces weak systems? WS result from undesirable behaviors (UBs) in computer systems design, development, implementation, operation, and use. When the various parties involved in the life cycle of a computer system from design to disposal fail to pay adequate attention to security requirements and protection, the result is a weak system. The causes of UBs include lacks of awareness, education, competency, due diligence, due care, and reward to behave well (ECDR). ECDR activities and their effects are often long term and continuous resource investments (RIs) are needed to develop and sustain them. However, organizations often do not see the benefits and underinvest in ECDR until losses and damages (LDs) are incurred and impact the business and/or its reputation. For example, Ernst & Young's 2004 Global Information Security Survey reports:

> We know from our observations and interviews that organizations don't act without the appropriate incentives. They often need some convincing that reducing risk by improving information security is worth the investment because the measure of value is elusive and the benefit is visible only through events that do not happen. Consequently, many organizations invest the minimum necessary to protect them. The result: a decrease in the overall security level for everyone on the network.

Since the Enron debacle (Holton 2006b) and other incidents, some regulators (like the US Securities & Exchange Commission), stock exchanges, and professional associations are stepping up the use of laws and regulations, such as the Sarbanes–Oxley Act (Bazerman and Watkins 2004), enforcements and policies (LEP) to mandate or encourage investments in ECDR programs and activities in an effort to reduce or eliminate undesirable behaviors and weak systems.

Massive viruses and worm attacks such as NIMDA (CERT/CC 2001b), and Code Red (CERT/CC 2001c, Krebs 2003) caused significant losses and damages to end users, business organizations, governments, and technology providers. They also prompted a change of emphasis on security education, competency, and innovation.[32]

A discussion of UAs leads to the question whether laws and regulations are adequate to address them. Are law enforcement agencies able to enforce the laws and regulations from capacity and capability perspectives? Are the penalties imposed adequate to deter future crimes? Are UAs ethically acceptable in the cultural context of society? Inadequacy in any of these areas means that UAs will be tolerated or largely disregarded and thus lead to more UAs. Investments in LEP initiatives and programs are key attributes for balancing an information security system.

From a system perspective, an increase in UAs will lead to increased LDs and prompt businesses to invest resources in information security. Similarly, when fewer WS exist after UBs and UAs decrease, fewer or no LDs will be incurred. However, this result may lead organizations to believe that no further security investments are necessary. As a result of decreased funding for ECDR and LEP activities, we will be back where we started.

Traditionally, as shown in Figure 3.6, businesses mostly consider resource investments in terms of business values. Investment increases are

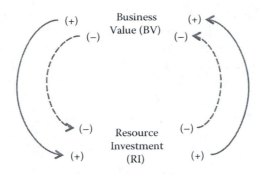

Figure 3.6 Traditional system of business investment focusing only on outcome of business value creation.

often justified by increases in business value. When an outcome is negative or not obvious, management reduces investments.

Organizations that do not encounter significant security incidents or breaches often feel safe and assume that security issues are minor. They may disregard undesirable activities that could impact business values. The business world now relies heavily on the trustworthiness of IT and must consider the influence of undesirable activities and behaviors inside and outside organizations. Resource investments directing at reducing UAs and UBs (Figure 3.7) are becoming critical for achieving positive business values.

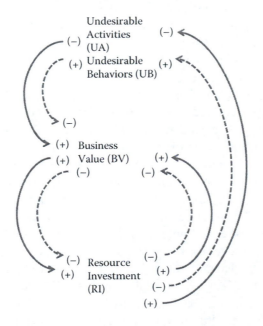

Figure 3.7 New system view on relationship of business values, resource investments, and undesirable activities or behaviors.

If an information security system is left on its own to operate in response to external events and developments, the inadequate resource investment over time will not sustain the proactive initiatives and programs required to reduce or eliminate UBs and UAs in the system. Instead of waiting for more losses and damages to trigger an increase in investments for ECDR and LEP, proactive steps are necessary to sustain the investments and keep the system balanced with the positive (solid) outcome cycle running instead of the negative (dotted) outcome cycle. Few or no LDs will result in sustaining or increasing the business value of IT because the information systems will be secured and protected and able to deliver the business needs at optimum levels of performance, quality, and reliability. By keeping a healthy level of RI for ECDR and LEP, the information security system will operate in a balanced condition that will manage the risks of attacks.

Awareness of the causal system is important but insufficient to drive information risk management requirements into stakeholders' immediate agendas. Organizations need a more strategic approach to achieve alignment so that a healthy level of resources can maintain ECDR and LEP related activities.

3.1.9 Summary of Issues and Dilemmas

The issues and dilemmas of information risk management based on practice at ALPHA and data from 30 practicing professionals may be summarized using Robert Flood's four windows systemic view (1999) as depicted in Table 3.1. The findings reaffirmed the issues identified in the current literature, as described in Chapter 2, and confirmed the presence of dilemmas (presence of multiple stakeholders, implications of noncompliance with regulatory and internal IT control policies, and competence deficits of IRM and various stakeholders). These findings revealed two main threads of inadequacies in the current model of information risk management.

One is the lack of consideration of the systemic aspects of the individuals and groups in the information security system. They based their actions on compliance needs and reacted to incidents without adequate preparation. Another inadequacy is the failure to consider the underlying assumptions and potential errors of the current risk assessment methodology, i.e., errors not identified in the risk assessment and lack of systems to accommodate changes in the business, technology, and risk environment.

In response to the research questions and findings from the initial action research cycle and related literature reviews, the research design was revised to approach the problem by developing and testing two approaches focusing on the findings. The first approach entailed the development and testing of a social–technical model, involving two organizational structures in response to the issues and dilemmas identified and focusing on the "soft" issues. Section 3.2 describes the two models of the social–technical approach

Table 3.1 Four Windows Systemic View of Information Risk Management Situation at ALPHA during Initial Action Research Cycle

Systems of Process (Efficiency and Reliability)	Systems of Structure (Effectiveness)
Processes (in form of pre-audit reviews) designed in response to audit and compliance issues, based on IT control policies; not based on sound information security or risk management principles Inability to detect emerging risk issues Inability to respond to changes in risk environment, including critical security events and resulting incidents	Issues involving IRM organization structure, roles and responsibilities, funding arrangement, physical location Fragmented structure, some IRM staff members continue to report to business IT and operations, others take instructions directly from IT services Geographical (location) requirements not met consistently Confusion of IRM roles, responsibilities, and value contributions Poor communication within IRM group, little learning and sharing of knowledge

Systems of Meaning (Meaningfulness)	Systems of Knowledge-Power (Fairness)
Lack of clarity of authority and ownership of information risk issues IRM pressurized by multiple stakeholders to focus on compliance to demonstrate value contribution Reactivity to audit and compliance issues Little learning for IRM members in information risk domain IRM member job security concerns bias activities toward needs of business managers to improve compliance rather than manage information risk	Governing ideas influenced by auditors, business functions, and global senior management, but not IRM IRM actions were issue driven and fell into flow of causal system if left unmanaged (as shown in Section 3.1.8)

Source: Flood, R.L. 1999. *Rethinking the Fifth Discipline: Learning within the Unknowable.* New York: Routledge.

including the outcomes of the testing, the main findings from the analysis, interpretation, and explanation.

The second approach focused on responding to changes in the risk environment. The piezoelectric principle surfaced during this phase and was subsequently adopted as the metaphor and model for developing and testing the approach. Chapter 4 discusses this approach and the related findings.

3.2 Social–Technical Approach

The social–technical approach introduced changes to the IRM system and practices by adopting social science and systems thinking techniques in understanding individuals and organizational behaviors and devising plans and action strategies that address key attributes identified from the knowledge acquired. Model A and Model B were implemented in three action research cycles to test the efficacy and suitability of the changes in addressing the issues and dilemmas discussed earlier.

The Model A approach set a new structure, operating model, and comprehensive program, evolving from the current practices and incorporating the social–technical elements necessary to address the concerns. The Model B approach differs from Model A in the organization structure and operating model, while maintaining the design of the IRM program. Model B was an incidental development arising from changes in the organization. This was inevitable and one of the known side effects of action research methodology whereby the workplace serves as a research environment.

In both approaches, IRM issues and dilemmas highlighted in earlier sections formed the basis for the design and testing of the models. This included addressing the theory-of-action issues identified among the stakeholders.

3.2.1   Model A Approach

The Model A approach for managing information security risk at ALPHA was tested and implemented in two action research cycles[33] as a continuation of the research study. The iterative nature of action research was used to incrementally improve the approach. The model included three main components:

1. An IRM organization structure with a centralized resource model cost funded by the various lines of business including IT services
2. An IRM operating model for clarifying roles and responsibilities
3. An IRM program incorporating:
    a. A subsystem for identifying critical business and IT systems for ongoing risk reviews
    b. A subsystem to conduct risk reviews on business applications and IT infrastructure systems
    c. A scorecard-supported system for performance measurement and management reporting
    d. A series of remedial action programs for stakeholders and issue owners
    e. An improved information risk awareness program with better tracking of participation and focused topics for addressing the awareness needs of various stakeholder groups
    f. A learning set for IRMs to enable them to utilize learning-based inquiries and share their learning experiences

The social aspect was the focus on individuals and group from a systems thinking perspective, using social science techniques to improve understanding of their needs and motivations, and influence their acceptance and subsequent actions in line with the objectives of IRM and the IRM program. The learning, analysis, and interpretation resulting from implementation of Model A resulted in the formulation of a five-level action strategies model (Figure 3.13 in Section 3.2.1.4) and a social science technique-enhanced IRM system known as the SECD4[34] system model (Figure 3.14 in Section 3.2.1.4).

3.2.1.1 Addressing Theories of Actions of IRMs and Other Managers

As shown in Figure 3.8, the normal practice environments in businesses and in IT operations were risk controlled through standards established in the organization's IT control policy and standards. The business users and IT systems were required to implement and practice the controls. From a systems thinking perspective, the theories in use of IRM members and business and IT managers reflected a "shifting the burden" archetype structure (Senge 1990, 2006). Security weaknesses in the business and IT systems were not, however, detected immediately, as indicated by the "delay" element in Figure 3.9. The CSA process was established to detect systems weaknesses and develop action plans for their resolution. This, in the theory espoused by the operational risk managers, should have improved the systems practices and behavior and led to a better risk-managed environment.

As indicated in Figure 3.10, the auditor, as an independent third party, was testing the integrity of the system periodically. When inadequate practices or security issues were detected, the business involved received a poor audit rating, and was penalized by an increase of its ORC. The penalty often led to pay freezes, cost cuts, and/or dismissal of staff involved in the security problems.

The theory in use of conducting pre-audit reviews was a symptomatic response to audit challenges. As shown in Figure 3.10, the introduction of new (mostly reactive) controls and the escalated use of the risk acceptance[35]

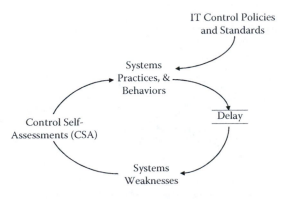

Figure 3.8 Information risk practice with CSA.

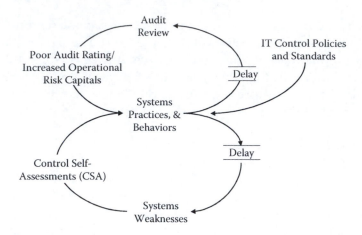

Figure 3.9 Audit review to assure adequate systems practices and behavior.

process created a balancing loop to the audit review. No action was introduced to strengthen the fundamental response to balance the loop. The side effect was not clear until the structure was redrawn (Figure 3.11).

The pre-audit review and risk acceptance activities formed a "shifting the burden" structure described by Senge (1990). The long term implication of this structure was an increase in complacency and a degradation of the IT control policies, as noted in Figure 3.11. The negative implications were revealed by the auditors' discoveries of issues caused by human complacency, failure to follow established procedures, and omission of crucial steps in execution of control procedures.

Risk acceptance procedures were misused. Controls that were difficult to implement were "risk accepted" and not handled. Business and IT users

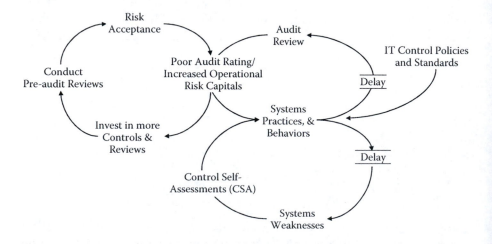

Figure 3.10 Symptomatic responses to audit interventions.

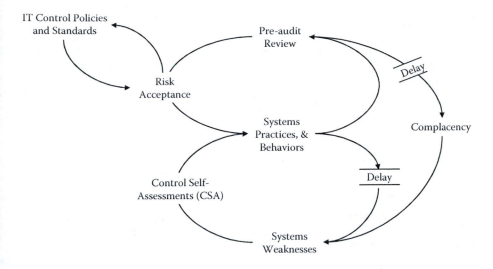

Figure 3.11 "Shifting the burden" structure enforced with symptomatic response.

waited for pre-audit review to identify issues, and addressed them only in time to meet the auditors' review schedules. Previous practices resumed when audit reviews were finished. This was evidenced by repeated mentions of issues in review reports. To make positive changes, Senge (1990) suggests the "principle of leverage" that allows actions and changes in structures to lead to significant enduring improvements.

> Often, leverage follows the principle of economy of means: where the best results come not from large-scale efforts but from small, well-focused actions. Our non-systemic ways of thinking are so damaging specifically because they consistently lead us to focus on low-leverage changes: we focus on symptoms where the stress is greatest. We repair or ameliorate the symptoms. But such efforts only make matters better in the short run, at best, and worse in the long run (Senge 1990, 114).

From a systems thinking view, the IRM program reinforced the actions as a fundamental response to the audit challenges by introducing two key processes to the system: (1) increasing awareness of risks and (2) conduct of ongoing risk reviews as depicted in Figure 3.12. The analysis showed that the IRM program was systemically sound and the results improved understanding of the differences between the new program and the previous practices.[36]

3.2.1.2 Addressing Auditors' Theories of Actions
The theories of actions practiced by the auditors were observed from their interpretation of the meaning of information risk management. In line with most practitioners' "no perfect security" view, the auditors agreed that

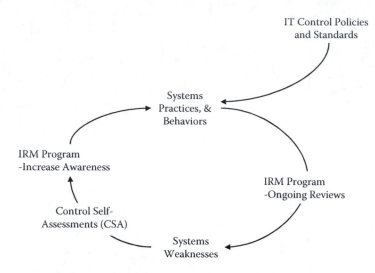

Figure 3.12 Enforcing fundamental response by IRM program.

a risk-based approach to managing information security risks was necessary. However, when a security issue that no solution was identified[37] and the resolution required a risk-based decision to be made, the auditors were often reluctant to accept it. The auditors often imposed lengthy processes and strict criteria for a risk to be accepted. They strongly enforced "compensating controls" using extensive manual procedures that were inefficient and ineffective.

Reflecting on the philosophical perspective of soft systems methodology and citing Checkland (1981), Jackson (2003) comments on "hard" systems paradigms:

> Hard approaches assume the world contains systems the performance of which can be optimized by following systematic procedures. These procedures involve establishing clear objectives and then using generalizable models, based on systems logic, to enable prediction and control of the real-world systems of concern so that the objectives are realized with maximum efficiency and efficacy. Unfortunately for hard systems thinking, logic is usually much less significant in terms of what happens in organizations than is the history, culture and politics of the situation (p. 185).

In contrast, according to Checkland and Holwell (1998), the soft systems paradigm "advocate[s] taking a more tribal view of organizations, and adopting a more interpretive approach to inquiry."

> An organization is to be seen at core as a social process, essentially a conversational process, in which the world is interpreted in a particular way which legitimates shared actions and establishes shared norms and standards (p. 71).

The auditors' theory in use of rigorously seeking mitigating measures regardless of the actual risks further suggested that they viewed information security as a "hard" problem, i.e., if there is a process that people follow, there is a solution to the problem and if there is no technical solution, there must be a procedural solution to compensate for it or resolve it. The soft aspect of the problem was disregarded. This contradicts my proposition that information security is a soft problem based on a synthesis of the literature reviewed in Section 2.7. Several facts may account for this contradiction:

- An organization's systems, in general, are based on the classical approach that is essentially a hard systems paradigm. Citing March and Simon (1958), Checkland and Holwell (1998) note that people in such organizations will follow the practice of seeing problems indicated by gaps between performance and goals; problem solving becomes a matter of closing the gap by finding a suitable means to achieve the goal that is already known.
- There is a general lack of awareness or appreciation of the concepts of hard and soft sides of information risk problems among practitioners.
- Soft issues are social issues that often require social trust before problem resolution. In this context, it required the auditors to trust the business users and IT staff to comply with established policies and procedures. This was fundamentally against the nature of their task of determining whether the practices were adequate.

As noted by Fukuyama (1995), the extent to which a person or group will trust another is a cultural bias. In an organization with a diversity of people from various cultural backgrounds, trusting people to address risk issues can be viewed as a challenge. Auditors may have exhibited lack of trust because they were not members of the departments audited and did not share many cultural norms with the individuals and groups involved.

Fukuyama (1995) adds that, "trust is the expectation that arises within a community of regular, honest, and cooperative behavior, based on commonly shared norms, on the part of other members of that community." A business organization may in essence be viewed as a community with a common interest (achieving business objectives) with a range of common norms. Examples are believing in the company's vision and mission statements and practicing its defined core values. Theoretically, based on the assumptions that the core values, common vision, and mission can become established norms and the organization has the ability to recruit honest people, the notion of trust is not entirely out of reach for a business organization. Nevertheless, the extent to which this can be achieved in an organization is subjective. The results are also often unpredictable because the many external and internal changes and relationships of individuals, groups, and organizations are highly complex.

While building trust among individuals and groups within an organization may improve business efficiency and information security practices by enhancing commitments, this approach was found unacceptable by the regulators. In a meeting held with a senior executive of a regulatory body, a major concern of the regulator was insider threat:

> Insider threats are the biggest threats to financial institutions. If an insider can gain access to customers' sensitive information, and use them illegally from the outside, they could cause massive damage to the institution. In addition, this could also affect the economy and confidence of the financial market in the country.[38]

From a risk perspective, the regulator highlighted concern about the impacts of an insider attack. Other attacks may produce similar outcomes. As long as an insider or external attacker can find a weakness to exploit, he or she can achieve a desired outcome. The outcome of the risk must be assessed from a number of angles. The nature or profile of an attacker is only one of many facets of an assessment. Other factors, such as the normal operating conditions of systems, the protection accorded, the rigor of monitoring, and the effectiveness of the response systems all play parts in preventing, detecting, and minimizing attacks and damages.

No organization has a guarantee that no insider attack will be possible in a fully controlled environment. As shown by Mitnick el al. (2002, 2005), and more recently in Richmond's account of a data theft incident (2011), humans can and often do fall prey to social engineering attacks. Outside attacks have increased due to the proliferation of network and system connectivities. Similarly, it has not been proven that a high trust society will necessarily lead to more insider crimes. On the contrary, Fukuyama (1995) notes that "the decline of social trust is evident on both sides of the law, in both the rise of crime and civil litigation."

> The decline of trust and sociability in the United States is also evident in any number of changes in American society: the rise of violent crime and civil litigation; the breakdown of family structure; the decline of a wide range of intermediate social structures like neighborhoods, churches, unions, clubs, and charities; and the general sense among Americans of a lack of shared values and community with those around them (p. 10–11).

Taking action to improve social trust in an organization is an important step for reducing security breaches and minimizing realization of information risks. Incorporating social science and systems thinking techniques in an IRM program is essential to the objective of improving social trust between the stakeholders and IRM and thus improve management of information risk in an organization.

The theory of action in which the theory in use differed from the espoused theory in these two groups of stakeholders further supports the inference of a possible "learning disability" (Senge 1990, Argyris and Schon 1991) problem that includes IRM staff members, as noted in Section 3.1.6. The IRM program that focused on improving social interaction involved ongoing dialogues with the auditors therefore helped to enhance their awareness and appreciation of the soft side of information security risk.

3.2.1.3 Competency and Trust

Two aspects of competency needed attention: (1) the competency of IRM, addressed in the action strategy directly, and (2) the competency of the staff members of stakeholders' functional areas. Peter Denning (2003) states that competency is important from a trust perspective: "Trust is an important assessment we make about others and others make about us. If others trust us, we will accomplish much. If others distrust us, we will accomplish little."

How do we build trust between IRM and the staff members of the lines of business and IT services? Taking steps to improve social trust in the organization was an important step to reduce security breaches and minimize the possible realization of information risks within the organization. To establish and build trust, Denning (2003) suggests a language action perspective:

> Trust is an assessment of confidence that an outcome will actually be accomplished and simultaneously an acceptance of the risk that it will not be. Trust is an emotional skill in which we align our intentions and our sensations of readiness for action.

Appealing to the emotional element of trust appeared to be a possible approach to obtain commitment and stimulate more positive action from the stakeholders and related staff members. They needed to change their focus on audit ratings and understand the consequences of their inactions or poorly executed actions that could affect the information risk of the organization. This approach, however, required IRM staff to communicate with the stakeholders on a one-on-one basis to review and resolve security risk issues in their respective areas. According to Denning (2003):

> Our trust in someone's promise is based on sub-assessments of competence, sincerity, and capacity. Competence means the person has the embodied skill to deliver what he promises. Sincerity means the person's private and expressed intentions are the same. Capacity means the person has the time, resources, and favorable circumstances to succeed. We won't trust someone whom we think is incompetent, insincere, or lacks capacity. We won't trust

someone who breaks promises. Simply knowing this can help us shape our actions so that we are seen as trustworthy.

This view relates back to the competency of the IRM members—a critical element in gaining trust and commitment from stakeholder staff members. Denning (2002) states:

> The term "embodiment" refers to knowledge "in the body," ready for immediate performance when the situation arises. This form of knowledge is distinct from conceptual knowledge, which is "in the mind," ready to provide explanation or description. An embodied capability includes a well-honed set of interpretations of the world, allowing the expert to immediately "see" what is needed in a situation and to act on it without thought.
>
> To many, the notion of putting the body into learning is unfamiliar. Most technologies rely on difficult intellectual abstractions. Mastering them appears to be the key to advanced education.
>
> In real life, we instinctively understand the difference between conceptual knowledge and embodied knowledge. We will choose the dentist who has crowned 100 teeth, the surgeon who has performed 1,000 procedures, or the pilot who has flown 10,000 flights.

An organization wants to recruit information risk managers who have prior experience in conducting risk assessments on different types of information systems in different contexts, have managed firewall networks, or administered security operations in a somewhat similar environment. IRM, however, needed time to gain the experience and acquire the embodied knowledge. Similarly, staff members of the lines of business also needed time and practice to become risk aware and manage risk in their areas. A common practice adopted by ALPHA was to define the competency needs as a standard in each IRM staff member's job description.

As noted by Hase and Tay (2004), "Standards have had a profound effect on how we consider issues of quality, selection, promotion, performance evaluation, training, and project management." Despite this,

> Standards seem to suggest linear thinking about performance. If a person, group, or organization can achieve a level of performance once, then it can do it again. That somehow the environment in which this happens is as predictable as the outcome.

As experienced in the research cycles conducted since the beginning of this study, the organizational environment in which IRM staff operates is essentially complex.

> Given the propositions of complexity theory, developing competency is a minimum standard for dealing with rational, linear systems. But, we need capable

people to deal with the unpredictable nature of complex environments. We also need to consider how to develop work environments that enable capable people to express their capability (Hase and Tay 2004).

A standards-based approach to establishing and building competency will therefore deliver limited capabilities to the IRM members and their constituents.

What we are interested in is how to go beyond this baseline to capability, the preparedness for applying standards and using competence in novel, complex situations rather than the familiar.

We suggest that the emphasis needs to be in the organizational processes that are used rather than the outcomes.

The difficulty is overcoming the need we seem to have to want to measure things, to predict. We cannot predict higher order abilities such as capability any more than we can predict creativity. We obtain the skills and knowledge to be a painter but a "work of art" is another issue.

The challenge is to implement processes designed to create optimum conditions for making decisions in the face of new and unforeseen problems. This can be described as fitness of purpose rather than fitness for purpose. Documenting the process so we can learn from it might be the best we can hope for (Hase and Tay 2004).

Evaluating the work of Dick (1997b, 2000, 2001), Davis and Hase (1999), Flood (1999), Revans (1980, 1982, 1998), Tay (2003), and Tay and Hase (2004) found action learning and action research suitable for achieving competency pursuits in complex environments. In another study, Denning (2003) evaluated the language action philosophy and established the importance of understanding how language acts in relation to competency and trustworthiness.

We all want to accomplish what we set out to do. Our accomplishments constitute our base of experience and allow us to move to higher stages of competence over time. The more competent we become the bigger the accomplishments we can achieve and can aspire to.

Language-action philosophy uncovers the truth that accomplishment cannot happen without commitments. Commitments are linguistic acts. The more we understand about the language acts in coordination, generation of possibilities, and disclosures, the more we will be able to organize ourselves to accomplish our goals. Most people report that the language-action perspective, by revealing new and effective actions, has enabled them to become more competent and trustworthy. They gain a competitive edge relative to others who lack this interpretation.

The language-action perspective illuminates many other phenomena of interest to professionals: for example, the meaning of innovation and how to produce it; the meaning of research and its connection to innovation; power and its influence on actions; entrepreneurship; design; and (for computing professionals especially) information (Denning 2003).

The establishment of an action learning session for the IRM staff was an appropriate step forward to instill knowledge sharing and learning. Formalizing the IRM program as a process from the beginning of the study provided an environment for developing IRM competency.

At the stakeholders' end in the lines of business, most staff members were committed to do a good job making sure that adequate security controls were designed, implemented, and/or delivered. However, they often lacked the competency to execute their commitments. Investing in training people and creating an environment conducive to gaining the competency were therefore necessary.

3.2.1.4 *Five-Level Action Map (FLAM)*

Reflecting on the results of the two action research cycles in implementing the Model A approach at ALPHA, a strategy action map for an information risk management system evolved as an initial outcome of the study. The five-level action map (FLAM), as the name suggests, consists of five levels of possible action strategies. The first three levels form a hierarchical structure, whereas the fourth and fifth levels exist in all the first three levels and are also interrelated, as shown in Figure 3.13:

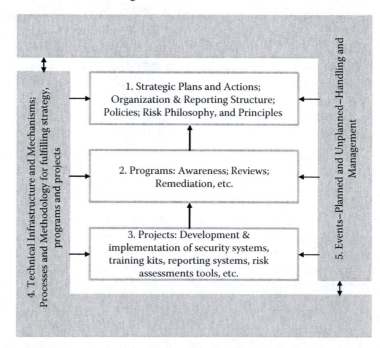

Figure 3.13 Initial five-level action map (FLAM) of information security risk management system.

1. Strategic or management level at which the organizational and reporting structure, roles and responsibilities, policies, risk philosophy, and principles of practice should be designed and developed.
2. Program level at which a series of programs should be identified and designed to address the current issues, with longer-term objectives of information security risk management.
3. Project level at which each program may encompass one or more projects and assign ownership, allocation of resources, determination of schedule, and implementation tasks so that the program will eventually become operational.
4. Technical and process or workflow level at which the technical infrastructure, components, and related processes and workflow are determined, developed, and implemented as projects within the programs.
5. Event level at which both planned and unplanned (emergency) incidents can be dealt with programmatically or through some form of organizational activity upon their occurrence within or outside the programs. The idea of including an event level in this action map was triggered by the learning from the SNMP and SPAM incidents discussed in Sections 3.1.6 and 3.1.7.

The action strategy at each level requires its own plans, personnel competencies, timeline and schedule, processes, and technology support to ensure its ability to meet its objectives, and collectively the objectives of the level above it.

Analyzing the application of the action map in Figure 3.14 revealed the need for an inherent relationship or influence between the technical and process level and the event level and vice versa. In other words, the technical infrastructure and processes implemented as part of the program will either support or hinder the responses and management of events. In essence, the second research question showed the need for this requirement (for events) to be addressed as part of the program because events are in fact the *changes* that affect a risk environment.

3.2.1.5 Combining Social and Technical Aspects of Information Security Risk Management Systems

Another outcome of the social–technical approach was rationalization of the systems of information security risk management practice into an integrated process as shown in Figure 3.14. The systems integrate the developed approach with the use of available tools and processes from premerger organizations and the measurement system implemented by the global IRM group.

A key difference between the information risk management systems depicted in Figure 3.14 and the previous approach (Figure 3.3) was the inclusion of the key stakeholders as part of the systems. The stakeholders were

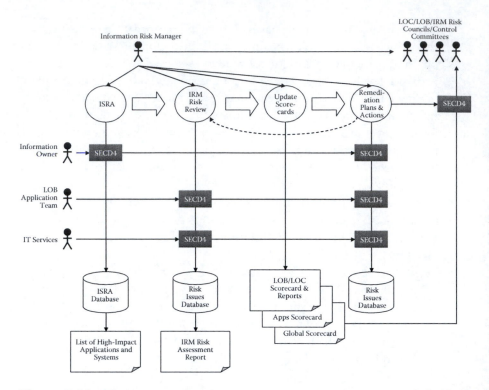

Figure 3.14 Information risk management system incorporating stakeholders' participation.

the information owner, line of business application development teams, IT services, and members of the various management-level councils and committees. The top of Figure 3.14 depicts the high-level processes for information risk management. The system starts with an information security risk assessment (ISRA)[39] process, followed by a risk review, scorecard update, and finally devising and acting on remediation plans. The cycle repeats with more reviews and regularly revisiting the ISRA to ensure that previous assessments of the individual applications remain valid or updating them if required.

The rectangular boxes in Figure 3.14 denote activities involving stakeholders and IRM. These boxes are critical junctures that involve both social and technical activities and require IRM to use social knowledge, tools, and skills to understand and address stakeholders' concerns and agendas and influence their acceptance and support to achieve the desired outcome at each stage. Techniques adopted included stakeholder analysis (S), entry and contracting (E), convergent interviewing (C), dialectic data analysis (D), and Flood's (1999) four windows systemic view (4) that were found to be effective to address the soft issues in the information security risk management systems processes. These techniques are labeled SECD4 in the boxes.

Before presentation of the scorecards and reports to the IRM Risk Council, LOB Technology Control Council (TCC), and LOC, the SECD4 social–technical process was updated as a way to socialize the scorecards and reports with the individual stakeholders in the groups and maximize their acceptance before the meeting. This step also minimized surprises to all participants. In Section 2.8, one of the propositions asserts that:

The two aspects— social and technical—were co-producers of the intended outcome of information security risk management. The distinctive characteristic of each must be respected or else contradictions will intrude and their complementarities will remain unrealized.

The analysis of the information security risk management system depicted in Figure 3.14 indicated that a social–technical integrated approach was possible and necessary to address the stakeholders' concerns and requirements throughout the system life cycle. As Peter Drucker (1990) asserts in the context of managing the performances of non-profile organizations:

I soon learned that [successful executives] start out by defining the fundamental change that the non-profit institution wants to make in society and in human beings; then they project that goal onto the concerns of each of the institution's constituencies (p. 111).

IRM's mission and goals were related to a fundamental change. The social-technical integration of IRM systems revealed needs for stakeholders' acceptance, commitment, support, and satisfaction by addressing "the concerns of each of the institution's constituencies."

3.2.1.6 *Communicating Information Security Risk Status*
We learned from the study on the implementation of Model A with the updated IRM systems shown in Figure 3.14 that one key element was the IRM scorecard[40] introduced as a tool to determine IRM performance at each line of business and location. A review of the scorecards of each line of business provided a high-level organizational view of information risk control status, particularly the state of implementation across the lines of business and locations, regionally and globally.

Using the scorecard as a focal point for performance measurement relating to risk control resolution at ALPHA's Tokyo office for three months helped reduce the number of high-risk (red) issues from twelve to three. This showed the stakeholders' focus on the issues noted on the scorecards and presented to the LOC.

The scorecards, however, captured only issues relating to IT control policy implementation and compliance. From a risk perspective, the controls specified in the policies reflected the risks assessed when the policies were formalized and did not cover risks that emerged thereafter from changes in the IT and operations environments. Risks arose from increased use of Internet-enabled applications, IT outsourcing, and offshoring of business operations. New security issues including those reported by the CIRT function that required security advisories could not be captured on the scorecards.

From a management perspective, there is a difference between control and controls. Peter Drucker (1973) made this point:

> In the dictionary of social institutions the word "controls" is not the plural of the word "control." Not only do more controls not necessarily give more control, the two words, in the context of social institutions, have different meanings altogether. The synonyms for controls are measurement and information. The synonym for control is direction. Controls pertain to means, control to an end. Controls deal with facts, that is, with events of the past. Control deals with expectations, that is, with the future. Controls are analytical, concerned with what was and is. Control is normative and concerned with what ought to be (p. 494).

This means that an organization's IT control policy essentially specifies the ultimate state of security that the organization aspires to achieve—a vision of control. However, policies are static and environments are dynamic—they change constantly. The scope of control covered in policies can encompass only known risks. Policies are limited to controlling known risk environments. They cannot accommodate new or unknown issues.

ALPHA's scorecard captured the status of implementation and compliance with the IT control policy, i.e., it measured the state of controls that had been achieved (amber and green items) or not achieved (red items) against a known risk environment. In other words, the scorecard did not provide the control desired from an IRM perspective. Effective IRM must address both known and not-yet-known issues (including emerging risks). The scorecard was effective in bringing focus to key risk issues.

A security control such as an incident response procedure may have been implemented and score a green rating on a scorecard. However, the lines of businesses and IT services might be unable to respond to a genuine security incident that involved an attack on a newly discovered vulnerability. In such cases a security patch may not have been devised or workaround (tactical security) controls were not in place. ALPHA faced such issues (the SNMP vulnerabilities and SPAM incidents) earlier but they could not be captured on scorecards because scorecards measure only against predetermined controls specified in policies. They are blind to new issues and therefore not responsive to change or reflective of the real risks faced by an organization.

The scorecards made a positive impact in gaining LOB stakeholders' support for the IRM program but their bias toward compliance raised new issues. Some stakeholders were more concerned about color comparisons with other operations than about underlying issues. This caused distraction and influenced the outcomes of scoring and the efficiency of the process. The influence on scoring affected the eventual remediation plan and action strategies. As a result, remediation plans and action strategies may be inadequate and important issues may be sidestepped through stakeholders' interventions and IRM staff members' failure to devise accurate and objective scores in the scorecard. If scorecard results showed consistent improvements (as in the Tokyo office's use of scorecards to assess performance management) in which IRM members actively made changes to bring about the improvements, the risk status of the business as reflected in scorecards would be indicative of IRM's contributions.

A question emerged when scorecards showed a decline in performance (more red and amber issues). Could IRM be one of the stakeholders accountable for the poor performance reflected in the scorecard results? This question required more evaluation before its relevance could be determined because a number of possibilities could account for the increased risk levels:

1. If the resolutions recommended by IRM members were ineffective, IRM should be accountable.
2. If the resolutions recommended by IRM members were effective but the outcome was affected negatively by errors in practice by end users, perhaps the end users are responsible. However, if the error was introduced as a result of an incorrect instruction from IRM (e.g., during a training session), IRM will be accountable.
3. If the lower performance captured on scorecards resulted from a changing environment or an increase of risk assessment activities that could not be reflected on scorecards, it will be difficult to assess the factors contributing to the negative outcome.

IRM's accomplishments certainly depended on other operations such as lines of business and IT services to fulfill their commitments to remediation plan and actions. Their failure to deliver could prevent IRM staff from meeting their commitments. Improving the organization's IRM performance and risk status requires more than establishing rules of practice for IRM. As noted in the discussion on competence and trust (Section 3.2.1.3), the ability to execute and deliver a commitment depends on the competency of participants. Their efficacies therefore cannot be measured simply through a reductionist approach such as a scorecard.

Even if these issues relating to negative outcomes could be resolved, the inability of scorecards to capture events arising from changes in the risk environment, particularly externally generated events, will impact an organization. Events caused by environmental changes make scorecards redundant but IRM will still be required to respond to help the organization manage the new risks. Using scorecards as performance management tools for managing efficacy is subjective and therefore limited, even when individual negative outcomes are investigated to determine the causes. Based on these limitations, an alternative method is required to respond to the research question about IRM performance measurement.

More importantly, the analysis above also showed that the scorecard system at ALPHA would continue to drive a culture of compliance, focusing on control-oriented security, but unable to deal with security challenges in a constantly changing environment. Thus, in response to the first research question in Chapter 1, the scorecard is not suitable as a tool for managing information risk.

3.2.1.7 *Limitations of New IRM Systems*

One key feature of the new IRM system introduced through the Model A approach was the introduction of the "proactive detection of weaknesses" process. The process was identified from a causal analysis of the IRM systems (as depicted in Figure 3.3.) Its objective was to provide a filter against complacency and ensure that the introduction of any new projects, technologies, and business initiatives would be risk managed before implementation. Other goals were to eliminate the pre-audit practice and ensure proactive management of information risk.

While *detection* appears in the name of the process, the actions are based on two sets of activities—a scheduled set of risk reviews and a comprehensive awareness program. The awareness program focused on developing and increasing awareness of information risk and commitment to practices that would help detect security weaknesses in business systems and practices without relying on IRM or other third parties to detect weaknesses.

While awareness is commonly suggested as a measure for improving security practices [Parker (1998), Hinson (2005)],[41] improvements resulting from awareness are subjective. They depend to a large extent on the contents presented and motivations for learning (Siponen 2000a). Wilson and Hash (2003) noted that, "The purpose of awareness is to focus attention to security.... Awareness presentations are intended to allow individuals to recognize IT security concerns and respond accordingly (pp. 8–9).

In many cases, learning about IT security through an awareness program cannot be quantified accurately or qualified unless the program focuses on a specific skill set relating to a well known set of risks or errors. Staff turnover and business environment changes require regular retraining to ensure that all members of an organization are updated and aligned. This means that the ability of individuals to detect risks will be subjective unless it is limited to a specific scope of known risks and regularly tested against a predetermined set of criteria. The effectiveness and efficiency of such efforts is therefore limited.

The literature review also identified this as a gap in the knowledge domain. The literature on detection focused on technical measures such as security monitoring and intrusion detection systems; see Graham (1998), Northcutt (1999), Bace and Mell (2001), Grance et al. (2003), Frahim (2005), and ISO/IEC (2006a, b). Published studies were not based on an information risk management perspective. They do not cover the roles of people and organizations in managing risks except to promote individual security awareness.

Siponen (2000a) discusses the motivation for security awareness training. The intent is to achieve an effective performance level measured against specific security guidelines or standards adopted by an organization to enhance security practices rather than improve risk detection capability. This plan does not deal with changes in the risk environment.

From a technical perspective [Ptacek and Newsham (1998), Bace and Mell (2001), Frahim (2005), and Timm (2010)], intrusion detection systems (IDSs) present several security limitations. An IDS may be based on rules or networks, systems, and behaviors. In both cases, only known attacks, patterns of attacks, suspicious or malicious traffic will be stopped. An IDS will fail to detect new attacks, especially those targeted at overcoming the IDS. Graham (1998), and Bace and Mell (2001) add that many IDSs are known to suffer from resource issues, problems operating in a switched network, and lack of accuracy and timeliness of their attack pattern databases. Clearly, relying on a technical approach for detection of security issues presents limitations. Technical solutions are inadequate for handling human behaviors such as complacency and management issues such as a failure to risk manage new projects and business systems adequately.

This analysis suggests that from a systemic perspective of information security risk management systems, a balanced (risk-managed) system requires more than introducing a continuous security risk review program and a security awareness program. Technology-focused solutions have also demonstrated limited effectiveness.

3.2.1.8 *Learning through Model A Approach*

At the end of the action research cycle on implementation of the Model A approach, a follow-up stakeholder analysis (Figure 3.15) revealed that more stakeholders supported the new IRM program. This demonstrated a positive outcome of the social–technical approach. While progress was made, the analysis also revealed that business resource constraints slowed the progress of implementation of IRM program activities in the lines of business where remedial actions were required. These findings further supported the need for IRM to continue engaging stakeholders in the lines of business more proactively, using more social techniques, such as entry and contracting (Dick

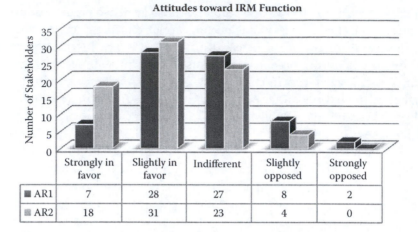

Figure 3.15 Progress in stakeholders' acceptance of IRM program.

2002a) skills to negotiate commitments, in addition to assigning roles and responsibilities in each cycle of the IRM review.

In the second action research cycle iterated within this phase of the study, the model was strengthened through an evolved approach for identifying key risks and addressing them in a programmatic manner. The approach encompassed the methods required to address the social aspects of risk management based on the social–technical system shown in Figure 3.14. The system incorporated a control scorecard system introduced by the global IRM group as a performance measure for tracking the status of control implementation in the organization. The scorecard used in the model was, however, insufficient for managing the performance and efficacy of the IRM program and related subsystems. The scorecard was limited to assessing predetermined controls specified in the IT control policies and was unable to encompass new and emerging risks in a changing business environment.

The outcome of this phase of the study was further influenced by more changes in the organizational environment. Outsourcing and offshoring initiatives required the IRM program and model to be more flexible and responsive. Change was again identified as a key attribute that influences the efficacy of an IRM program. The implementation study revealed certain shortcomings that constrained the applicability of the model to situations where the risks were known and documented:

1. Although the model incorporated a component to address unplanned events (from the learning about related incidents during the earlier research cycle), a method for realizing this could not be found or developed at this stage. This was partially due to the organization's focus on the remediation of known risks and audit compliance. No

suitable methods could be found in the literature or from other practitioners to address this need.

2. For detecting emerging risks, the Model A approach relied on awareness as the main mechanism to identify and report observed unusual
events in work areas.

3.2.2 Model B Approach

Several key stakeholders attributed the inadequacies of Model A to a reporting structure discrepancy. A revision designated Model B was proposed and
implemented. Model B focused on the organization structure, decentralizing
the IRM function into individual lines of business. The regional and corporate
(global) IRM functions served as coordination points to ensure consistency
of practice and help resolve risk issues that crossed lines of business.

3.2.2.1 IRM Organization Model

The primary motivation for and outcome of the change in the IRM structure was the cost model for supporting the function. On the surface, the risk
management model was not impacted. The various initiatives that supported
the strategy remained the same but the lines of responsibility and accountability were transferred to the LOBs.

From a global organizational perspective, the decentralized model was
really two models in one. At a global level, the model exhibited a form of
"federated organization" described by Handy (2002) characterized by a small
core (corporate IRM) and multiple subsidiaries (IRMs within LOBs). For a
federated organization to work, Handy notes that two principles must be
understood and practiced: "The first is subsidiarity: the principle that the
larger and higher body should not exercise functions which can be carried
out efficiently by smaller or lesser bodies." The corporate IRM function in
our study was similar to the higher body. Handy also states that, "The second
principle refers to those in the subsidiaries: they must want to increase the
range of activities in their roles."

The LOBs were receptive to including the IRM function within their
businesses. The global LOB IRMs were willing to increase their ranges of
activities according to the revised scope of work. Thus, the new IRM organization model satisfied these two principles at the global level. As noted by
Pugh and Hickson (1996), for the federated model to work:

A considerable amount of trust and confidence is required. The centre cannot
be sure if the subsidiary organization can carry out the function efficiently
before it has actually done so. But, in a catch-22 situation, if it uses this lack of
experience as an argument against allowing them to try, then subsidiarity will
never occur (pp. 41–42).

The second principle implies that a model provides "more discretionary opportunities in the job, which no one has specified, but, if carried out effectively, will be regarded as showing appropriate initiative" (Pugh and Hickson 1996). There were clear benefits to IRMs in the LOBs if the model was well executed.

At the regional level, IRM would have liked to believe that similar autonomies existed for each LOB IRM subgroup in the region. In reality, the LOB IRM members in the region belonged to a larger LOB IRM group at the global level. They did not have the prerogative to make decisions and set directions locally, and had to follow the strategies and plans of the global IRM head within the LOB. This was essentially a decentralized and hierarchical structure within each LOB IRM organization.

The regional IRM group that formed loosely through the matrix had three reporting lines for each IRM: (1) the global head of LOB IRM; (2) the RIRO; and (3) the regional LOB CTO or head of IT. The RIRO as the main coordinator for IRM activities of the region had to synchronize them with seven global heads of LOB IRM while ensuring that the seven regional LOB CTOs were agreeable to the initiatives. This created substantial complication and communication needs for the IRM organization.

Using the dialectical analysis approach for collected data, as in the previous research cycles, a number of shortcomings were identified and compared with the structure in the Model A approach. The following shortcomings were recorded in my research journal:

1. While cost management was one of the motivating factors for change, the implementation resulted in additional headcount cost (directly incurred by the businesses). The seven global heads of LOB IRM were re-leveled from vice president to senior vice presidents. The LOBs could no longer work on a partial headcount basis by sharing IRM resources with other LOBs. The minimum IRM staff in an LOB was one. Before the reorganization, several LOBs funded half or fewer headcount resources for the regional IRM group.

2. Although the total number of IRM members in the Asia region after the reorganization increased (from 14 to 17), the group could not be scaled to cross support different LOBs. Some IRMs at less critical LOBs had fewer activities due to the lower number of business applications and the static nature of the applications (like accounting and human resource). Other IRMs continued to be challenged by more changes in business applications and regulatory compliance. IRM members at one LOB had no motivation to provide support for another LOB because they would be held accountable for negative outcomes but not recognized for positive results. The resource-sharing issue was played out when one LOB based

in Hong Kong was required to conduct a security review for an outsource service provider (OSP) in Singapore. A number of other OSPs used by the investment banking LOB were also located in Singapore. In the Model A approach, an IRM member in Singapore could simply be assigned to review all the Singapore-based OSPs without concern for cost issues relating to a specific LOB. After reorganization, the IRM in Hong Kong (who were not part of the investment banking LOB) had to justify a single trip to Singapore for the review, and the Singapore-based IRM (who were part of the investment banking LOB) could not extend assistance to perform the review. From a risk management perspective, the division of IRM by LOBs limited the IRMs' views of risks relating to OSPs. The IRMs had to gather views separately through the global IRM scorecard process.

3. Maintaining consistent IRM practices across different LOBs emerged as another issue. In Model A, every LOB IRM was already planning a specific approach to manage risks, mitigate gaps, and use various reporting and assessment tools. Much time and many resources were invested to promote consistency. The change meant that LOB IRMs would be more focused on fulfilling the demands of the regional CTO and the global head of LOB IRM, instead of ensuring consistency of practice across IRM. Although a global IRM Technology Risk Council (TRC) was established to promote consistent practices, the council's recommendations were not enforceable from accountability and resource perspectives. The council could only influence the principles of practice in general, but could not determine how they would be executed.

4. The inconsistency of practices had the potential to create confusion among the businesses and auditors. It could also lead to different interpretations of policies.

5. As the number of IRM staff in each LOB was limited, each LOB IRM would have a broader scope of responsibility and coverage. This gave little room for specialization. IRM staff members would become generalist risk managers and require more external assistance for dealing with new issues. This would impact IRM career development and increase the cost of risk management.

6. The global LOB alignment also meant that every risk decision in a region (within an LOB) required consultation with the global head of LOB IRM. This increased the turnaround response time for IRMs. When priorities on the global side started to shift, the region's attention would be affected. Essentially, if an LOB IRM could not tap into other local or regional IRM resources, the LOB risk exposure could increase.

7. As a direct cost to LOBs while reporting directly to CTO in the LOBs, IRM members would have to focus more on business results. While this might provide a better understanding of the businesses they served, it also meant they would avoid contentious issues that could be seen as not producing business results. This arrangement was also vulnerable to habituation (see Section 3.2.2.2 below).

Analyzing using the four windows systemic perspective of Flood (1999), the issues revealed had the potential to affect all four window areas unfavorably:

1. Practice consistency, increased cost and reduced scalability of IRM resources, increased reporting complexity and bureaucracy, and increased decision dilemmas could affect the structures of the systems and hence the effectiveness of the IRM group.
2. The issues of cost versus scalability and increased bureaucracy would affect the process systems and hence the efficiency and reliability of the IRM group.
3. The difficulties of cross-LOB support would reduce interactions of IRMs and prevent them from learning from other LOB IRMs. Furthermore, the limitations on IRM development and the generalization of IRM expertise diminished the meaningfulness of the IRM function.
4. From a system of knowledge power view, the fairness of the new organization to the LOBs along with the increased cost of managing information security risks had to be considered. Was it fair for an LOB IRM at a local level to undertake a much greater range of responsibilities without adequate resources to execute the responsibilities? The LOB IRM recommendations for resolving risk issues identified at the LOB also had to be questioned because of the bias of LOB IRM reporting and the reward system in the new organization.

From the four windows perspective, the change did not add significant value to the IRM systems. Model B introduced several new issues and dilemmas without substantial benefits when compared to the Model A approach.

3.2.2.2   *Learning through the Model B Approach*
The implementation and execution of Model B raised a number of questions as shown by the discussion of the IRM organization model above. The findings showed that the approach was ineffective for improving the risk status of the organization and the systems for managing information security. More critically, the analysis of the changes whereby IRMs become part of the LOBs organization, like the CSA process, had the potential of introducing the risk of habituation as described in Section 3.1.4. When such an

organizational model is in use, additional measures are required to counter the habituation challenges.

The knowledge gained from negative cases evidenced in the research cycle rejected the Model B approach from an information risk management perspective and from a cost and resource management perspective. Model A evolved over the period of the study and its various components provided a practical framework to address the social–technical information risk issues and dilemmas in the organizations. However, it did not address the responsive requirements.

3.2.2.3 Learning from SQL Slammer, Blaster, and SARS Incidents

The real test of any approach to information risk management is the onset of a significant security or non-security related event that affects an organization's risk status. During the study's action research cycles in which the two social–technical models were tested and implemented, ALPHA faced the (1) SQL Slammer network worm; (2) the Blaster network worm; and (3) the SARS epidemic.

3.2.2.3.1 SQL Slammer Worm Infection In January 2003, an unknown perpetrator released a network worm program on the Internet. According to CERT/CC (2003a):

> The self-propagating malicious code exploits a vulnerability in the Resolution Service of Microsoft SQL Server 2000 and Microsoft Desktop Engine (MSDE) 2000. This worm is being referred to as the SQL Slammer, W32 Slammer, and Sapphire worm. The propagation of this malicious code has caused varied levels of network degradation across the Internet and the compromise of vulnerable machines.

A software patch for the security vulnerability (Lanza 2002) exploited by the worm on the structured query language (SQL) database server system was published on July 24, 2002 (Microsoft 2002), more than five months before the incident emerged. The worm program required access to a specific network service (UDP[42] Port 1434), which in most situations was blocked by perimeter network firewalls against external network access, particularly from the Internet. ALPHA's network was attacked and the worm program managed to propagate to the database server systems in Australia. The worm greatly degraded internal network services and affected access to various critical business and office applications.

A day before the worm propagation to the network in the region, IRM's CIRT engineer received a security advisory about the emerging threat. He immediately notified IT services and the line of business application development teams to block access to the relevant network services and apply the security patch as soon as possible. The IT and business stakeholders did not, however, respond to the security alert in a timely manner. The result was a significant service impact the next day.

I later learned from global IRM members that a consultant was responsible for introducing the SQL Slammer worm to the organization's network from his infected machine, albeit accidentally. He was connected to ALPHA's corporate network via its virtual private network (VPN) remote access service from a hotel in New York where he worked remotely. As a result of this incident, the IT control policy was revised to require all external consultants and vendors to use only certified computer systems equipped with security software before they accessed the organization's network environment.

3.2.2.3.2 Severe Acute Respiratory Syndrome (SARS) Epidemic   In early March 2003, an outbreak of a new disease known as SARS emerged in Asia. By April 1, 16 deaths in Hong Kong and 4 in Singapore were reported. More than 1,000 people were quarantined at home and in hospitals. Because the cause of the infection was not fully known and the number of victims escalated, organizations started taking precautionary steps to minimize outbreaks among staff members. ALPHA partially activated its contingency plan in locations like Hong Kong and Singapore. Staff members worked from more distributed locations (their homes or business continuity sites) to prevent overcrowding in the offices and minimize the potential spread of the virus.[43]

The most critical requirement from an information security perspective was the need for secure remote access. Because many employees worked remotely from hotels during business trips or from their homes, a secure remote access infrastructure was already in use in the region and globally but it needed additional components. Users needed tools for their laptops or home PC desktops to connect securely to the corporate network from remote locations to continue their work. They also needed access to the corporate information systems, and the ability to network legitimately. This required more than maintenance of the usual office-based access. The lack of these tools created a bottleneck in the implementation of contingency plans.

Suddenly, ALPHA faced a surge of requests for new remote access accounts, IDs, hardware, and software to facilitate access. This became a challenge to the IT services that had to deal with the surge. More problems emerged when IT services encountered a shortage of hardware to meet users' contingency needs. Most importantly, the new remote access users had to learn to use the new security tools before they started working from home.

Another realization concerned network capacity—the number of remote connections the VPN infrastructure could support. The infrastructure was designed to support about 25 percent of the user population in the region and could serve up to 50 percent of the employees working remotely in Hong Kong and Singapore if needed. If a need arose for more employees to work remotely, the remote access network would reach its threshold and the contingency plan would not be fully deployable.

The outsourcing of all operations support functions to a third party occurred on April 1, 2003. It should have been a blessing to the organization since the third party presumably could leverage its resources from other locations to meet the sudden surge of demands from ALPHA. The provider was, however, also supporting the IT infrastructures of other organizations affected by the SARS outbreak. ALPHA's hope of continuing operations using the outsource service provider's infrastructure simply faded away. Instead of gaining leverage from the outsourced service provider, ALPHA faced a resource competition problem and the service provider was not equipped to handle the unplanned simultaneous demands.

The epidemic continued through late July 2003. The consequences of the epidemic were profound. The economy of the region and the financial performances of many organizations were crippled (Song 2003, Prystay 2003). Fortunately, no major security attacks or frauds were found at ALPHA during the SARS epidemic.

3.2.2.3.3 Blaster Worm Infection

In early August 2003, another network worm program known as W32/Blaster or simply Blaster was reported on the Internet. Blaster exploited a known vulnerability of the remote procedure call (RPC) interface on Microsoft Windows operating system platform (CERT/CC 2003b, Finlay and Morda 2003). Public notification of the vulnerability and related security patch was circulated on July 16 (Microsoft 2003b), 25 days before the outbreak of Blaster worm, which was detected globally on August 11, 2003.

Blaster looks for Microsoft's NetBIOS[44] network services (at ports 135, 137, and 139). NetBIOS was used widely on Microsoft Windows operating system networks for file sharing within a network environment. In most organizations, file sharing using NetBIOS will be blocked at the network perimeter[45] by network firewall devices since the sharing service was for internal network use only.

While ALPHA had a managed network infrastructure with multiple tiers of firewall systems, the NetBIOS network service was open to external connectivity. While the security patch was available, it was not applied to the IT environment and the network was infected with Blaster. All the desktop PCs, laptops, and server systems running Windows were almost immediately affected. This caused network congestion and continuous shutdowns and restarts of machines.

The incident escalated to Severity 1 status. That meant IT services stopped all other activities and immediately deployed the patches, blocked service port 139 at the network perimeter, and ran antivirus software to eradicate the malicious program. More than a week of remediation activities was needed to clear the IT infrastructure of the network worm infection. All IRM members were activated to support the Severity 1 process by participating in crisis conference calls and providing risk management advice on demand.

On the Monday after a declaration by IT services that the worm had been eradicated, it reemerged on the network. An investigation established that the laptop of an employee who was on vacation became infected while connected to his home network. The worm was not eradicated from the laptop and spread to ALPHA's network when the employee returned to the office. The second infection was limited to a small number of PC systems that had not been patched and was resolved a few days later.

While the social–technical (Model A) approach was able to help address the soft issues, the techniques focused on understanding stakeholders' perspectives and gaining their commitments and not on preparedness or readiness for change events and other incidents. Therefore, when Blaster and other incidents occurred, the responses were again reactive and focused on recovering from rather than limiting the damage. Along with a poor state of preparedness, these incidents revealed a lack of capability and capacity to respond.

Following the SQL Slammer incident, the global IRM group proposed an update of the IT control policies that would require third party access to the corporate network only from "certified" computer systems. However, no technology was available to detect an authorized connection to a network then. The only possibility was to use a fixed network address, and/or a fixed hardware identifier for the network access card on the system. This was found impractical from an administrative view because of the number of computer systems on a network serving more than 100,000 staff members worldwide. No policy can be enforced (or certification implemented) unless an organization has the capability of detecting violation. Nevertheless, certification was still under discussion when the Blaster incident occurred (more than seven months after the SQL Slammer incident).

For convenience and expediency, contractors, consultants, and even staff members continued to connect any machine that would help them deliver services to ALPHA's corporate network. They faced monetary penalties for not delivering services, but the chance of tracing a virus or worm attack back to them was low. Some claimed ignorance of the policies and certification process when they were found to be using uncertified systems on the network. If a certification body is to perform validation work, it must provide evidence of proper validation and machine configuration upon completion. However, this process cannot ensure that a user will not add or remove other software and devices after certification is completed.

Another policy concern was the definition and implementation of a "secure build" required to ensure that third party computer systems connecting to the network were not infected, malicious, or vulnerable in an effort to prevent spread of their problems to other systems in the corporate network. Ideally, a secure build should be able to detect both new and known risks on a system to be connected to the network. The available technical measures including software and configuration at the time of this research cycle (2003), were limited to those that prevented known risks of attacks.

Antivirus software, which was the main security technology then, could only detect previously known viruses and worms, not new strains just "released in the wild." Heuristic non-signature based virus protection capability tended to take a more precautionary approach and often sounded false alarms. Their sensitivity to the differences was reduced in an effort to gain user acceptance—another form of habituation (Section 3.1.4). The new policy, even with a certification procedure and secure build requirement, was not sufficient to provide the controls needed to respond to unplanned events.

Both the SQL Slammer and Blaster worms exploited vulnerabilities that required access to network services (NetBIOS and SQL) that should not have been open to the public on the Internet. A commercially availability security solution for providing those services in a secure manner (for example, via an application proxy) to prevent external exploitation was not deployed. This showed a failure to consider security during the design of applications that require network services to be opened publicly. In both cases, security patches were available many weeks before the worms were released but were not applied. This showed the ineffectiveness of the patch management systems used by IT services and the failure was confirmed in the post-incident review.

The post-incident review after the Blaster incident also noted that ineffective communications and inaccurate IT asset inventories and policy implementations were the major obstacles to effective response and recovery. These findings should have surfaced in the SQL Slammer incident, but no post-incident review was conducted by IT services. Again, this indicates a possible learning disability (Senge 1990, Argyris and Schon 1991) in the organization, as discussed in Sections 3.1.6 and 3.2.1.2.

When a perpetrator develops an exploit code and launches a virus or worm program to attack vulnerable systems on the Internet (behind or outside the corporate firewall networks), other perpetrators will copy the attack pattern. From an information risk perspective, we should expect similar attacks to recur and organizations must be prepared to handle them. Recurrences of similar events are not coincidences. As Burger and Starbird (2005) emphasize, they are "expected coincidences" since such attacks are widely publicized and their results and impacts have been demonstrated.

> Coincidences *do* happen, and when they do, we take note. Any particular coincidence is indeed an extremely rare event; however... what is rarer yet is for us to experience *no* coincidences at all. Basically, the moral is to expect the unexpected (p. 4).

Besides handling "expected coincidences," organizations must expect the unexpected like the SARS epidemic that lasted several months and affected infrastructure systems in ways ALPHA did not anticipate. The SARS epidemic should have been considered an expected coincidence because the avian influenza (bird flu) incident occurred in Hong Kong in 2002 and led to the killing of more than 170,000 chickens to eliminate all virus strains from evolving into epidemics (CNN 2002). The business continuity management (BCM) function did not anticipate in 2003 that a disease epidemic could impact business organizations directly after the bird flu incident of 2002. The SARS epidemic thus became an unexpected event that no organizations including healthcare providers and medical professionals were prepared to handle.

In a global information security survey involving more than 1,300 respondents, Ernst & Young (2005) reported that organizations, on the average, allocate only 15 percent of their time and budgets for incident response-related activities when attacked, 38 to 41 percent for daily routines, 18 percent for compliance, 6 to 7 percent for other activities, and 18 to 22 percent for strategy.

In the same survey, Ernst & Young also noted that 60 percent of respondents named "compliance with regulations," 31 percent named "worms and viruses," and 55 percent named "meeting business objectives" as the main driver that most significantly impacted or would significantly impact their organizations' information security practices. In later surveys, compliance remained one of the top drivers for information security—50 percent in 2006 (Ernst & Young 2006), 68 percent in 2008 (Ernst & Young 2008), and 64 percent in top three priorities in 2012 (Ernst & Young 2012b)—even though more respondents pay more attention to new technology and social media risks in recent years.

In contrast, priority on incident preparedness remains low in Ernst & Young survey results—10 percent in 2011 and 48 percent in 2012. In 2008, "only 24 percent of the respondents ran crisis management testing that involved business and executive management" (Ernst & Young 2008). Business continuity planning that should include incident preparedness ranked among the top three priorities of only 55 percent of the respondents in 2012 (Ernst & Young 2012b).

The lack of focus on incident preparedness or readiness was a common problem in the industry and not peculiar to ALPHA. From an information risk management perspective, these incidents substantiated the need for an event level action strategy in the information risk management model developed in the earlier research cycles. Putting these issues in today's context as cybersecurity risks evolve rapidly, the need for incident preparedness has become even more urgent (Ernst & Young 2012a).

3.2.2.4 *Business Continuity and Disaster Recovery Planning*

While the SQL Slammer and Blaster incidents revealed ALPHA's inadequacies in responding to information security risk issues, the SARS epidemic provided new insight into the workings of business continuity management including ALPHA's business continuity plan (BCP) and disaster contingency and recovery plan (DCRP).

As shown in Figure 3.16 and discussed in Section 2.4, the traditional approach in information security planning was often based on a strategy of protect, detect, and respond or react. Most organizations such as ALPHA, however, placed significant focus and emphasis on the protective element in view of the regulatory and auditor pushes for compliance. While incident detection, response, and management were covered in the IT control policies, the systems for detection focused mainly on known events and the systems for response management focused on recovery.

In most cases, as at ALPHA, recovery of IT infrastructure and application systems was regarded as a facet of IT management and therefore handled as a subfunction of the IT services division focusing on DCRP or disaster recovery planning (DRP). Recovery of business-related services was the responsibility of the BCM function as part of the BCP process.

As shown in Figure 3.16, IRMs can implement many security measures to prevent an incident but many cannot react on their own after an incident occurs. If a security event affects the IT infrastructure or systems, IRM must call upon the disaster contingency (severity management) process, with actions determined by DCRP management. In the event of a business operation or service issue, the IRM's reaction or response will be to route the incident to BCM to determine what business continuity steps are to be taken.

The role of IRM takes a backseat, providing on-demand advisories, mainly whether the IT control policies can be relaxed to meet the needs of the

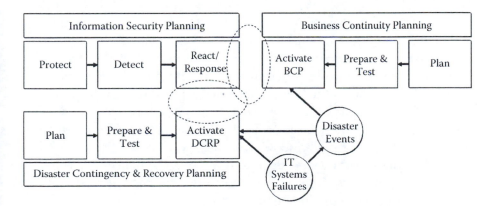

Figure 3.16 Lack of synergy of IRM, BCP, and DRP systems and processes.

situation. IRM plans and actions before an incident do not provide guidance or activate any systems or processes that can facilitate response or hasten recovery. Conversely, DRP and BCP pay little or no attention to information-security related risks and incidents. They assume that IRM will handle risks and incidents within the scope of their practice, only to be surprised when their plans were activated because of such incidents.

These were the outcomes experienced after the series of incidents that occurred during the research study. Clearly, the incidents revealed gaps and a significant lack of synergy among the three roles that were responsible for unplanned events affecting the organization. We could have asked IRM to work more closely with the BCM and/or IT on DRP or vice versa, but if the systems of approach remain different and separate for each function and compliance and prevention of risk are primary concerns, an integrated approach would still be an unlikely outcome from a collaboration.

3.2.3 Summary of Issues and Dilemmas and Research Outcome

Table 3.2 summarizes the key issues and dilemmas analyzed in the phase of the study that tested the Model B approach. The outcome of the study of the development and implementation of the social–technical approach revealed the following points:

1. Incorporation of social science and systems thinking techniques into an IRM system was possible. Based on a subsequent stakeholder analysis, the positive outcomes were acceptance of the IRM program and commitments of stakeholders to implementation. Causal analysis of the new IRM system also showed it was capable of addressing theory of actions issues among stakeholders.
2. The FLAM framework and SECD4 process that evolved from the learning of the social–technical approach provided a set of tools suitable for understanding existing IRM systems and devising action strategies for improving information risk management systems.
3. Care should be taken in deciding an organization structure. The implementation of the Model B approach showed that a fully decentralized model with full LOB ownership of the IRM function may not necessarily be efficient, effective, meaningful, and fair, when evaluated from a four windows systemic perspective.
4. The series of security incidents showed that the focus on the soft aspects of IRM is important, but not sufficient. The focus does not address the changing nature of the information risk environment, in view of the discrepancies analyzed in the current risk assessment methods and the limitations of a compliance-oriented approach. The

Table 3.2 Four Windows Systemic View of Information Risk Management Situation at ALPHA during Action Research Cycle on Model B Approach

Systems of Process (Efficiency and Reliability)	Systems of Structure (Effectiveness)
Decentralized organization model (Model B) increased overhead in resources; concentrating decision authorities in global groups could impact efficiency and reliability of IRM in each LOB in region	Model B lagged in flexibility by requiring all decisions to be made at the top of the organization hierarchy and added new layers of coordination and communications requirements regionally and globally
Existing systems of processes unable to detect emerging risk issue; incidents indicated systems of processes were not ready to respond efficiently and reliably to critical security events	Multiple incidents showed that existing system focus on protection and prevention with little to no attention to responsiveness led to significant losses in productivity and long period of recovery
Gaps in process integration and synergy among IRM, BCP, and DCRP with regard to incident response and management	Changes in organization structure did not resolve need for increased local planning and action strategies; changes reduced effectiveness of IRM and LOB in addressing risks in business and IT environments

Systems of Meaning (Meaningfulness)	Systems of Knowledge Power (Fairness)
Different modes of communication required for different stakeholders for IRM program to be meaningful to each group	Possible bias of IRM assessments and resource focus and unfair demands on regional IRM members' time and resources resurfaced from design of IRM reporting line and organizational structure
Meaningfulness of IRM scorecard was evaluated and value was limited to compliance measurement and focus on key issues that were predetermined and documented in IT control policies	Decentralized organization structure concentrated power in global groups, requiring use of influence in region to gain commitment and motivate IRM performance
IRM program was unable to provide or support meaningful outcome in critical incident situations	Diminishing authority and autonomy in location and region reduced focus on local requirements and issues

Source: Flood, R.L. 1999. *Rethinking the Fifth Discipline: Learning within the Unknowable*. New York: Routledge.

incidents also highlighted discrepancies among the IRM, BCM, and DRCP functions when the requirements and focus intersected at the response element.

These outcomes suggested the need to further improve the model and add a requirement to address both planned and unplanned change events in the organization's information risk environment.

Endnotes

1. ORC is funding a financial institution must set aside annually. In the event of operational risks that affect the organization, the funds can be used to cover the losses incurred. ORC was intended only for operational risk issues including systems and information risks. The amount was based on the operational risk managers' assessments of the potential exposures (or risks) faced. The audit result (rating) was a factor in allocating ORC because it should demonstrate how well the controls performed in managing exposures and risks. In the case of ALPHA, the factors were 0.85, 1.00, 1.25, 1.50, and 2.00 for ratings of A, B, C, D, and F, respectively. If a department rated C, D, or F in an audit, its operating budget for the year was reduced by the appropriate audit factor. For example, if the ORC for a department were computed at US $1 million, a C rating for the department would increase the ORC to $1.25 million. This would normally lead to cost cutting, reduction or elimination of bonuses, and even staff changes to provide the ORC adjustment required. Conversely, the ORC of a department that achieved an A audit rating will be reduced by 15 percent and provide additional budget for operations, bonuses, and other items. Audit ratings are therefore key motivators for making a group compliant.

2. Asia also included Australia and New Zealand. However, no significant IRM activities were reported for New Zealand since it was supported by staff in Sydney. My data collection process included interviews of stakeholders in Sydney, Singapore, Hong Kong, and Tokyo.

3. The activities of Asia IRM team members had direct impact on other stakeholders' perception and results on IRM deliverables and future development. In addition, IRM's practice, ongoing business support and future function and focus will be affected by stakeholders' acceptance of IRM deliverables and perception of IRM's value contributions.

4. The global corporate IRM determined the main direction and agenda for the IRM team. This impacted my plan and also provided a channel for escalation of issues from the region.

5. Asia did not have a dedicated IRM function for business lines. Resources in the region were shared across business lines then.

6. One may argue that such attitude of stakeholders could result from a lack of information security risk awareness, and that improving awareness would escalate priorities for information risk activities. While education and awareness help, they do not replace group and individual immediate short term goals and agendas. The effects of education and awareness are often long term. It is therefore essential to review other approaches for adding information risk issues and activities to stakeholders' agendas, instead of simply relying on education and awareness. Despite this, education and awareness were incorporated into the IRM program throughout the study because such activities eventually produce longer term cultural and practice changes.

7. CSA was a process designed and directed by the ORM department. Information risk was one of the components assessed. A semiannual checklist-based process required the business manager for each department to identify any missing controls or potential control issues in their areas. The results were entered into a central database and periodic reports were generated to give management a

comprehensive view of the statuses of all business systems from a control perspective. Every checklist item was marked green (complied), amber (action taken to comply, not fully implemented), or red (not complied, no planned action) to indicate the status of compliance. CSA was not specific to ALPHA practices; it was a common tool used by central banks in several countries to ensure that their organizations practiced some form of risk management and control.

8. If an auditor identified an issue that was not captured in a CSA report, a business department would receive a poor audit rating for failing to perform a thorough or accurate self-assessment.

9. In one of the heritage firms, IRM was organized as a business aligned function reporting directly to a business manager (or business application development manager) whose main task was to handle the CSA and audit-related activities. In another heritage organization where R&C was practiced, IRM focused only on providing technical security advice for addressing control issues. However, IRM was also engaged by the R&C function to help conduct security (pre-audit) reviews a few weeks before the major audit to ensure that control issues were addressed prior to the audit. The IRM performed audit coordination functions during audit processes.

10. IRM is a back-office function that does not contribute directly to an organization's revenue or profitability. Having seen several layoffs after the mega merger in 2000 and 2001, IRM staff and managers were concerned about job security and were eager to demonstrate their value contributions. As a result, they willingly undertook pre-audit activities that could demonstrate their contributions (through satisfactory or higher audit ratings). Conversely, successful elimination or resolution of risk issues not related to compliance would produce a "no security incident" result—a nonmeasurable nonevent.

11. A check of the knowledge background, training, and experience of IRMs revealed that more than 50 percent of their staffs had no formal information security or risk management qualifications, training, or job experience before joining the teams. They were mostly project managers or auditors before transferring to IRM.

12. To understand the scope of the security risk management issues and dilemmas in BETA's customer organizations (government agencies, financial institutions, and other business enterprises), I designed a mini-survey of 37 questions and used it as a basis for further data collection with the stakeholders of the organizations. The questionnaires were used to guide a series of structured interviews with 30 respondents to determine the similarities and differences of their security risk management challenges and their strategies and plans in managing the relevant issues and dilemmas. The interviews and survey responses provided new insights on the issues and dilemmas of information security risk management.

13. In one heritage organization, IRM functioned within a business group known as business-aligned IRM (BIRM). The IRM reported to the head of operations or head of business application development and the payroll cost for the IRM was fully absorbed by the business group. BIRM is a global organization within a business organization. For example, the investment banking business maintained a global BIRM team. Each region and business center in a strategic geographic location was supported by a local BIRM. The manager served only his or her own business department. In other words, an IRM from the investment

banking business would not do work for a retail bank operation and vice versa. This ensured business specialization and focus for IRM operations.

14. In another heritage organization, IRM was part of IT and grouped as a centralized, shared pool of resources to serve all businesses. To fund resources, the businesses were charged at the end of each year based on their utilization of the IRM. The funds were allocated based on previous year utilization. This model enabled better scalability and a greater variety of work for IRM members. However, it prevented business specialization. An IRM was required to understand the information risk issues in various businesses.

15. In the newly merged organization, a slightly modified pooled resource model was adopted. An IRM team was established to focus on helping the businesses manage their information risks. A team of security engineers was assigned to support IT services in infrastructure security and business application development. The regional team had two lines of reporting, one to the regional head of IT services and another to the region's COO. The Global CIRO's rationale for this reporting was to ensure a balance of power and allow for business issue escalation to the COO when necessary.

16. ALPHA regional centers were in Singapore, Hong Kong, Tokyo, Sydney, and Mumbai.

17. An LOC was set up in each operating location in a region to monitor and address all operation-related issues including problems found in the systems used by the lines of business in the location. The head of business operations of one of the lines of business chaired the LOC. Its members included the chief control officers (CCOs) of all lines of business, and the heads of compliance, audit, IT services, and business application development for the location. Committee agendas covered regulatory and compliance issues and requirements.

18. This risk did not materialize, as the COO did not take an active interest in managing the regional IRM function. The COO was responsible for agenda items that required assistance from IT and therefore preferred to let the head of IT continue to be the primary reporting line for IRM in the region. The parallel reporting was redundant.

19. The SNMP is a network management component of the Internet protocol suite that allows devices and computer systems on a network to report the status of their well-being, and configurations to a requesting station in a standardized manner. Weakness or vulnerabilities of the SNMP could potentially allow a perpetrator to gain information about device configurations that would allow him or her to compromise the security of information and systems on the network.

20. SPAM refers to unsolicited electronic mail messages sent by advertisers and marketers to solicit recipients' visits to their websites or purchase their products. In 2002, SPAM messages were mainly annoyances to the recipients because they quickly filled mailboxes and deleting them took time. In 2003, SPAM was used to carry malicious programs that often tried to take control or steal data including sensitive business and personal information from users' computers (Byrum 2003, Moeller 2004, Egan and Mather 2005).

21. A security exploit is a computer program or series of procedures (computer-based or manual) devised by a perpetrator to exploit a vulnerability to gain unauthorized access to computer systems or information or disrupt access.

Some security researchers develop such exploits to demonstrate the criticality of vulnerability, while perpetrators develop and use them for fraudulent or criminal purposes.

22. Build is a common IT term that denotes the version or makeup of an application or operating system for a specific environment. A build integrates the base components of an application or operating system (supplied by a vendor) with other environmental and system variables such as devices used locally, number of users supported, language used locally, level of patches applied, etc., to create a system specific to the environment.

23. The NIST Risk Management Guide for IT Systems (*Economist* 2003) cites nine steps for risk assessment. The first involves systems characterization—grouping systems as part of the asset identification step. Threat and vulnerability analyses were separated into two steps, and additional steps covering countermeasures, control analysis, and results documentation were suggested and in essence encompassed the four steps described.

24. Knowles categorized the criticality of identified risks into three materiality levels: group materiality, strategic business unit (SBU) materiality, and low materiality.

25. The problem is asymmetric. We do not know what the potential attackers already know but they can find out what we know because our methods are open and often based on common or standard practices and available technology solutions.

26. The Hurricane Katrina disaster struck New Orleans and the Gulf Coast areas of the US as a Category 4 (and at one point Category 5) storm in late August 2005. It killed tens of thousands of people, destroyed infrastructures, and left many more homeless.

27. Malware is generally used as a short form for malicious software—programs that encode malicious intentions that may harm users or organizations that use the programs.

28. The Organization for Internet Safety (http://www.oi-safety.org/) is an example. It was established by technology vendors to promote the principles and practices of responsible disclosure.

29. The analysis outcome was published in the Journal of the Professional Information Security Association, Hong Kong (Kang 2005a).

30. The dotted lines show a negative influence along the direction of the arrowhead. The solid lines show a positive influence. The plus (+) and minus (-) signs at the beginnings and ends of arrows show the respective increases and decreases of each point in the system. For example, an increase in undesirable behavior would lead to an increase in the number of weak systems and vice versa. An increase in education activities would lead to a decrease in undesirable behavior and consequently a decrease in the number of weak systems.

31. Weak computer systems have security weaknesses that have not been patched when patches are available or have inadequate security configurations (e.g., disabled firewall, no account policy setting) that make them vulnerable to attacks. A weak system is an insecure system.

32. Microsoft's Trustworthy Computing Initiative (http://www.microsoft.com/mscorp/twc/) focuses on ECDR to reduce UB. It also invests in other industry activities in the LEP area to help law enforcement and governments reduce UA.

33. See Figure A.2, Appendix A.

34. SECD4 is a collection of social science inquiry techniques, which includes stakeholder analysis (S), entry and contracting (E), convergent interviewing (C), dialectic data analysis (D), and Flood's four windows systemic view (4)

35. Risk acceptance (known as RA at ALPHA) was a formally documented process included in the IT control policies to permit the information owner to accept identified risks under specific conditions. One requirement was formal documentation of a risk if the costs and resources required for mitigation were too high. RA also required compensating control procedures (using manual means) to be implemented to minimize the possibility of exposure to the risk involved. In practice, however, RA was misused frequently to bypass control measures that were too time consuming or difficult to follow. For example, a request for a generic ID required for application access to database systems was preceded by the submission of a RA form in which the issuer (from IT) could account for the issuance without the need to validate the need for the request. This was clearly a misuse of the procedure. A subsidiary project was initiated to eliminate this practice.

36. This analysis and the series of systemic diagrams were tools for explaining the benefits of the IRM program to the stakeholders.

37. An example of such control issues included legacy application systems' non-compliance with security settings (such as minimum password length) required by the IT control policy. To gain compliance, either the legacy application had to be replaced, or custom-built security systems had to be developed. Both options were costly and unjustifiable from a business view. Such issues therefore required risk decisions to be made.

38. Briefing by the Monetary Authority of Singapore (MAS) on February 8, 2002.

39. The ISRA process documented as part of ALPHA's IT control policy requirements involved identification of information assets (including application systems) and business owners, asset classification, and a high level assessment of the potential threats and impacts of the assets.

40. The IRM scorecard was a two-dimensional table with the X axis listing all the required controls specified in the IT control policy and the Y axis listing the LOBs and core infrastructure system components of ALPHA. Each cell in the table reflected the status of compliance of LOB units or infrastructure components with required controls in green (fully compliant), amber (partially compliant), or red (not compliant).

41. A comprehensive review of the literature in this area is discussed in Section 2.5.4.

42. A user datagram packet (UDP) is used in broadcast network services. UDP-based network services are known to be more vulnerable to attacks. Internet-based applications generally do not require UDP network services. Other more secure methods can also be used in place of a UDP. It is normal practice to block UDP-based network services at a network perimeter.

43. The steps were taken based on advisories from the health authorities that included advice for travelers. For example, see the advisory of the Singapore Ministry of Health (2003).Technical advisories were also available from professional organizations, but limited in content and appropriate response instructions due to the nature of the incident—the first in Singapore's history. See Goh (2003).

44. NetBIOS is a set of networking services for computer networking. NetBIOS can be implemented on top of a number of various networking protocols such as TCP/IP (Transmission Control Protocol/Internet Protocol).

45. A network perimeter is a logical partition for delineating the Internet (or other public) network from the internal corporate network. The perimeter is normally defined by a network-filtering device (firewall) that enforces a security policy. In most corporate networks, the perimeter network involves several firewall systems designed to provide layered defenses against attacks and information leaks. The policy defines the types of permitted and expressly prohibited network services. Network engineers are normally responsible for configuring firewall systems based on policy and monitoring for violations. Information security engineers and information risk managers normally work with application development teams to define appropriate security policies for implementation at network perimeters.

Responsive Security

4

The initial research cycles established that responding to change was an important issue in the IRM system. Also, the evolving program at ALPHA was inadequate to address this need. The need for IRM strategy to focus on preparedness and hence, readiness to respond, did not become obvious until the SNMP vulnerability incident, and was reinforced when the SPAM, SQL Slammer, and Blaster incidents followed. However, as the study then was implementing and testing the social–technical approaches to address the soft issues of the program, developing a response-focused approach was deferred.

In realizing the limitations of the approaches taken for BCP and DRP in Section 3.2.2.4, I noted that the response process intersected the IRM, BCP, and DRP systems. The response process was where we found the common goals with possible leverage and collaboration among the three functions.

The two paths of discovery—literature review and reflexive analysis and interpretation of the practices through action research cycles—reinforced the need for responsiveness. The iterative discourses, case studies, and implementation testing of an evolving approach focusing on responsiveness through the subsequent action research cycles in the study affirmed that the validity of responsive security had not been disconfirmed.[1]

This chapter discusses the reflexive analysis and interpretation involved in the final research cycles, validates and refines the concepts, framework, and methodology of a responsive approach for managing information security risk in a constantly changing risk environment.

4.1 Piezoelectric Metaphor

In an informal discussion with Boon-Hou Tay, a fellow action researcher, about the need to be responsive, he introduced a sensor that is commonly used in the electronic and electrical engineering domains. The device is called a piezoelectric sensor and it exhibits unique characteristics that are typically not found in other sensing technologies. *Piezo* is a Greek word that means *to squeeze*. When piezoelectric elements are strained by an external force (a squeeze or a push), displaced electrical charges accumulate on opposing surfaces (PCB Piezotronics 2002). This means piezoelectric elements have many practical uses in industrial applications as pressure sensors, force sensors, and accelerometers.

The phenomenal behavior of the piezoelectric sensor is interesting in that the charges are displaced uniformly—all positive charges on one surface and all negative charges on the other—in response to the exerted force. The sensitivity of the material to the external pressure triggers the change (accumulation of charges on opposing surfaces) in the internal state of the material. The change of state involved in this phenomenal behavior can be summarized in three distinct steps: (1) squeeze; (2) trigger; and (3) alignment. When the pressure is released, the sequence is: (1) relax; (2) trigger; and (3) de-alignment.

In human organizations in the normal state, individuals focus on their respective tasks (like piezoelectric charges during a relaxed state). When an incident exerts an external pressure on a working environment, individuals who are near the event are likely to respond. Unlike piezoelectric materials that are subject to the rules of physics, human responses will be subjective and personal although their actions or inactions may be influenced before and during an event by other individuals or personal factors. The collective responses of all the people involved in an event may range from chaotic to uniformly coordinated (like piezoelectric sensors).

Chaotic response occurs when an incident has no precedent or bears little resemblance to the prior experiences of the people in the situation. Chaos ensues when individuals pursue their own response actions without consulting or coordinating with others. If an incident is a repetition of a prior situation and the people affected were trained to respond to it, we will likely see the organization behave similar to a piezoelectric material. Responses may vary, depending on the willingness and capabilities of individuals to respond consistently. Nevertheless, every incident tends to be different. The probability of uncoordinated responses increases with the extent of dissimilarity to prior incidents experienced by participants. A small change in an event or series of events has the potential to produce a completely different incident based on nonlinear feedback (Stacey 1992).

To simplify the discussion and analysis by omitting the feedback loop of the system, we can envisage the state changes from normal to fumble (or confusion) to chaotic resulting from the escalation of external and internal incident variables that advance a situation from normal to critical to catastrophic.[2] The amount of effort (or level of difficulty) in responding to an incident will increase as the number of variables increases. The effort required will likely reach a plateau when the outcome is already chaotic. It may even fall drastically at the chaotic stage if no one can do anything at that point. Further changes in the forms and variables of the incident beyond this point are highly unpredictable as are the potential impacts of the responses. As Ralph Stacey (1992) notes:

When a system operates in chaos, it is highly sensitive to small changes. It amplifies tiny fluctuations or disturbances throughout the system, but in a complex way that leads to completely different, inherently unpredictable forms of behavior. Because tiny changes, so tiny that we could never hope to notice or measure them all, can so completely alter the behavior of the system, its long-term development depends in effect upon chance (p. 63).

When a change occurs, people tend to work on personal priorities or respond only to their psychological states of mind in deciding whether to help someone else out of the situation, to work themselves out of the situation, or simply do nothing. According to Stacey (1992), "The behavior of an individual component of a system can have a profound effect on the future of the whole system."

If individuals in organizations can respond consistently, with close alignment and coordination of each other's responses, a behavior similar (or almost similar) to that of a piezoelectric material may be possible. This requires preparation. Preparedness or readiness of the individuals will also make response to a situation easier. The more prepared an organization is for various incident scenarios, the less difficulty it will experience in responding.

The above analysis infers that an organization's responsiveness (alignment of resources) to handle anticipated and unexpected behaviors (triggers) of adversaries[3] or the onsets of information risk events relates inversely to the outcome of the actions of adversaries or events. If this is true, an organization that is not responsive to adversaries' actions and related information risk events will more likely experience a more severe impact than one that is more responsive. While this appears logical, we cannot be sure that an impact is more or less severe because the nature of the incident was unpredictable in the first place. We therefore need to determine whether an organization is better off being responsive or unresponsive.

In essence, response is an action (or set of actions) for aligning organization resources to handle a change event. The efficacy and reliability of a response depend on (1) awareness of occurring or emerging change and (2) awareness of what to do (preparedness) and how to respond (competence). As noted in McGee (2004), the choices of actions available for responding to a change event diminish with time. As an event unfolds into an incident, the options for responding become more limited. Early awareness of a change event and the preparedness or readiness to act that enable an organization to align to the new situation resulting from the change will make a difference in the outcome.

A changing situation in an organization environment features three attributes similar to what a piezoelectric material can detect and respond to: (1) change events; (2) situation awareness; and (3) critical alignment, as shown in Figure 4.1. These three attributes are key elements of a responsive

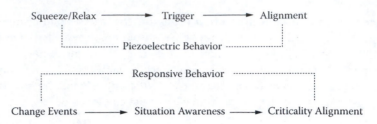

Figure 4.1 Mapping piezoelectric behavior to responsive behavior.

approach. In other words, to be responsive, an organization needs to be able to (1) detect and identify the triggers to discover change events; (2) prepare the systems (people, processes, and technology) to respond effectively and efficiently to each different type of trigger to increase situation awareness or visibility of risks; and (3) coordinate the activities and communicate status of the evolving situation to align people, processes, and technology to respond and manage the incident and provide business continuity by focusing on the critical systems and components involved.

Analyzing this against the past security incidents to which IRM and the various stakeholders were not able to respond effectively and the business and IT infrastructure changes caused by the outsourcing and offshoring plans, it was clear that the changes had to encompass external and internal events and not focus only on potential internal security events.

BETA was a complex system. While internal changes were implemented, events that could produce severe consequences could have arisen from external events affecting the information systems, network, and people in the organization. The span of coverage across the infrastructure and application systems was broad. A balance of focus from business could be achieved if and only if information risk management focuses on criticality of the information risks. The mechanisms for managing risk must be able to adapt to the criticality status of the systems and environment that vary over time and by event type. To bring focus, an understanding of what was critical to the business and the supportive services was needed. The potential estimated impact of an event or incident affecting the security or reliability of the systems should contribute to a criticality assessment.

While this approach appears logical, as gathered from further dialogues with external practitioners, questions about its applicability in an actual organizational environment were raised:

1. How can we detect and identify triggers that will lead to significant events?
2. If the events are unknown, how can we plan and prepare the organizational systems to be ready to respond?

3. How can we measure the performance of this strategy to know that the organization is ready, since it is too late to learn about performance after an incident?

Answering these questions requires more understanding of the characteristics of security incidents and analysis of the forms of past incident responses. These questions were considered as part of the plan and action strategy after completion of the action research subcycles, conducted at BETA and GAMMA.

4.2 BETA's Approach to Emerging Risks and Attacks

In May 2004, another network worm program emerged and began attacking computer systems that were not adequately protected or were exposed on the Internet. The Sasser worm (Microsoft 2004a, Symantec 2004b) was named after the Local Security Authority Services Server (LSASS) where the worm exploited a known vulnerability. Similar to the SQL Slammer and Blaster exploits, the LSASS vulnerability was publicly known (Rafail 2004), and a security patch was already available for deployment on April 13, 2004, more than two weeks before the worm was discovered on the Internet.

According to eEye Digital Security (2004), the LSASS vulnerability was discovered by eEye Research and reported to Microsoft for remediation on October 8, 2003. This meant a gap of 188 days between the discovery of the vulnerability and the availability of the security updates.

While the Sasser worm attack was widely publicized, its actual impact was comparatively smaller than those of the Blaster and SQL Slammer worms in 2003. One BETA customer organization in Singapore and two in Australia suffered significant impacts from the attack. Most other BETA customer organizations fumbled but managed to contain or update their systems against the worm without significant losses.

BETA was directly involved in the Sasser attack in two ways. Like ALPHA, its network was targeted and the organization had to ensure that the internal network and systems were resilient and responsive to the attack. Furthermore, it needed to ensure its customer organizations using its technology systems were similarly protected against the attack.

The swiftness with which BETA was able to respond to the Sasser worm (Symantec 2004b, Microsoft 2004b) incident was unlike the situation when ALPHA dealt with previous worm attacks [SQL Slammer (Microsoft 2002) and Blaster (CERT/CC 2003b)] discussed in Sections 3.2.2.3.1 and 3.2.2.3.3. Within a few hours of detection, each regional center and subsidiary business location around the world assembled a local response team to disseminate the security alert to all staff and provided instructions on how to inform customers of the security situation, receive and handle feedback, and manage infections reported by customers for prompt resolution.

The local response centers communicated with the global response center via a conference call system and also e-mails. A global security alert mailing system generated alert messages to millions of security contacts in the customer organizations to ensure that they received the security alert promptly to begin taking appropriate actions. The efficacy of the response resulted in similar swift follow-up actions from most of the customers contacted and effectively blocked the worm program from propagating. In less than two days, the worm attack diminished to a limited number of local incidents.

Within BETA, all users installed the security patch for the vulnerability that the worm exploited through a mandatory updating process prior to the worm propagation. The internal network was safe from the attack. The network team, however, stepped up monitoring of the network to ensure that no other attacks would emerge during the period when everyone else focused on helping customers to respond to the attack. A study of BETA's practices and recent developments established that:

1. There were no formal security response processes prior to the NIMDA worm incident in 2001. Subsequently, a simple process was established, involving only the security engineering groups and related product groups at corporate headquarters.
2. When the SQL Slammer attack emerged, the response team had difficulties in reaching out to subsidiary and regional business locations. The security engineering group then began to improve the response process to include dissemination of information to regional and subsidiary business contacts.
3. During the Blaster incident, given the scale of the attack, the security engineering response group found it necessary to send security alerts to all customer organizations directly. It was then discovered that the mailing program did not respond quickly enough. E-mail to the last customer contact was sent out more than 48 hours after the first alert message.
4. Not all customer contact information was fully updated, and or no security contact was listed. Most alerts went to procurement and business executives who were not aware of security measures or the criticality of the alert. Sales and marketing staff in the subsidiary businesses were not aligned to the security situation promptly to alert and help customers with attack issues. Some sales executives were still calling customers' executives to sell their solutions when they should have been involved in stopping the worm propagation on their networks.

5. The scale and speed of the Blaster worm showed that a much more responsive process than the existing security engineering response process had to be established.

6. After the Blaster incident, the response process and supporting tools were revamped. A security lead was appointed at each regional and subsidiary business location. Depending on the size of the business, some security leads were appointed to full-time positions; others handled security as a secondary role. The main responsibility of a lead was to ensure security readiness of the region or location.

7. The objective of security readiness was to ensure that the subsidiary and regional offices were all ready to respond to the next security-related incident that would affect the organization and/ or its customers. Readiness involved identifying security contacts at each customer organization; establishment of a virtual security team and a security response team to handle incident- and nonincident-related security issues locally; ensuring mandatory security awareness training to enable staff to understand their roles and responsibilities during a security incident; disseminate monthly security updates to all staff (via the virtual security team); and conduct regular drills of the response process to ensure staff readiness. During a security incident, the incident response team would meet and establish close communications with the local staff and globally with the security engineering response team. The local staff was to ensure all customers under their care received the security alerts and took appropriate actions. Any issues at the local level were then escalated to the local security lead and the global security response lead.

8. In addition to the security readiness program implemented worldwide, response tools were also revised with the addition of a new mailing system and database to support simultaneous and immediate dissemination of millions of e-mail alerts to customers.

9. In each product group, the engineering and development processes were revised to include a mandatory response process to prepare the developers and program managers to respond to security vulnerabilities and exploits discovered on the products they managed.

The efficacy of the changes made at BETA after the Blaster worm incident was visible during the Sasser incident. The main outcome of the changes was the significant improvement achieved in communications and message dissemination during the response process. The change was also intended to improve the perception of BETA's security. Until BETA appointed individuals to focus on security readiness, communicating security alerts and other messages within local subsidiaries and to customers was ineffective.

The alignment and preparation of all staff to be ready to respond to new and emerging security incidents resembled piezoelectric behavior. During the nonincident stage, internal information security risk management activities were geared toward two major steps:

1. Addressing requirements for compliance with the organization's corporate IT security policy. This included the use of security technology designed to improve the status of compliance and enable better use of IT systems. This is a continuous effort aimed to address known risk issues and reduce their chances of becoming incidents.
2. Preparing individuals and groups at all locations and regions across the world to be aware of ongoing security issues, understand the structure, format, and contents of security notification messages (with different levels of criticality), and practice the actions relevant to the levels of criticality of security alerts. The latter was performed as part of the incident response drills that were conducted at least twice a year and prepared the organization to handle emerging risks and discover unknown risks that had the potential to develop into incidents.

These actions were performed during daily activities of individuals and groups and could be compared to the normal un-squeezed (*relax*) state of the piezoelectric sensor.

When a security incident emerged, alert messages were first sent to the security response leads in each location and region to step up their awareness of the situation—*situation awareness*. Once an incident was confirmed, established communications mechanisms were activated. Security alert messages ready for distribution to all staff and customers were promptly prepared and sent. The global security response team was on 24-hour standby to receive calls and e-mails to gather feedback and reports from customers and staff across the world. In parallel, the product engineering team worked on the security workaround and updates. Suitable solutions to the incident were incorporated in the security notification messages and updated when new findings emerged. This stage is similar to the "squeezed" state of the piezoelectric sensor in which individual and group activities *aligned* with the needs and actions required to respond to the emerging incident. The progress of a security incident resembles the pressure asserted in the "squeeze" of a piezoelectric sensor.

When a security incident has been technically resolved via workarounds and/or updates and less support is required, individuals and groups begin to stand down as necessary. The global security response team continues to work with the local security leads to consolidate all reports and lessons learned from the incident to evaluate the effectiveness and efficiency and devise improvements. This stage resembles the gradual release of pressure exerted on a piezoelectric sensor; the system eventually returns to its normal "un-squeezed" state.

While BETA did not base its action strategies on the piezoelectric theory, the motivation and learning that led to the development and implementation of a global system of readiness and response were similar to the learning and understanding I gained at ALPHA. That learning led to the formulation of the piezoelectric theory of information security risk management: when managing information security risk, the action strategies must encompass a system of readiness and response along with addressing the known information security issues to achieve a state of management control as defined in the organization information security policies.

Comparing the action strategies undertaken at BETA against piezoelectric sensor behavior, it was clear that the control actions at BETA constituted a subset of the possible control actions in the piezoelectric theory to address known issues. Similarly, the readiness and response actions at BETA for dealing with emerging and new security incidents were similar to the possible action strategies in the system of readiness and response of a piezoelectric device.

The action strategies of BETA achieved readiness, response, and control. It follows that the action strategies were subsets of the action strategies of the piezoelectric theory of information security risk management. In other words, BETA's actions were in line with the piezoelectric theory of information security risk management and showed that a responsive approach to managing known and unknown security issues made a difference in achieving a positive outcome.

The experience and learning from the readiness activities and responses of BETA found no disconfirming evidence that disapproved the construct validity of the responsive approach and demonstrated how a focus on responsiveness was possible for addressing both known and unknown security risks. They showed that when resources and focus were placed on a system of readiness and response actions, an organization can manage a security incident more effectively and efficiently than it did before such a system was in place. As the incidents unfolded, BETA saw the enactment of the piezoelectric metaphor in real life—the alignment of individuals, groups, processes, and technologies that (unintentionally) paralleled the paths of electric charges within a piezoelectric material. This similarity validates the efficacy of the responsive approach.

The differences in outcomes (impacts experienced) by organizations including BETA that were ready to act on the worm alert by distributing security information and patches supported the claim that an organization that is not responsive to adversaries' behaviors and risk events will more likely experience a more severe impact than an organization that is more responsive. In addition to not disapproving the validity of the responsive

approach, BETA's action strategies related to readiness and response provided further insights on specific actions for implementing such an approach
in other organizations:

1. Establish a structured organization of people, processes, and tools
   to be ready to respond to any unplanned events. The basic elements
   should include an updated internal and external contact list; assigning individual responsibilities for security alert communications;
   and establishing the appropriate tools for crisis communications
   (e-mails, facsimiles, phone calls, and other suitable means). Social
   media that have gained widespread use in public and private online
   environments are also useful for such mass communication needs.
2. Provide regular training and awareness briefings to all employees.
3. Conduct drills to test the accuracy of data (internal and external
   contacts) and readiness of employees to execute their individual
   roles based on the situation. Scenario planning can serve as a tool to
   enhance the readiness and responsiveness of all involved.[4]
4. The need for a stand-down process as an incident is handled, as
   described below.

A typical incident has three major stages (normal to critical and back to
normal). Triggers along a timeline can signify the emergence of a security
incident. Detecting and identifying these triggers are critical steps to ensure
effective and efficient responses because the choices of actions available
diminish as an incident unfolds (McGee 2004).

Every incident eventually reaches a plateau stage at which the level of
significance no longer rises over time. After this stage, the significance level
starts to decline. If individuals who respond to an incident remain at the
same level of alertness (alignment), they would be subjected to undue stress.
Resources spent on this stage are wasted if an incident is resolving and staff
members remain in response mode instead of resuming their daily activities.
Fatigue may also cause errors and produce other unintended consequences.
De-triggering is an important step that allows the gradual stand down of
people responding to an incident. Concern about returning to normal activity was one of the concerns expressed by the subsidiary office teams at BETA.
The lack of communication about resolution of the incident kept them on
high alert longer than necessary.

Conversely, if individuals stand down before the de-trigger point, an
organization will run a risk of being unprepared and possibly face much
more exposure since the level of significance of the event may be near or at
its peak at that point. An effective responsive approach must therefore incorporate appropriate standing-down actions with active monitoring of possible
de-triggers to ensure a smooth and genuine stand down to normal condition.

We see also potential for synergy and leverage of the BCP and DRP functions to ensure integrity of data collected, use of common tools and reporting systems, and consistency and alignment of processes. BCP and DRP scenario planning and drills may also include information security-related incidents to provide end-to-end coverage for business continuity.

4.3   Learning from Tsunami Incident

On December 26, 2004, at 7:59 a.m. local time (12:59 a.m. GMT), an undersea earthquake emerged north of Simeulue Island, off the western coast of northern Sumatra, Indonesia. The magnitude of the earthquake was reported to be between 8 and 9.3[5] on the Richter scale, and lasted about 10 minutes. Besides causing local destruction in the surrounding villages, the quake generated a tsunami[6] that spread over most of the Indian Ocean. According to Caritas India (2005):

> The tsunami the quake generated washed off the shores of Indonesia, Sri Lanka, South India, Thailand, and other countries with waves up to 30 meters. It caused serious damage and deaths as far as the east coast of Africa, with the furthest recorded death due to the tsunami occurring at Port Elizabeth in South Africa, 8,000 kilometers away from the epicenter.

Updated news of the destruction continued to be broadcast on various television channels.

> By the end of the day more than 150,000 people were dead or missing and millions more were homeless in 11 countries, making it perhaps the most destructive tsunami in history (*National Geographic* 2004).

Earthquake experts later reported that Indonesia had no early warning system in place to detect earth movements in the area or under the ocean. Authorities had no way to send early warnings to potentially affected countries to prevent the disaster from causing a massive loss of lives. The irony was that Japan's experience with tsunami disasters and the efforts of US Geological Survey had made a disaster monitoring and alert system available and an early warning message was disseminated (CNN 1998a, b). Cities with more than a million people are susceptible to more fatalities when such a disaster strikes (Roach 2003). The importance of implementing such a system was therefore recognized. The required alert system and related technology were, however, not implemented, as there was no prior incident of this nature in the affected countries. Because of this, such a potential disaster response issue was not brought to the attention of the national leaders concerned, for them to give it priority and resources for implementation. After the incident, the Cable News Network (CNN) reported:

Although National Oceanic and Atmospheric Administration scientists at the Pacific Tsunami Warning Center in Hawaii issued tsunami warnings as soon as they heard of the huge earthquake off Sumatra, the waves outran communications at jet speeds of 500 mph (804 kph), catching hundreds of thousands of people unaware (CNN 2006).

The timeline of the tsunami captured by CNN (2006) and the US National Oceanic and Atmospheric Administration (NOAA) (2004) indicates that early warning was in place but not all countries affected by the disaster were members of the system and did not receive warnings.

False alarms are always concerns when early warnings are issued. According to NOAA, "75 percent of all tsunami warnings since 1948 have been false" (CNN 2005a). Consequently, while Thailand was a member and received the alert, it decided not to act in view of a prior false alarm. Charter 2000-Aliran (2004) in Malaysia also noted that the local media failed to pick up the news of the early morning earthquake in Indonesia that many suspected may have contributed further to the losses.

While the tsunami tragedy highlighted the dire consequences of inadequate early warning systems and preparedness against disasters of such scale, several lifesaving anecdotes were reported. National Geographic noted that:

In several places the tsunami announced itself in the form of a rapidly receding ocean. Many reports quoted survivors saying how they had never seen the sea withdraw such a distance, exposing seafloor never seen before, stranding fish and boats on the sand. Tragically the novelty of the sight apparently stoked the curiosity of the people who ran out onto the exposed seafloor. Tourists in Thailand were seen wandering around photographing the scene.

People who knew geography knew what the receding ocean meant. Survivors who knew it meant trouble reported how they ran for high ground, rounded up family and friends, and tried to warn people who were drawn to the water's edge. Experts say that a receding ocean may give people as much as five minutes' warning to escape to high ground. That may have been enough time for many of the people who were killed by the 2004 tsunami to save themselves, if only they knew what to do (National Geographic 2004).

According to the British Broadcasting Corporation (BBC), a teenage girl who was on vacation in Thailand saw the waves and recalled a geography lesson about tsunamis and alerted her family and other tourists and saved them from the disaster (BBC Online 2005, Telegraph 2005). An Indian national working in Singapore watched the early morning news of the earthquake in Indonesia and called his home in the Nallavadu village in India. His sister, who answered the call, noted that seawater was seeping into their home. The man realized what that meant and urged his sister to run out and warn the rest of the village. The villagers used a public address system set up to announce sea conditions to fishermen and broadcast the warning across the village. Their vigilant and responsive actions saved more than 3,500 lives (Chin 2004, UNESCAP 2006).

These incidents clearly showed the importance of disaster awareness and emergency preparedness. New initiatives were developed to improve responses and prepare for future incidents (Handwerk 2005, Lubon 2006).

Disasters are often unpredictable. However, the tsunami incident in December 2004 came as a shock to most people although signals of its emergence appeared hours earlier. Despite the warning signals, countries that received them did not respond. Most countries assessed that risk as low or insignificant compared with other disasters they experienced despite the well-known tsunami disaster in Japan and the preparation measures Japan implemented.

The tsunami incident showed the human tendency to assess risk based on past incidents and local experience. If people have no prior local experience with a risk, they usually assess it as low. This confirms the observation in Section 3.1.4 that highlighted the importance of making subjectively assessed risks more explicit and bringing attention to risks that are largely unknown. A change in information security risk strategies in an era of constant changes and uncertainties is expected and required.

While the lack of preparedness had cost the lives of many across the region, the fisherman's experience and the school pupil's timely recall of geography lessons saved many lives (Chin 2004, BBC Online 2005, *Telegraph* 2005, UNESCAP 2006). These positive outcomes illustrated the power of knowledge and strengthened the importance of situation awareness as a fundamental requirement of effective and efficient response. Again, the difference in outcome between those saved by responsive people (like the fisherman and school pupil), and those who had no responsive parties to help was significant. This further supports the claim that an organization that is not responsive to the adversaries' behavior and actions will more likely experience more severe impacts.

4.4   Revealing Uncertainties and Making Risks Visible

Among cities with bad weather, Beijing, China's capital, is well known for its smog, i.e., polluted fog that completely blurs vision. As in many other big cities, meteorologists are well equipped to forecast the weather. Before the arrival of heavy smog or fog conditions (like typhoons in coastal cities like Hong Kong and Shanghai during monsoon seasons), the media announce pending events and broadcast frequent updates. They publicize the arrival of the event, the expected duration, and protection measures. Anyone who drives in foggy weather or heavy rain feels very vulnerable because of the lack of visibility. A driver will slow down, turn on the headlights, and turn on the radio to get weather information.

Visibility is an important aspect of situation awareness. It influences our responses to risks. However, most information risks in the online environment are invisible. An important step in managing uncertainties is to provide visibility so they can be recognized. Disregarding them may produce dire consequences as demonstrated in the analysis in Section 3.1.7. Unknowns must be made explicit even if they remain unknown. Knowledge of their existence provides a basis for management attention, discussion, and decision before strategies can be devised. Drucker (1990) suggested a similar approach for managing risk:

> The main goal of a management science must be to enable business to take the right risk. Indeed, it must be to enable business to take *greater* risks— by providing knowledge and understanding of alternative risks and alternative expectations; by identifying the resources and efforts needed for desired results; by mobilizing energies for contribution; and by measuring results against expectations, thereby providing means for early correction of wrong or inadequate decisions (pp. 511–512).

As discussed by Styles (2005), attention is closely integrated with perception, and most effective when visual perception is provided. One possible representation of unknown risks is adding a third plane (or axis) in the risk chart in Figure 4.2. A third axis indicates unknowns and uncertainties in risk assessments. The follow-up strategy for managing the risk will therefore have to address unknowns and uncertainties explicitly.

A parallel of this issue of making unknowns visible can be drawn from Hilary Lawson (2004) who discourses about "saying the unsayable" when she questions the relationship between openness and closure:

> The problem with the notion of 'the world' is that it makes it look as if the world lies already differentiated awaiting the descriptions of the language; as if the task of the human kind is to find the right description, the one that accurately names the bits of the world and their relationships; as if diligent scientists could uncover the ultimate building blocks of matter and we would know what the world is made of (p. 284).

This concept is imposed on the managers in a similar manner. They are expected to be able to identify and assess all information security risks within their organizational contexts and/or information systems comprehensively and accurately with specific methods and tools.

> Instead, I wish to propose that we hold the world as open. It is we who make sense of it through closure. We who, through the process of closure, hold

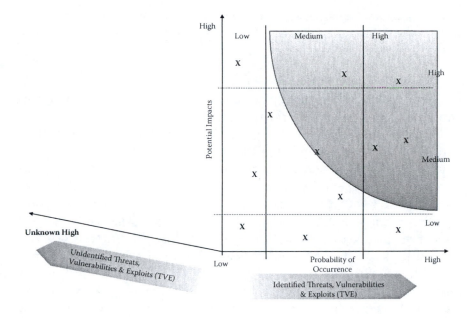

Figure 4.2 Element of uncertainty creates invisible plane on risk chart.

openness as a complex array of things. Closure can be conceived therefore as a process that enables the flux of openness to be held as differentiated bits. Closure is the process of realizing identities, of realizing things. It is the mechanism by which we hold that which is different as one and the same (Lawson 2004, p. 284).

The method by which common risk assessment is conducted further promotes the ideal that all risks that must be known can be known and assessment is only a matter of identifying, describing, and assessing their criticality.

The objects of science, the particles and laws, are not true descriptions of the world but are ways of holding openness, ways of making sense of openness so that we can intervene to effect. All of our sensations, all of our perceptions, all of our descriptions of the world are the product of closure and they have the characteristics of closure. They are not openness, nor do they have anything in common with openness (Lawson 2004, p. 284).

The risk assessment method that we use provides only a form of closure of the risk environment that allows us to intervene. It does not necessarily represent the openness of the risk environment because the environment changes constantly. We therefore should not confine ourselves to a single closure.

At a simplistic level, the framework of openness and closure provides an explanation for our inability to describe the world. We cannot describe the world, because the world is open. Since openness has nothing in common

with closure, if we pursue any individual closure, it is seen to fail. Each closure may offer a way of holding openness, but openness is something other
(Lawson 2004, p. 286).

The effectiveness of the common approach to risk assessment has been
questioned. Evidence from our research study illustrated its limitations,
particularly for dealing with emerging and unplanned risk events. Lawson
(2004) adds that "failures do not tell us how the world is, but the manner
of their failure tells us something about how the world is not." The limitations of the risk assessment and management methods similarly did not provide information about the risk environment, but demonstrated that it was
not limited to what the tools and methods assumed it to be. In other words,
our analysis showed that the risk environment exceeds what a common risk
assessment method can identify. There is a difference between the world view
of the risk assessment method adopted and the openness of the risk environment. The analysis triggers the idea of a third axis (hidden plane that must be
made visible) to provide another closure to the openness of the risk environment to allow for intervention. This is in line with Lawson's theory of closure:

> The strength of the theory is that it offers a description of how it is that
> although we are unable to describe openness we can nevertheless intervene in
> the world. It is this step that allows us to move on from the otherwise relent-
> less circling of the self-reflective paradox (Lawson 2004, p. 287).

In addition, Lawson asserts that:

> Philosophy does not need to remain confined in the strategies of avoidance.
> We do not need to think that we should avoid the attempt to answer the ques-
> tions that puzzle us most deeply. We do not need to conclude that because it
> is unsayable it should be avoided. For in some sense, everything is unsayable
> (p. 289–290).

The third axis that contains the unknowns should not be unsayable and must
not be avoided. By making the third axis visible, we define a new closure to
the openness of the risk environment. As Lawson (2004) stated, "Although
each of these closures [may ultimately] fails in the limit, they are powerful
nevertheless." With this visibility, the closure is "capable of changing how we
think and what we can achieve" (p. 290).

4.5 Responsive, Reactive, and Proactive Strategies

Similar to the practices followed at BETA, analysis of the interviews and survey results from 30 practitioners showed that many organizations had begun

practicing more response-oriented information security risk management even though they continued to espouse defense-oriented strategies. The survey established that:

1. Security monitoring and disaster recovery were among the top three priorities in about one third of the responses. This reflects attention to preparedness (respondents' theory in use). This finding was supported by the votes on the role of IT security during the emergence and occurrence of a security incident and their above average to high level preparedness of their security staffs to handle security incidents. The heavy emphasis on patch management (73 percent) and change management (67 percent) further showed that their practices slanted toward a responsive system of information security risk management.
2. The responses on the level of preparedness and the type of worms and viruses that caused major impacts on respondents' organizations showed an inverse relationship between the two areas. Low preparedness caused greater impacts when unplanned or unknown security events emerged.
3. Conducting drills on security incident response was not in the top three priorities of the security plans of any respondents. However, when security incident response was considered in another context, testing was performed by at least 47 percent of the respondents. A much higher state of preparedness therefore could be expected if preparedness for security incidents were considered one of the top three priorities of a security plan.

This theory in use phenomenon can be explained as a defense-oriented security strategy that is generally perceived as proactive—"prevention is better than cure"—and projects better control and leadership over the issues and concerns involved.

When the responsive security approach was first presented and discussed with information security practitioners outside ALPHA in an effort to seek disconfirming evidence, questions arose about the viability of the approach. Some respondents were concerned that the approach would be too reactive. They mistook *responsive* to mean waiting for something to happen instead of dealing with information risk proactively. The responsive approach is not reactive.

In the context of strategic management, Russell L. Ackoff (1999) identifies reactive, preactive, and interactive planning as important for different needs. The type of planning would also influence the future of an organization and the environment in which it operates in:

> Reactive planning is bottom-up tactically oriented planning. What strategy it contains is implicit, a consequence of numerous independently made tactical decisions. It begins with the lowest or low-level units of an organization identifying the deficiencies and threats they face. Then they attempt to return to a preferred earlier state by designing projects intended to reveal the causes of these deficiencies and threats and to remove or suppress them. Next, using cost-benefit analyses, priorities are assigned to projects. Finally, using an estimate of the amount of resources that will be available for work on projects, a set of them is selected starting at the top of the priority list, working down until all the expected resources have been allocated. The set of projects thus selected constitutes the unit's plan (p. 103).

Reactive planning is therefore issue oriented, specific to an information security risk manager's response to auditors' comments, regulatory compliance requirements, and security breaches.

> Preactive planning is top-down strategically oriented planning. Objectives are explicitly set but tactics are left to the discretion of individual units. Such planning has two parts, *prediction and preparation,* of which prediction is the more important. If a prediction is in error, even good preparation for what it predicts may be in vain.
>
> The preactive planning process begins at the top of an organization with preparation of one or more forecasts of the future. These are analyzed for the threats and opportunities they present. Then a broad statement of overall organizational strategies for dealing with these threats and opportunities is prepared. The predicted future(s) and the strategic "white paper" are then passed down through the organization. Each level adjusts the forecast and the analysis to its own specific environmental conditions, and selects objectives and goals that are compatible with those of the organization as a whole. Programs to pursue these objectives and goals are formulated in general terms (Ackoff 1999, pp. 104–105).

Information security risk managers who adopt a continuous risk assessment approach to determine new and emerging risks in response to organizational events such as changing business systems and processes and introduction of new information technology are in fact preactive in their planning. In general, this is often regarded as being proactive (anticipating issues before they arise).

> Interactive planning is directed at gaining control of the future. It is based on the belief that an organization's future depends at least as much on what it does between now and then as on what is done to it. Therefore, this type of planning consists of *the design of a desirable future and the selection or invention of ways of bringing it about as closely as possible.*
>
> There are aspects of the future that we cannot anticipate; for example, natural or political catastrophes, or technological breakthroughs. We cannot

prepare for these directly, but we can do so indirectly through *responsiveness (interactive)* planning. Such planning is directed toward designing an organization and a system for managing it that can quickly detect deviations from the expected and respond to them effectively. Hence responsiveness (interactive) planning consists of building responsiveness and flexibility into an organization (p. 107).

A responsive approach is beyond being reactive and preactive. In line with Ackoff's definition, it is future oriented, and more importantly, anticipates unknowns and is designed to allow the organization and system to be responsive and flexible. Adopting a responsive approach in information security risk management ensures that an organization's information security system is future-oriented, capable of detecting deviation in the risk environment, and responds effectively. Preparing to respond means putting necessary processes and resources in place and practicing their use regularly. Organizations become more alert to changing situations and less reactive overall. The idea that being responsive is interactive (beyond preactive or proactive) is important to also drive a positive perception for the piezoelectric theory.

It is also important to note that the responsive approach does not eliminate the existing practice of proactively resolving and addressing known security issues. Instead, it highlights the inadequacies of preventive aspects and deals with issues relating to the lack of responsiveness of an organization. When an organization deals only with known issues and expends all the available resources on dealing with known issues, as experienced at ALPHA, it is often surprised by new or emerging security events. Such surprises require more "fire fighting" than preventive plans anticipate.

The concepts of readiness and response were introduced as a new work item proposal at ISO/IEC JTC 1/SC 27/WG 4,[7] and the proposal was discussed at the sixth RAISE[8] meeting in August 2007 (Kang 2007). The discussions led to the development and publication of international standard ISO/IEC 27031 on "ICT Readiness for Business Continuity" (ISO/IEC 2011a).

4.6 Criticality Alignment

Section 3.1.7's discussion of information security risk analysis and management revealed that risk assessment is subjective, filled with uncertainties and unknowns. An information security officer from a major financial institution participating in a security conference commented that "it is so subjective that we are just guessing all the time, and often not sure whether we are doing the right thing."

If risk assessment is not practical due to its subjectivity and ineffective for addressing security issues, what alternative is available to an information risk manager? Furthermore, based on constrained business resources and the business objective focus of management, how does an information risk manager gain the agreement and support of management to direct needed resources to risk management? This situation is similar to a business negotiation in which one or more conflicts of interest exist even though management may acknowledge that information security risks must be managed.

According to *The Strategy of Conflicts,* Thomas Schelling's classic work (1960), one possible strategy is to look for "prominent" solutions that both parties can recognize to provide a focal point for establishing commitment (p. 58). This relates to the notion of criticality alignment—one of the three key stages of the piezoelectric behavior metaphor. According to Section 4.1, the proposition for criticality alignment is that:

> A balance of focus from business could be achieved if and only if information risk management focuses on criticality of the information risks. The mechanisms for managing risk must be able to adapt to the criticality status of the systems and environment that vary over time and by event type.

Criticality alignment defines and provides a focal point from which the boundaries of systems can be identified—where business interests and risk issues intersect. Based on the principles of piezoelectric behavior analyzed in the earlier research cycles, criticality alignment was identified as an area where an information risk manager should focus to align risk management with business needs and respond to issues emerging from changes in organization systems and critical areas. This extends the notion of criticality used in other approaches, such as Knowles's (2005) "materiality" of risk[9] and the criticality of risk at BETA that provide only indicators of the importance of an asset involved.

Alignment relates to outcome. Criticality alignment requires action to produce a desired outcome. Criticality alignment is business directed and business aligned. It focuses on business undertakings (projects, initiatives, programs, uncertainties, sensitive or critical data such as intellectual property, or applications and related supporting infrastructures) that can impact a business and require management to act.

Using the four windows systemic view of Flood (1999), an organization may consider fairness a desirable attribute or requirement for criticality alignment. In Ernst & Young's 2012 Global Information Security Survey, alignment of information security initiatives with business is noted as one of the four most critical areas that has shown little improvement and in fact demonstrated stagnation and even erosion (Ernst & Young 2012b).

The criticality alignment of the business consists of two types of issues. One is the intersection (or overlap) between business-critical concerns and the results of a risk assessment, i.e., potentially high impacts of risks on business-critical information assets. The other is a business concern not detected by risk assessment, for example, a third party service that is critical to certain business processes, but not risk assessed, or did not exhibit identifiable high-impact risks upon risk assessment.

At higher management levels, regulatory compliance is often a business concern. From an information security risk assessment perspective, compliance is a regulatory rather than an information risk. Through the process of identifying and assessing criticality alignment requirements, regulatory compliance may thus surface as a concern requiring focus by information risk managers. At a minimum, in the course of responding to incidents, an organization must remain in compliance with laws and regulations and corporate policies. While this alignment requirement needs to be considered, its criticality depends on the triggering events.[10]

A business environment changes constantly and the criticality alignment requirements of an organization are therefore not constant. The methods for discovering and affirming criticality alignment needs of an organization should allow for changes. The outcome of an initial process should be considered and used to trigger the next round of evaluation and action strategies. An action research approach that is dialectic and iterative is preferred over a static process. The dialectic variation (Dick 2002b) of the soft systems methodology (SSM) (Checkland and Scholes 1990, Sankaran et al. 2004) may be used for this purpose. The SSM-based dialectic approach (illustrated in Appendix B) provides added benefit by the introduction of the ideal world model to compare with the existing environment. The model allows participants and researchers to gain more clarity through the comparison before determining where improvements should be focused.

The approach of using criticality alignment as the focal point for justifying information security systems in organizations was found to be more acceptable from a business perspective, as reflected in an interview with the CIO of a multinational logistic company in Singapore: "The focus [of the logistic company] is on using IT to automate more of their business processes and create more value to the business, and implementing information security, if it is part of the product/systems that they get without paying, they will do it. Otherwise, they will have to consider it more carefully."

Based on the efficacy of using criticality alignment to gain stakeholder agreements and identify a focus for information security risk management, it may appear that risk assessment is redundant but that is not the case. Risk analysis and assessment are still relevant and necessary, even though they are subjective. Risk assessment is part of the criticality alignment identification process and identifies known and perceived risks. Despite the subjective aspect of risk assessment, the list of risk items it identifies constitute a logical starting point for approaching the stakeholders to reach a consensus on criticality alignment requirements. Without a list of risk items, the stakeholders will not understand the risks faced and how they relate to the business and the criticality alignment needs would be impossible to identify.

The list of risk items may not, however, be the only tool that is available. As discussed in Sections 4.9.1 and 4.9.2, failure mode effects analysis (FMEA) may provide a more directed list of critical assets and potential failure modes and address the inadequacies of a risk assessment. FMEA was also introduced as a possible tool in ISO/IEC 27031 (ISO/IEC 2011a).

4.7 Testing Responsive Approach at GAMMA

An opportunity to implement and test the validity of the responsive approach arose in June 2005 when I worked with the chief security officer (CSO) of GAMMA, a retail bank in Thailand. The responsive approach presented a new perspective for addressing the challenges of managing information security risk. GAMMA faced a series of virus and worm program attacks that caused significant business losses. All major banking applications except the automated teller machine (ATM) system that was on a separate network and operating system were unavailable for two weeks.

The case study of GAMMA revealed another limitation[11] of existing risk assessment methodologies such as OCTAVE (Alberts and Dorofee 2002), ISO/IEC 13335 (ISO/IEC 2004, 2005a), ISO/IEC 27005 (ISO/IEC 2008), and various commercial methodologies as described by Moses (1994). Most consultants and GAMMA used such methodologies. There was an assumption in those methodologies that the existing risk assessment identified risks relating to the existing system. When a new system was considered, the methods based on the existing system became inadequate. Information security officers and risk managers would have to wait for the information system designers to complete at least a first draft of their design before the IRM staff could conduct a risk assessment of the draft system. This made risk management a reactive approach and required changes after the risks of the original design were identified, assessed, and analyzed.

Conversely, the CIO wanted the CSO to produce a set of security recommendations including requirements and action strategies to be included as part of the new infrastructure and information systems design. These recommendations could then be incorporated in a new system that integrated security needs.

Instead of using risk assessment as the basis for determining security requirements, a framework-based approach was adopted for GAMMA's needs. The IRM framework (described in Appendix C) was based on the Singapore Standard SS493 developed to capture similar requirements for use in the standards development area.

The IRM framework and the SSM-based Dialectic Model of Systems Inquiry (DMSI) enabled the information security team to sieve through many aspects of the organization to identify the critical information assets, key business requirements, essences and ideals of those requirements, and the implementations feasible to derive the FLAM. The outcome of the FLAM was a comprehensive security plan that addressed the known security risks and key requirements. It also served as a foundation for the CSO to build a more responsive system for preparing against the unknown and unexpected security issues that would likely emerge thereafter.

The concept of criticality alignment was able to identify and align the critical business needs of the CIO and business managers with the IT security concerns and achieve a common focus and the necessary resources to implement the security plan. Unlike traditional security plans that addressed only the known (or identifiable) risks, with minimum or no preparation to deal with the unknown or unexpected, the new plan at GAMMA met the response needs so that the organization became more responsive to planned changes and unexpected changes in the risk environment.

The final dialectics of implementation involved evaluating the results of the external security tests conducted on the new security infrastructure based on the responsive approach. The dialectics focused on the vulnerability management system that addressed known risks and the security updating system designed to mitigate a critical range of newly discovered issues. While a real-time continuous monitoring and performance measurement system was not implemented in this test (it was not feasible due to resource constraints) to measure the responsiveness of the organization, the security readiness of GAMMA reflected an acceptable state of responsiveness for the issues considered. The security readiness of GAMMA was demonstrated by the following:

1. The new IT infrastructure incorporates the component systems required of a responsive approach, namely a system for distributing and installing security updates and malware signature updates as and when the updates are made available by the providers and approved for deployment by the CSO's security operation staff member.
2. GAMMA implemented a process that collects and tracks occurring events. A team of operation staff evaluates the events and gets ready to respond if they develop into security incidents. The process was further supported by the implementation of an incident response and handling procedure. The operational staff members were trained on the operation of the new IT security systems, event monitoring, and incident response procedures.
3. GAMMA engaged a third party security company to conduct security penetration (attack) tests on a periodic basis. The objective is

to ensure that the IT infrastructure can withstand an organized attack by external perpetrators, using known vulnerabilities commonly found on IT systems and applications. GAMMA passed the initial test that established that the new security infrastructure was up to date with security patches and anti-malware signatures, and the operation of the IT infrastructure did not provide weaknesses for commonly known attacks to perpetrate successfully.

The IT systems, operation processes, and testing indicated GAMMA had the minimum necessary infrastructure systems and processes in place and was ready to respond to both known risk issues and a critical range of newly discovered issues. The updating would enable GAMMA to be more responsive than it was before the initiative. The minimum infrastructure systems and processes are important foundations for introducing the more comprehensive responsive strategy model and related strategies (discussed below) to enhance the readiness and responsiveness of the organization.

The testing of the initial responsive approach provided an ecological validation indicating that use of the approach in organizations that had different social and practice values other than those found at ALPHA and BETA was possible.

4.8   Learning from Antinny Worm Case Study

In April 2004, the public website of a computer software intellectual property protection agency (ACCS) in Japan was attacked by a network worm program. ACCS found it was the act of a group of hackers whose purpose was to make the site unavailable to the general public—a denial-of-service attack. The network worm known as Win32/Antinny (Microsoft 2005, Sophos 2006), or simply Antinny, spread by means of an executable file in a Japanese peer-to-peer (P2P) network known as Winny. The worm program displayed a number of variants. Generally, when a user opened a file, the worm installed itself into the systems area to make sure that the program was loaded automatically whenever the computer systems restarted. It then played a video file and displayed a graphic image. Some known variants of the worm were also reported to steal personal information, including names, e-mails, and files, and send it to a file-sharing network (Symantec 2004a).

According to MicroWorld (2006), top-secret military information, business documents of hundreds of corporate firms, personal and confidential data on thousands of patients, complete information from the Yahoo shopping mall, high profile information of the Liberal Democratic Party, and thousands more records were floating on the Internet, creating an enormous information leakage in Japan.

One of the variants of the Antinny worm attacked the ACCS website by sending a large number of illegal system query commands to the website. The nonstandard conformance syntax of the commands created a huge utilization of system resources on the website server. As hundreds of thousands of users simultaneously sent such illegal query commands to the website, the server slowed and eventually stopped. This made the site unavailable to the general public. A specific characteristic of the Antinny worm that attacked ACCS was that it attacked only on a Monday or zorome[12] day and has been attacking since April 2004.

Telecom-ISAC[13] of Japan is a consortium of telecommunications and Internet service providers (ISPs) in Japan. In early 2004 it established a centralized monitoring system to detect exceptional network traffic behaviors and security events at the edges of the providers' networks. The Antinny attack on ACCS caused an upsurge of network traffic and was quickly detected at the network monitoring center. The worm program utilized an estimated total network bandwidth of more than 300 Mbps—three times the speed available in a typical enterprise network environment.

According to a published report of the incident (Nakao 2006), in April 2004, the monitoring center had no suitable security measures to deal with Antinny or other forms of denial-of-service attacks. Telecom-ISAC's immediate response was to revise the network routers and firewall system filtering rules at the affected ISPs' network gateways to block the illegal commands, based on the target's network address (the ACCS website). This was quickly found ineffective because of the number of network gateways involved. When the filtering rule was applied, the ACCS website became inaccessible even to legitimate users.

Since the Antinny worm used the ISPs' domain name systems (DNSs) to resolve the network address of the ACCS website before sending the attack commands, the response team assessed that a simple deletion of the A (network address) record of the DNS would make the worm ineffective. While this approach resolved the attack on the ACCS website, it caused an upsurge of query traffic to the DNS servers at the ISPs, by a factor of six, making the DNS unavailable even to legitimate queries. This unintentionally led to denial-of-service attacks on the DNS servers.

After two weeks of research, the response team decided to use Sinkhole (Mirkovic et al. 2005), also known as Blackhole networking technology, to reliably redirect the bad traffic to a separate network segment for analysis and allow legitimate network traffic to reach the website.

The Sinkhole network approach was implemented about two months after the detection of the attack. It proved effective in protecting the network and ACCS website against the attack. However, the sources of the problem had not been addressed. The worm program used the P2P software to proliferate without end users' knowledge and the users lacked security practices that would have prevented such malicious software attacks. As long as the end users' machines were not disinfected, the attacks continued even though the targeted website remained unaffected. This situation translated into high network loads on the ISP networks.

To address the underlying issues that made the worm attack possible, the team at the Telecom-ISAC monitoring center engaged an industry-led security consortium to increase security awareness activities through seminars and distribution of information pamphlets to the general public. Where specific subscribers' systems could be identified, the ISP called or e-mailed them to inform them of the worm infection and advised of the mitigation steps necessary to disinfect and protect against a reinfection.

In November 2006, according to Nakao (2006), only about 70 percent of the infected systems in Japan had eradicated the Antinny worm infection. Many inadequately protected systems and unaware users remained vulnerable.

Two key points emerged from studying this incident. The first was a lack of preparedness or readiness to respond to security incidents among the ISP community in 2004 in Japan despite several earlier security incidents involving network worms and denial-of-service attacks [CERT/CC (2003a, 2004a, b), Legon (2004), Lemos (2004), Microsoft (2004b), Pelline (2004), and Symantec (2004b)]. The paradox was that the key stakeholders provided security support as shown by the creation of the Japan Telecom-ISAC[14] program in early 2004 that signified their awareness and commitment to addressing Internet security risks.

The focus of the Japan Telecom-ISAC program was on monitoring and detection and after-incident reactive measures, instead of responses to emerging security incidents—a critical but often missed area between detection and reaction. Consequently, the attack was able to continue for a prolonged period even though it had been detected. In concluding remarks about the lessons learned from the incident, Nakao (2006) recommended the implementation of a "measure for evasion against DDoS attack" and capability to "predict and foresee, so that [responsive] controls can be deployed in the early stage [before the occurrence of an incident].[15]

Another important learning from the Antinny incident relates to the availability of technology ready for deployment to respond to the needs of ISPs. In this case, the Sinkhole (Mirkovic et al. 2005) networking approach was developed after denial-of-service attacks were assessed to be significant threats for businesses operating on the Internet. Its adoption, however, has been limited because it is not useful under normal operating conditions. When no offending network traffic threatens, the Sinkhole network simply idles and consumes resources to stay alive. The principle of piezoelectric behavior is therefore important from a strategic planning perspective. Planning must incorporate a responsive technological infrastructure to manage changing IT risk environments. A large investment based only on a risk-based approach (no past denial-of-service attacks) would make no sense if it targeted only low risk events.

Besides the Sinkhole network for responding to threats of Internet attacks, a number of security technology and concepts aimed at providing better capability for detecting and identifying new and emerging attacks that use new techniques and exploit vulnerabilities that are widely known or reported have been developed. Honeypot (Amoroso 1999, Honeynet Project 2002, Takakura 2006), Honeynet (Honeynet Project 2002), Strider HoneyMonkey (Wang et al. 2005), and Darknet (Bailey et al. 2004, Bailey et al. 2005, Owano 2012) are some of the innovations that may improve an organization's responsiveness to new attacks on the Internet.

While revising this chapter in March 2013, I tried to access references previously saved on Evernote,[16] a free Cloud-based note-taking application available on the Internet. For the first time in a long while, it prompted for my password, stating that it could have been changed from what the application stored locally. After two unsuccessful tries, I accessed the Evernote website. Evernote (2013) had in fact published a blog entry the night before alerting users that its site might have been attacked. Although it did not find specific compromises of payment data and premium accounts, it learned that "the individual(s) responsible were able to gain access to Evernote user information, which includes user names, e-mail addresses associated with Evernote accounts and encrypted passwords."

Evernote was quick to acknowledge and communicate information about the attack, and more importantly, promptly blocked all user access until it completed an online password reset. A password reset will effectively make the stolen encrypted passwords useless to the perpetrators, even though it does not address the specific weakness that allowed the successful intrusion. The responsive action served as a quick stopgap to prevent further losses while the company addressed the underlying weakness. The incident demonstrates that more organizations, especially those that operate online services on the Internet, now focus on incident preparedness, quick responses, and resecuring their systems upon discoveries of attacks.

While the responsive approach for information security risk management was not the basis for the development of responsive security technologies and incident readiness in organizations like Evernote, the nature of the technologies and the focus on incident preparedness and response in their design and deployment all point toward better detection and response capabilities of the organizations using them. A responsive approach that promotes a responsive strategy for managing information security risk in an organization is therefore desirable.

The responsiveness achieved by applying responsive security technologies and focus on incident preparedness further illustrate that the construct validity of the responsive approach has not been disconfirmed. In other words, the development of responsive security technologies adds to the responsive approach in defining the technology elements and processes for improving security readiness and response.

4.9 Refining Responsive Approach

Our understanding of the limitations of common risk assessments techniques such as the ISRA method used at ALPHA and the inclusion of a third axis representing unknown risks to the analysis raised the question of how to implement these factors in a practice environment.

4.9.1 Risk Forecasting

It would be impossible to reflect unknown risks graphically on a third axis (Figure 4.2). The complexity of an organization and its environment make advanced planning for dealing with the unknowable not feasible. According to Flood (1999):

> Complexity theory questions whether long term intended action is possible. It points out that the way things unfold is inherently unknowable to the human mind, emerging through spontaneous self-organization originating from some distant detail, rather than advanced planning. The most we can do is to manage what is local, whilst appreciating the incomprehensibility of global complexity. Managing what is local entails continually considering outcomes that extend over a small number of interrelationships, very few stages of emergence, over only short periods of time into the future. This is what I meant by learning within the unknowable. We learn our way into a mysterious future (p. 90).

In other words, to be meaningful to risk managers, business management, and specialists like meteorologists who forecast weather, the third axis should reflect the risks faced. The risk information is then used to determine suitable responses and action strategies.

Open systems theory states that all systems have permeable boundaries and are therefore open to their environments. Some systems may also have relevant task environments lying between the social environment and the system. For a system to be viable over time, it must (1) constantly scan the relevant environments for changes that might affect its viability; and (2) actively adapt to new information it receives in a way that influences its environment (Emery and Devane 1999). Appropriate sources should be consulted to obtain useful data for the risk forecast required for the third axis.

The analysis of information security risk management at ALPHA revealed causal behaviors similar to those of open systems. To deal with internal and external changes, we had to design and implement attributes that enabled ALPHA to detect relevant changes in environments and actively adapt to the new information received in a way that would influence the environments. Traditional monitoring systems focus mainly on past event records instead of looking for emerging changes in the environment. As a result, incident response, disaster recovery, and business continuity management elements often focus on investigation and recovery instead of changing the protection systems to respond to changes detected.[17]

Implementing and managing information security risk in an organization must deal with internal and external changes. These changes have characteristics that are at times similar to those experienced by other organizations or may be specific to an incident. The methodology employed to manage information security risks should be ready to deal with common challenges and the organization's information security requirements.

Understanding change is a critical aspect of forecasting risk. Understanding requires continuous and rigorous monitoring of critical parameters that affect the security of existing systems and environment. It requires more than learning from past events. New events and their emerging characteristics must be understood and linked to the critical alignment needs of the organization. Specialized risk forecast data are available on the Internet. Examples are the Internet Storm Center operated by the SANS Institute,[18] the University of Michigan's Internet Motion Sensor (Bailey et al. 2004), and the Japan Telecom-ISAC Internet Monitoring Initiative (Nakao 2004, 2005).

Ideally, continuous assessments of current status against past similar patterns of behavior or attributes should project the likelihood of an adverse event. However, unless an extensive database of past security events is available and appropriately coded to permit real-time pattern matching to expected developments, an estimation of probability of an adverse event in real time is not possible (Blakley et al. 2001). A database must be context dependent in order to be relevant to an information security environment. In practice, such databases are costly to build and maintain. More importantly, the approach still relies on past known events.

Based on what we can access from both internal and external information sources, at least four categories of information may be tapped for information risk forecasting (Figure 4.3):

1. Technology (including products and applications) vulnerabilities and attack data available from external sources including security and patch advisories, patterns of network traffic, detection of viruses and worms in the public domain such as those reported by SANS Institute[19] and the Telecom-ISAC (Nakao 2004, 2005) as cited earlier.

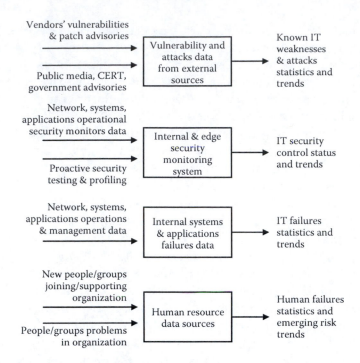

Figure 4.3 Sources of information for information risk forecasting.

2. Internal and edge (perimeter) network security monitoring based on systems, security logs and network traffic data (e.g., Netflow[20] data) captured on the network and reviewed by intrusion detection systems and/or near-real-time behavior-based malicious event detection systems. Increasingly, more organizations are deploying behavior-based capabilities to detect new or emerging attacks (Dempsey et al. 2011).

3. Internal systems and applications failure data (security and non-security-related failures) available from IT and applications teams. Incident reviews of failure events, in particular, unexpected events, should be conducted frequently and soon after an unexpected event occurs to capture the fresh memories of participants. Prompt reviews also reduce the opportunities of employees to alter their stories to show that they took appropriate actions and were not responsible[21] (Weick and Sutcliffe 2001, p. 66).

4. Human resource related data covering new hires and departures, contractors' visits, visitor profiles and access frequencies, and identification of disgruntled employees. Such data can reveal potential risks from people in the organization.

Instead of plotting graphs for presentation purposes, a list of emerging issues that details statistics and trends in those four areas will provide a view (forecast) of the potential risks ahead. The individual items in this list can then be traced to see whether they match any of the criticality alignments shown in Figure 4.4. This activity will generate a list of key risk indicators (KRIs) that match the emerging risks to the requirements for criticality alignment (RCA) and a list of residual and systemic risks that are not directly matched to specific security needs.

When a match occurs, an action strategy may be devised to prepare a response for forecasting the emerging risk but the strategy will have to be accepted by the management in order to gain its support and commitment. Techniques that proved effective in the social–technical approach (the SECD4 model in Figure 3.14 in Section 3.2.1.5) can be applied to achieve this desired outcome. The action strategy is therefore based on sound principles and accurate data.

4.9.2   Scenario Planning and Development

The responsive approach is about addressing unknowns. While we can draw lessons from related literature about organization and business management, no literature specific to information security risk management presently exists. In analyzing the history of system failures, Paul Ormerod (2005) concludes that, ultimately, all systems will fail one way or another. He also rationalizes that:

> No biological species, with the exception of humanity, is able to anticipate the future and to plan its strategy accordingly. In reality, extinction is a pervasive feature for biological species, as it is for firms. Yet the people in companies are able to think about strategy, they are able to make decisions which will affect the ability of the firm to survive, and still extinction is an evasive feature (pp. 186–187).

If we can identify potential failure situations early, we can devise actions to try to prevent them. In a worst case scenario in which a failure cannot be avoided, we can still prepare for survival. FMEA was one of the earliest systematic techniques developed by the US military in 1949 to analyze malfunctions of military systems (NASA 1966). The process generates a list of potential failure modes, effects, related events that may be used to determine critical event indicators that must be monitored, and appropriate responses[22] (Fadlovich 2007).

Failure analysis is not risk-based; it focuses on understanding the system assessed from technology, process, social, and other perspectives. It includes events that are critical but not necessarily security concerns. Different attack methods may produce the same failure in a system and trigger similar critical events for response. Monitoring critical events and preparing to respond

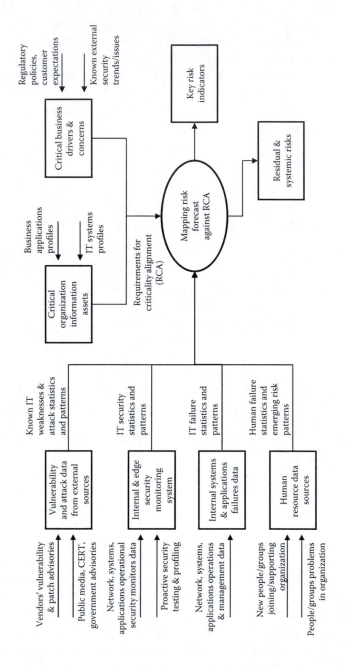

Figure 4.4 Mapping risk forecasts against requirements for criticality alignment.

will raise an organization's chance of being able to detect and respond to new or previously unknown attacks. However, uncertainty is always present in complex systems and organizations, as Ormerod (2005) notes:

> We have encountered many examples of situations in which it is extremely difficult to penetrate the curtain of uncertainty, which shrouds the future. From simple games to more complicated ones like chess to the real-life world of decision-making in business and politics, no matter how carefully researched and planned, the future consequences of decisions made today are frequently surprising. To have the intention of securing a particular outcome is usually no guarantee at all that it will be achieved. Intent is not the same as outcome (pp. 186–187).

Although the intention may be different from the outcome, intention will drive actions and affect readiness and the outcome. If we take no action, an event will run its course. The lack of action as a result of unpreparedness or poor planning constitutes waiting for a disaster to happen and is undesirable. The readiness of an organization will make a difference when a disastrous situation arises. Ormerod (2005) asserts that, "Knowledge and innovation are the keys to survival, to prolong the period to extinction." Ralph Stacey (1992) commented about dealing with the unknowable in a complex organization:

> The long-term future of an innovative organization is unknowable: it cannot be predicted to any useful extent. This follows from what scientists have discovered about nonlinear feedback systems, of which a business organization is one. The unpredictability arises from the very structure of the business system, not simply from changes in markets and technology (p. 13).

To deal with the dynamics of a complex organization and handle the unpredictable and unknown, Stacey (1992) suggests:

> Innovation and new strategic directions, however, require the development of new mental models— new maps— for new situation. In other words, no person, no book, can prescribe systems, rules, policies, or methods that dependably will lead to success in innovative organizations. All managers can do is establish the conditions that enable groups of people to learn in each new situation what approaches are effective in handling it. There cannot be comprehensive installation, only piecemeal intervention at sensitive points in the system (pp. 15–16).

This raises the question of how to develop the required mental model if people in an organization have no prior experience with security incidents or related situations. As we learned from the tsunami incident discussed in Section 4.3, the pupil and the fisherman who saved many lives were able to relate what they learned previously and use the knowledge to make a difference. What they knew about a tsunami was not completely similar to the actual event but the information they had was sufficient to allow them to relate and respond. The knowledge was useful even though it was not a perfect match to the situation. This form of knowledge is similar to an "imaginative leap into the future." The scenario planning technique of Peter Schwartz (1996) and colleagues utilizes this principle:

> Scenarios are *not* predictions. It is simply not possible to predict the future with certainty.... Rather, scenarios are vehicles for helping people learn. Unlike traditional business forecasting or market research, they present alternative images of the future; they do not merely extrapolate the trends of the present.
>
> Scenarios allow a manager to say, "I am prepared for whatever happens." *It is this ability to act with a knowledgeable sense of risk and reward that separates both the business executive and the wise individual from a bureaucrat or a gambler* (p. 6).

Tay and Lim (2004) provide additional insights on the use of scenarios and how scenarios affect levels of awareness and competencies. At the Mass Rapid Transit Corporation (MRTC) in Singapore, training of new customer services officers to operate a train system in preparation for responding to safety and emergency situations was a major issue. Forgetting was identified as a major and common problem and fell into several categories: forgetting as a failure to retrieve; forgetting as fading of memory; forgetting as distortion of the memory trace; and forgetting as a result of interference. To solve this problem, Tay and Lim (2004) devised a scenario-based training system that incorporated several cases that trainees could select for practice.

> Each case is a model of an expected sequence of events that can happen in a railway service. It serves to bring out the context within which a trainee can explore and experience. This adopted training system enables each trainee to appreciate and understand the expected performance should an actual situation arise.

Critical modules in the proposed system were mandated as part of the basic training package. The main objective was to achieve clarity, involvement, and achievement:

> Clarity aims to extract and abstract from the physical environment a set of objects and background pictures with a view to give the user a concise and clear understanding of the intended scenario setting such that he/she is able to direct his/her activities within a scenario posed by a given case study.
>
> Involvement is user's participation in the proposed system.
>
> ... Involvement provides an opportunity for the trainee to critique both the action he/she takes, in relation to his/her desired result, and the rationale he/she has for taking the action in the first place.

Achievement in the proposed system refers to the log activity with true or false status by the proposed system.... By reviewing past activities or steps taken, a trainee is able to question/reflect his/her familiar/unfamiliar answers in order to determine to the next subsequent step. This feature helps to lead the trainee to a deepened appreciation of the given situation. As a trainee will be tested upon on a few selected case studies in a given assessment, this feature also helps the trainee develop an awareness of his/her style of thinking, his/her strong points and weakness in a given case study such that he/she is able to improve in the remaining case studies detailed in the system (Tay and Lim 2004).

Tay and Lim demonstrate that the use of scenarios in training systems led to several important outcomes that non-scenario-based training systems were unable to accomplish. Besides overcoming the forgetting problems, scenarios provide a framework that enhances trainees' situational awareness, illustrates context of a situation more explicitly than text learning, promotes andragogical[23] learning, and makes available a system that allows responses to be practiced and tested as many times as needed.

Testing via a scenario-based training system provided a means to measure the responsiveness levels of trainees to be measured (comparing their test results to predetermined criteria) during non-incident situations and in critical incident scenarios. Although the scenario-based training system project was not specifically for information security risk management, the problem situations were similar. Customer service officers were required to respond to incidents in which they may or may not have had experience. Traditional classroom training was found ineffective. Similarly, security staff members may be required to respond to unfamiliar security incidents. Evidence from the case studies in Sections 4.2, 4.3, and 4.8 showed that:

1. The level of responsiveness has a direct relation to levels of awareness and competencies. To improve responsiveness, we must improve the awareness and competencies of individuals.
2. Scenarios provide a proven method to improve awareness and competencies.
3. In situations that are impractical for scenario drills in actual environments as in the North-East Line mass rapid transport system (Tay and Lim 2004), technical simulation systems may be applied to improve learning and achieve better awareness and competencies.

In a conversation with my brother-in-law who is a pilot captain for an international airline, I asked how airlines ensure that their pilots are able to handle emerging situations such as extremely bad weather or turbulence, flight deck disturbances, and other critical situations they could not plan for or anticipate before taking off. In fact, pilots often face challenges because weather forecasting is not perfect. Also, their operating conditions may change due to environmental, human, or technical factors. A pilot cannot wait for a situation to erupt and then decide what to do. At a minimum, he or she must activate certain minimum safety measures, make use of the nearest control units on the ground, and work with ground officers to determine the best course of action. In the midst of a sudden chaotic situation, communications may be severed and participants in the situation may panic and fail to act appropriately.

To prepare pilots to be ready and responsive to changing situations, they undergo regular scenario-based simulation training, exercises, and testing. They listen to audio recordings captured by "black boxes" recovered from catastrophic flights to analyze the unfortunate incidents and review the related actions and communications. Experienced pilot captains go through these exercises to keep current on recent incidents, life saving actions, and other aspects of situations that may arise during their flights.

Scenario-based training and critical incident analysis are key activities for improving responsiveness in information security risk management. These activities are not entirely unfamiliar in the information security field although their use is usually limited to certain groups, such as CIRTs and CERTs. We can learn much by adopting practices such as the periodic drills that improve the readiness of CERT and CIRT organizations (APCERT 2010, 2011, 2012, 2013).

One way to improve responsiveness to information security risks is to identify relevant security scenarios that may have critical impacts, i.e., require criticality alignments when similar scenarios materialize. Security scenarios may be built from failures and attacks, FMEA results, analysis attack trends, technology advances, and internal and external business and social trends and changes. Research reports on these subject matters [Kienzle and Elder (2003)] may be used to ensure that the scenarios are realistic and relevant. Heijden (1996), Ringland (1998, 2002), and Schwartz (1996) provide useful teachings and insights for developing scenarios and using them for strategic planning.

Remember, however, that scenario-based training addresses only the people aspect of managing information security risk. Security is also affected by technology implementation in infrastructure and application systems and also by the processes that operate and support them. Integrating responsiveness in technology and processes is also required.

From a technological perspective, along with scenario-based training (Tay and Lim 2004) and analysis of the Antinny incident (Section 4.8), numerous technology advances in networking and security are in fact trending toward responsiveness. The Sinkhole network has no use during normal operations but becomes valuable when a denial-of-service attack emerges.

The Sinkhole thus provides responsiveness. Similarly, the concepts of network isolation (Clark et al. 2006, Chapple 2007) and segmentation (Smith 1998, Norton 2001) allow easy segregation of networks into application or service zones so that attacks or technical problems can be contained and kept from affecting other network zones. This allows a business to focus its responses on affected zones while continuing its business in other areas. Designing and implementing a suitable technology infrastructure and understanding plausible risk scenarios are fundamental. If these measures are not effective, investing in technology readiness will be unjustifiable.

4.9.3   Responsiveness Requirements and Action Strategies

Knowledge of the KRIs, residual and systemic risks, and security scenarios collectively can meet an organization's responsiveness requirements. These tools also provide useful input to determine the action strategies necessary to improve resilience and responsiveness. In addition, a set of assurance action strategies is required to track progress, establish the state of readiness, and ultimately make an organization confident that it can respond effectively and reliably to the next information security event.

These action strategies may be developed using the FLAM planning framework derived in action research cycle 2 (Section 3.2.1.4). These collective actions as shown in Figure 4.5 define a system model for implementing a responsive approach to information security risk management. Note also in the system model (Figure 4.5) that the action strategies are implemented through two final components: the policies and program.

4.9.3.1 Information Security Policies

It is important to note that a responsive approach to managing information security does not preclude the formulation of policies or rules of operations in an organization. On the contrary, rules and policies are critical to responsiveness and responsiveness requires the identification and formulation of rules and policies and resulting control measures to be more rigorous and promote responsiveness rather than stifling it. As noted by Malcolm Gladwell (2005) about "thinking without thinking," rules form an important foundation for competitive game players and artists. Rules allow them to respond effectively and efficiently during competitive or high stress situations that cannot be simulated completely.

Rules and practices enable players and artists to learn their roles and responsibilities, understand their strengths and weaknesses, and benefit from exposure to practice-made scenarios. Rules and practices allow them to polish their skills to respond effectively and efficiently to changing environments. At a certain point, the players and artists can proclaim their readiness or preparedness to deal with the uncertainties of a competition or live

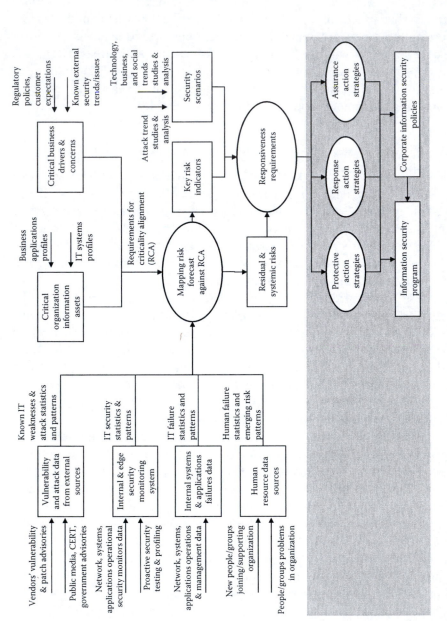

Figure 4.5 Information risk management system model based on responsive approach.

performance (Gladwell 2005). However, rules and policies that remain static are ineffective when an operating environment or situation changes. They are also ineffective if they focus only on preventive controls. As shown in Figure 4.5, information security policies should be regularly updated (updating is in essence a response to change) to reflect current concerns and support the information security program necessary to execute the strategies.

4.9.3.2 *Information Security Program*

The program constitutes another critical component of an action strategy. It involves designing suitable activities for improving protection, responsiveness, and assurance within the bounds of laws and regulations and information security policies and rules.

An information security program should consist of at least three components. The first is a program for addressing known risks, as in the Model A approach (Section 3.2.1) implemented at ALPHA. This may leverage the IRM framework (Appendix C), the SECD4 system (Section 3.2.1.5), the five-level action map (FLAM; Section 3.2.1.4), and the dialectic model of systems inquiry (Appendix B) that have been found to produce reasonable outcomes (see Sections 3.2.3 and 4.7).

The ISO/IEC 27001 ISMS (2005e) may also serve as a foundational risk management system in conjunction with the other tools for strengthening the outcome. Standard 27001 has the advantage of being widely recognized in the industry and this helps gain management buy-in. Its popularity, however, does not necessarily translate into effectiveness and reliability because organizations tend to focus on gaining the certification rather than ensuring that their practices are aligned with the objectives of ISMS.

The next component is preparation for meeting unknown risks based on the processes and technology, developing the security scenarios, and training staff to achieve the system model depicted in Figure 4.5. Based on the security scenarios, regular drills should be planned and conducted to train staff and test their readiness.

The third component of the program is to support the assurance action strategies. As noted earlier, this involves tracking progress of the first two components, establishing a state of readiness, and assessing the level of confidence in the ability of the organization to respond effectively and reliably to the next unknown event. This component provides the performance indicators and replaces the scorecard system of the Model A approach that was found ineffective and unreliable.

4.9.3.3 *Readiness Assurance*

The response readiness assessment in the assurance component provides two important sets of indicators to management and stakeholders. The combined indicators can act as a *responsive index* or *readiness index* to show the overall state of response readiness of an organization.

One set of indicators reflects the state of readiness of the information infrastructure for detecting potential internal and external information security risks that could impact critical information assets. Indicators should reveal the operational status of the monitoring systems highlighted in Figure 4.3 and the subsystem for identifying and tracking the criticality alignment of the organization shown in Figure 4.4.

Next, based on the set of security scenarios applicable to risk forecasts, a set of indicators should be developed to indicate the preparedness of the organization (technology, processes, and people) to respond to the onset of the risk scenarios (Figure 4.5). The state of preparedness may be measured by analyzing resource readiness and outcomes of drills and tests involving scenarios.

4.10　Responsive Learning

The initial study on the issues and dilemmas of IRM at ALPHA (Section 3.1) revealed that the single-loop learning behavioral model was dominant. Policy compliance, risk mitigation, a control orientation (zero risk tolerance and no reconciliation of the governing variables with the consequences of the risk management actions) constituted a common theme during the initial action research cycles. According to Argyris and Schon (1991):

> Under conditions of little public testing of assumptions, low risk-taking, and the resulting high probability of self-sealing processes, we believe there will be little attempt to question the governing variables of model I. The learning behavior according to model I encourages learning that preserves the governing variables of model I and the behavioral world generated by model I; this is single-loop rather than double-loop learning (p. 79).

To foster double-loop learning, a social–technical approach to managing information security risk was desired. Through the first and second action research cycles, a revised approach incorporating five key elements: stakeholders (S), entry and contracting processes (E), convergent interviewing (C), dialectic data analysis (D), and Flood's four windows view (4), designated SECD4, evolved from the initial approach devised as part of the initial research cycle (Figure 3.14, Section 3.2.1.5).

In the course of the research and a series of security incidents, we observed and reviewed the limitations of the SECD4 social–technical approach. Although the approach was able to address stakeholders' concerns and influences, the responsiveness of the organization to emerging and new risks remained a major constraint to managing information security risks. This led to the development of the responsive approach (Figure 4.5).

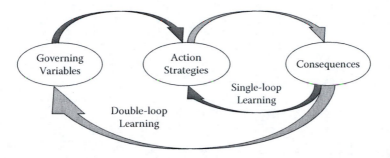

Figure 4.6 Concept of single- and double-loop learning. (Adapted from Argyris, Chris and Donald A. Schon. 1991. *Theory in Practice: Increasing Professional Effectiveness.* San Francisco: Jossey-Bass.)

From a macro perspective, comparing the model for the responsive approach (Figure 4.5) to Argyris and Schon's single- and double-loop learning model (Figure 4.6), it shows in Figure 4.7 that the governing variables and action strategies are inherent in the responsive approach, with the outcome of one influencing the input and outcome of the other.

Responsiveness is a key element in this model. Data sources such as those depicted in Figure 4.7 provide relevant information about the changing risk environment and form key components of the model. The information about changing situations is checked against the governing variables and then used to develop action strategies and evaluate the consequences of the strategies.

As illustrated in Figure 4.7, the changing situations within and outside an organization serve as inputs and are evaluated against the governing variables for determining the information security and responsiveness requirements to update the action strategies. Similarly, execution of the action strategies will create changes in the organization systems through outcomes or consequences that are not necessarily the sole products of the action strategies. Ongoing changes in systems, environments, and behaviors will continuously affect outcomes.

Changing situations and governing variables are linked as are changing situations and action strategies and changing situations and outcomes. Figure 4.8 depicts these linkages over the Argyris and Schon (1991) single- and double-loop learning model.

These linkages show more than the influences between changing situations and governing variables, action strategies, and outcomes (or consequences). From a learning perspective, the sensitivity and responsiveness of an organization and its people to the changes around them enable them to evaluate the governing variables, action strategies, and consequences against the changes.

This form of learning exhibits both single- and double-loop dynamics. Single-loop learning involves responding to changes, mostly at the micro

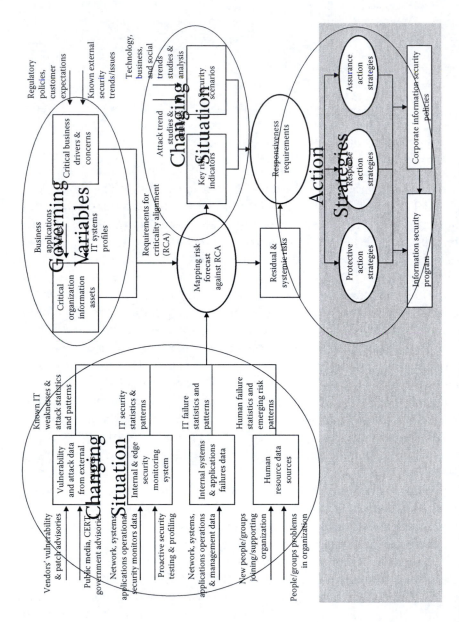

Figure 4.7 Macro view of responsive information security risk management systems model.

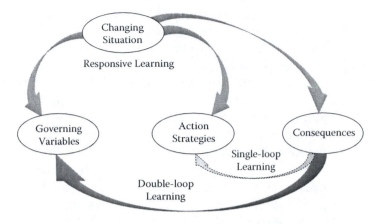

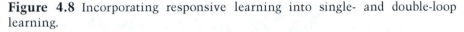

Figure 4.8 Incorporating responsive learning into single- and double-loop learning.

event level, during the execution of the action strategies, making real-time or near-real-time changes to actions based on emerging risks identified and the changes detected. This cannot be a double-loop process because a double loop would stall the execution and response. In a dialectic conducted with Tay (2003) on the successful fault diagnostic expert systems, we learned that the operators of machines needed to be responsive to emerging faults when the machines were in operation and single-loop learning was therefore necessary for efficiency.

On the other hand, when designing action strategies and revising them for improvement after an incident or scenario-based testing, governing variables must be evaluated carefully. Double-loop learning based on macro changes within and external to the systems (individuals, groups, behaviors, threat and technology trends, and business directions) are necessary to ensure that the governing variables are challenged and updated.

Improvements in the design and execution of action strategies should lead to enhanced readiness and, as evidenced in this study, improved responsiveness to internal and external changes. Improvements of action strategies should also increase sensitivity to ongoing changes in the risk environment. This process, called responsive learning, leverages single- and double-loop learning with a focus on changing situations at both micro and macro levels.

The emergence of responsive learning within a responsive strategy leads to an integrated performance evaluation process. Through the single- and double-loop learning processes, the performances of an IRM and the entire organization become clear. Three aspects of effectiveness may be measured by scenario testing and drills. One measures the completeness and accuracy of the data available from risk forecasting and situation awareness systems discussed in Section 4.9.1 in supporting the identification of emerging security events and the criticality alignments of the organization.

While the actual performance cannot be determined until an actual incident occurs, responsive learning enables the performance of IRM and the organization to be revealed through scenario testing and drills included in the responsive model (Figure 4.5). A poorly[24] designed plan, action strategy, or badly[25] executed action will likely result in undesirable outcome of scenario testing. A poorly devised scenario (based on lack of understanding of the risk environment) will also likely result in negative feedback from the participants (Tay and Lim 2004, 2007). The effectiveness of the risk forecasting systems (Section 4.9.1) may also be measured with scenario testing and drills. Incomplete or inaccurate data will likely produce poor performance in detecting emerging events and limit the scopes of scenarios that may be developed and used.

In an incident involving poor preparation, as evidenced in this study (compared with the outcomes discussed in Sections 3.2.2.3 and 4.2), any impact would likely be more significant. However, proper planning and execution of action strategies of a responsive security model (such as the model in Figure 4.5) would make the likely outcomes of scenario testing and drills more positive. The performance data collected from the scenario testing and drills will also provide a basis for measurement against real incident outcomes. If an incident occurs, the outcome based on IRM and organizational responsiveness may be measured or estimated. The results could then be compared with those from the scenario testing and drills to analyze discrepancies and make adjustments to improve subsequent performance. The performance measurements from scenario testing and drills and responsive learning translate into better readiness and responsiveness.[26]

This approach to information risk management will impact the outcomes of incidents instead of counting the incidents and help control compliance gaps. The responsive learning process used in conjunction with the responsive model (Figure 4.7) within a responsive strategy will provide a viable approach to address the performance measure issues raised in research question 3 (Chapter 5).

Endnotes

1. Note that in empirical research such as this study, we can only affirm from observations made that the validity of the theory has not been disconfirmed in the study, but not claim that the theory is valid just because we did not find disconfirming evidence. This is a problem of inference as pointed out by Popper, also known as the Black Swan problem.
2. This phenomenon was also discovered in social situations involving movements of people, as noted in Schelling and cited in Robert Dodge (2006).
3. An adversary is anyone whose actions could result in the realization of a security threat to an organization. The initial outcome of an adversary's action is the emergence of a security event that may or may not be obvious and may result in a security incident.

4. Scenario planning was, however, not used for readiness preparation at BETA. Testing efforts at BETA were focused on validating collected data. Actions were explained in security messages (for example, alert e-mails) to instruct individuals of their responsibilities and actions required during incidents.

5. The media reports of the earthquake magnitude varied but fell between 8 and 9.3 on the Richter scale (National Geographic 2004b, Caritas India 2005, UNESCAP 2006, CNN 2006).

6. Tsunami is a Japanese term for a series of waves generated by strong movement of the earth. Waves may be as long as 60 miles (100 kilometers), travel thousands of kilometers, and be spaced hours apart (National Geographic 2004b).

7. ISO/IEC JTC 1/SC 27/WG 4 is the working group that identifies and develops international standards on security controls and services to support the implementation needs of ISO/IEC 27001 and emerging technology not covered within Subcommittee 27 of Joint Technical Committee 1 of ISO and IEC. I was the founding chairperson for WG 4 and chaired the group from September 2006 to August 2012.

8. The RAISE Forum is a regional gathering of information security professionals in the Asia Pacific region. The group meets semiannually or annually to share updates on information security standards and information security-related issues and developments in each member economy. The proceedings are published in print and online (http://raiseforum.org/).

9. Criticality in Knowles's context indicates the significance of an information security risk to an organization to bring attention to and gather the resources to manage it. Criticality was used to manage emerging risk at BETA to indicate the seriousness of a security event that had the potential to unfold into an incident. Criticality is risk focused, but not necessarily business aligned. Furthermore, the materiality and significance of risk are still subjective, based on assessment by a risk analyst regardless of the terminology used.

10. In the external survey, business continuity rated as the top reason for implementing information security, with 22 percent of responses, 3 percent higher than regulatory compliance. Ernst & Young (2012b) reported that 51 percent of the organizations surveyed rated business continuity as a top priority, but only 17 percent considered compliance monitoring a top priority. One reason for seeing a low priority for regulatory compliance relates to the nature of the industry where an organization operates. For example, in a security workshop conducted for a telecommunication company in Indonesia, the IT manager reported that no regulation in his country (during the period of the study) mandated information security management and practices. In those situations, regulatory compliance is not a driver for implementing information security risk management. Ernst & Young (2012b) attributes the change from compliance focus (in 2006) to business continuity (in 2012) to maturing of risk strategies.

11. See Sections 2.3.6.1 and 3.1.7 for a discussion on other limitations such as subjectivity, lack of consistency, and focus on mitigation.

12. On a zorome day, the day of the month coincides with the numerical value of the month, for example, April 4, May 5, June 6, etc.

13. Information Sharing and Analysis Center (ISAC) is an initiative to improve information exchange, cooperation, and collaboration within an industry, in this case, the telecommunications sector, to counter cybersecurity challenges

arising from Internet use. The initiative was formed to help deal with situations a lone organization would not be able to address effectively because the Internet is a shared space and as weakness of any entity could lead to attacks or breaches of security affecting other entities. Collaboration, cooperation, and information sharing about security events and issues on the Internet, even between competitors, are beneficial and necessary. Japan Telecom-ISAC is an independent organization established in 2002 to foster such activities and promotes a high level of trust among member organizations.

14. Japan Telecom-ISAC is a consortium of major ISPs in Japan. The group was established to allow information sharing and analysis of security events and incidents affecting Japanese ISP network. Information is available online (https://www.telecom-isac.jp/about/index.html).

15. The text in brackets was based on a verbal clarification from Koji Nakao at a meeting in Singapore on November 3, 2006. The meeting also confirmed the accuracy of the incident-related information and the validity of the analysis.

16. For information about Evernote, see http://www.evernote.com/

17. Mandia et al. (2001) and international standards ISO/IEC 18043 (2006a), and ISO/IEC 27035 (2011b) provide guidance on incident responses focused on establishing processes for collecting evidence and investigation activities.

18. For details of the Internet Storm Center operated by the SANS Institute, visit http://www.sans.org/

19. Information about the SANS Institute is available at http://www.sans.org/

20. Netflow is a network protocol developed by Cisco Systems for collecting Internet Protocol (IP) traffic information on an IP-based network. As an industry standard, it is widely supported by network vendors. Netflow data provides traffic monitoring and incident investigation. Basic Netflow information is available on the Cisco website: http://www.cisco.com/en/US/products/ps6601/products_ios_protocol_group_home.html.

21. The aim of a review should be to learn from the failure rather than find a scapegoat to bear the consequences. However, individuals may feel guilty about their actions and change their statements to deflect responsibility.

22. The FMEA method was adopted in ISO/IEC 27031 as a possible methodology for assessing failure scenarios. An outline of the process can be found in Annex C of the standard (ISO/IEC 2011a).

23. The andragogical mode of learning addresses five issues, namely, the reasons for learning, the methods of learning, enabling learners to relate to their experiences, the readiness and motivation for learning, and overcoming inhibitions to learning (Carlson 1989, Tay and Lim 2004, Adams 2013).

24. A poorly designed plan or action strategy in this context lacks the essential elements and input required of a responsive strategy, for example, not considering the inputs and elements depicted in Figure 4.5.

25. Badly executed actions take many forms such as a lack of coordination, lack of prior training, and/or lack of information dissemination to ensure participant awareness and competence to execute the desired actions.

26. Do not mistake our focus on responsiveness as a quest to complete the response to an incident as quickly as possible. We want early detection of a security event or series of security events that may evolve into an incident. The less time needed to achieve discovery, the better will be the response and damage

mitigation. We need to minimize the time between discovery and response. The time between discovery and closure is another matter. A measurement of this "time to closure" may not necessarily drive the desired behavior of a responder. If a low threshold (short time period) is established, a responder may scan the event information and handle the response superficially to meet the time target (against which his or her performance is measured). Time issues may negatively impact the effectiveness of a system. When selecting and implementing performance measurements, we must assess the potential side effects just as we do when deciding security controls and approaches. The four windows view (Flood 1999) evaluates effectiveness and reliability and also efficiency, meaningfulness, and knowledge power (or fairness) and would be useful for such analysis.

Conclusions and Implications

5

Answers are merely places to rest for a moment. They are not final.

Richard Paul and Linda Elder
The Art of Socratic Questioning

5.1   Summary and Results

The four major action research cycles along with their outcome analyses and interpretation led to the development and validation of social–technical and responsive approaches to information security risk management. The approaches incorporated supporting frameworks and tools for answering the three research questions cited in Chapter 1. The research questions were confirmed as significant issues based on the gaps noted in the literature review presented in Chapter 2. The nature of these research questions encouraged the use of social science methods of inquiry. Action research was found suitable and therefore adopted for the conduct of the research study.

A fundamental challenge to information risk management is the circularity problem arising from the common principles identified in Chapter 2. The circularity problem highlights a common discrepancy in the current principles in which weak links[1] prevail in the final outcome of their application, resulting in uncertainties in the information risk environment.

A primary outcome of the research study was the discovery of the piezoelectric behavioral metaphor that led to the development of a substantive theory or concept called the piezoelectric theory of information risk management. The piezoelectric theory recognizes the existence of uncertainties and notes that complete identification and elimination of weak links is not a practical objective for information risk management. A primarily preventive- or protection-focused approach does not deliver the desired outcomes because unknown risks are always present and emerge as the environment and systems undergo change.

Based on the findings of the study, the theory asserts that an organization's responsiveness to the anticipated and unexpected behaviors of adversaries and impacts of change events relates inversely to the potential impacts of the actions of adversaries or events. In addition to the current approach of adopting baseline standards (such as the ISO/IEC 27001 standards) and related principles and controls, an organization should strategize information risk management with a focus on change events, situation awareness, and criticality alignment.

Change events may be planned, unplanned, or unexpected changes that commonly result in "focusing events" (Birkland 1997). Situation awareness alerts individual and groups to emerging risks and the need to respond before they worsen into disasters. Criticality alignment involves aligning those actions with the needs of critical systems, areas, objects, or components to be protected or segregated from an impacting event. This approach prepares an organization to deliver the necessary piezoelectric behavior to improve its readiness to respond systemically to the actions of the adversaries and to planned and unexpected changes in the risk environment.

An organization that fails to be responsive to adversaries' behaviors and actions and change events will experience more severe impacts than an organization that is ready and responsive (Sections 3.2.2.3 and 4.2 compare outcomes from a set of security incidents that occurred during the study period). In a best-case scenario for defending an organization, its responsiveness will deter the strategies of external and internal adversaries.

A responsive organization is ready to handle an event actively in a timely manner, thus expending the adversaries' resources and minimizing impacts. An example is the use of the Sinkhole network against the Antinny worm attack discussed in Section 4.8. The readiness position is far more beneficial than an inability to act even when a changing risk situation is expected. When readiness is not a focus item in an organization's information risk management strategy, valuable resources will continue to be used to address only known risks in an effort to comply with internal or regulatory policies or both. Management will be constantly surprised when attackers breach the security of information systems (as discussed in Section 3.1.6 and 3.2.2.3).

The principle of the piezoelectric behavior, supported by the findings of the research study, provides a possible resolution to the circularity problem depicted in Figure 5.1. The principle supports and expands existing techniques by improving risk readiness status.

Based on the literature review in Chapter 2 and the issues and dilemmas cited in Chapter 3, an information risk management strategy must be responsive to changing events, maintain a focus on stakeholders' interests, and influence their commitments. The initial research cycles established that a social–technical approach leveraging existing social science inquiry techniques and systems thinking tools was suitable for gaining the required understanding of stakeholders' concerns and agenda. The research led to the development of integrated tools such as the FLAM and the SECD4 risk management process and resulted in implementation of action learning sessions as part of the IRM program.

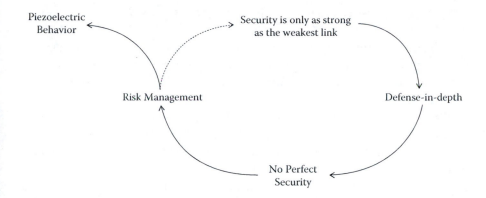

Piezoelectric Behavior — Security is only as strong as the weakest link — Defense-in-depth — No Perfect Security — Risk Management

Figure 5.1 Resolving circularity problem of information security principles by introduction of piezoelectric behavior or responsive security principles.

Using the criticality alignment segment of the piezoelectric theory developed in the final action research cycle of the study improved organizational ability to further engage stakeholders. Criticality alignment is similar to establishing the focal point cited in the bargaining theory of Schelling (1960) and Dick's (1997a) dialectic analysis technique to dissect disagreement to establish agreement (see Appendix B). Unlike a bargaining situation, the ultimate outcome of information risk management remains the delivery of effective, reliable, efficient, and fair information security that benefits the business (and not the IRM function). The use of strategic bargaining should not be misconstrued as a two-sided win-or-lose contest between IRM and business interests.

Criticality alignment establishes a common focal point between IRM and business management that will help resolve disagreements about critical risk issues facing an organization. This approach addresses a common shortcoming in traditional risk management that was revealed in the organizations studied. Concerns about business resources and uncertainties about significance of risk issues often resulted in a trade-off between business and risk management. This win-or-lose situation fails to address the underlying risks when business "wins." In reality, the adversaries are in a better position to "win" from such a trade-off. The social–technical approach engages the key stakeholders to gain their understanding and support. Most importantly, trust is a critical component of the responsive approach.

The validity of the responsive approach and the social-technical approach was not disconfirmed through the action-research cycles.[2] The responsive approach exhibited a form of responsive learning (see Section 4.10) that incorporated single- and double-loop learning behaviors to meet the needs of various situations. The combination of these principles, concepts, and tools developed through the study addresses the three research questions.

5.2   Conclusions about Each Research Question

Research Question 1: What should an information risk manager do differently or change in a strategy for managing information security risk so that the result will not be a compliance-driven and/or control-oriented security culture?

The research study revealed that the traditional approach of information risk management practiced in the organizations studied relied primarily on baseline standards, and used subjective outputs of risk assessment methodologies to devise and implement controls to resolve identifiable information risks was problematic and did not provide the desired outcomes. The study showed that the piezoelectric theory of information risk management allowed information risk managers to adopt a responsive approach in developing an information risk management strategy and plan. The responsive approach directs management focus to readiness of the organization's systems to respond to changes including unexpected security events and planned changes in the risk environment. The approach improves situation awareness by identifying and implementing criticality alignment. To be ready, an organization needs to utilize action strategies and activities including scenario planning, testing, and drills to prepare individuals and systems to respond to unexpected changes while complying with policies for addressing known risks based on risk assessment.

The responsive approach does not replace or diminish the needs for other tools and methods because they are necessary for meeting regulatory and policy requirements and addressing known risks. Closures of known risk issues through traditional approaches such as ISO/IEC 27001 ISMS will provide more resources and focus on readiness for unexpected events and related risk issues. The result is a new meaning for traditional risk management beyond addressing known risks and achieving policy and regulatory compliance.

Research Question 2: How should information risk managers deal with information risks in a constantly changing business and IT risk environment, for example: (1) managing security risk development in an IT arena that could disrupt the business and/or IT operations, and (2) implementing changes in the business and/or IT strategy that could significantly change an organization's risk posture?

Severe effects on business continuity and IT services availability arose from events described in the early research cycles. The relevance of this research question in practice has been reaffirmed. The responsive approach was developed as a result of the research findings. Organizations always face uncertainties that cannot be identified and controlled by traditional approaches. Readiness to respond to any event is therefore a logical approach to address change.

Change events: (1) unexpected security events and their impacts and (2) planned changes noted in the research question are key aspects of piezo-electric behavior. The responsive approach based on the piezoelectric theory involves developing and implementing strategies and plans that detect change events, improving an organization's awareness of changing situations, and preparing to respond systemically based on the need for criticality alignment. As discussed in Section 4.6 and earlier in this section, criticality alignment is one of the three key elements of piezoelectric behavior. It allows business management and information risk managers to agree on an approach ensuring that the systems and resources most critical to the organization are aligned for adequate protection and responses to anticipated and unexpected changes.

To manage information risk in a constantly changing business and IT environment as noted by this study, information risk managers should implement a responsive approach. They should establish a clear understanding of the business risk environment including the social–technical aspects. This may be achieved through the IRM framework (Appendix C) and the dialectic model (Section 3.2). This understanding of the business risk environment will enable an information risk manager to develop suitable strategies through specific programs and projects that will achieve the information risk management objectives in line with stakeholders' agendas. The study developed the FLAM (Figure 3.13) and the SECD4 social–technical process (Figure 3.14) and tested their applicability in a practice environment with positive outcomes.

An information risk manager should also understand how critical systems fail and utilize methods such as FMEA to identify potential triggering failure events that will require criticality alignment. The potential failure events should be monitored and systems should be designed to address their onset and suitable (criticality alignment) responses.

The action strategies and related IRM programs should be updated constantly based on data gathered from the changing risk environment (emerging events and results of actions of adversaries). The IRM systems model (Figure 4.5) which evolved from the outcomes of the study and provides an initial model for establishing a continuous flow of risk information for analysis and updating of the action strategies in response to changing events. In addition, IRM should provide the necessary education and training to improve situation awareness and competencies based on individual and group roles and responsibilities in relation to the potential risk scenarios and known risk patterns revealed by learning experiences. Scenario-based training and drills can be adopted to fill the need for situation awareness.

Research Question 3: How should organizations resolve the conflict between measurement of the performance of an information risk manager and the outcome of a security incident? Should the information risk manager's performance reflect the security risk status of the organization? In other words, what should the relationship be between the manager's performance and the security status of the organization?

As discussed in Section 3.1.8, a systemic analysis of causality revealed that after a risk situation improved (reduction of damage or loss), the tendency was to reduce investments in information security-related activities. Similarly, when information risk managers' strategies improve risk status and reduce or eliminate incidents or when security events are well managed sufficiently to prevent negative impacts, the outcome is "unaccountable."[3] The lack of outcome should not be a factor in determining the competency of an information risk manager because the event that produced the lack of outcome never existed. Management will also be skeptical about the need to continue allocating resources to security.

Conversely, when an organization's information risks are not managed adequately, breaches are likely to occur. As this study has shown, an organization in that situation will suffer losses and damages from anticipated and unexpected security events and will question the performance of its information risk managers. In that situation, using risk status to measure information risk manager performance is paradoxical.

Using a social–technical approach supported by the use of a scorecard system (Section 3.2.1.6) in our study, we demonstrated that a control- and compliance-based scoring system could not measure the risk status of an organization effectively and using such a system to measure performance was unfair to information risk managers.

Instead of measuring risk or compliance status to determine performance of information risk managers, the study concluded that a responsive approach utilizing scenario testing and drills provided more effective, meaningful, and fair measure of performance of risk managers and security readiness of the entire organization. Furthermore, using such metrics as baselines against incident outcomes will reveal discrepancies (between drills and actual events) and enable adjustments to be made to achieve continuous improvements.

As shown by the piezoelectric theory and the study findings, an organization's responsiveness is indirectly proportional to the significance of the impacts resulting from a security event or a focusing event. The capability of the organization's people, processes, and technologies to respond to and align with a changing risk situation will demonstrate the organization's responsiveness and also provide a systemic metric for measuring the security readiness of the organization, the performance of its information risk managers, and relevant stakeholders. Such metrics can be obtained from scenario planning, testing, and drill processes used to improve readiness. An organization that is not ready is less responsive and, as shown in this study, will suffer larger impacts. An organization's readiness to respond can be tested by various methods such as scenario-based exercises and drills. Readiness can be improved by IRM strategies, plans, programs, and actions that should involve stakeholder participation. The reverse is also true. A direct relationship exists between an organization's readiness to meet risks and stakeholders' actions. Measuring readiness (and hence responsiveness) is meaningful and fair to the stakeholders (including the information risk managers).

In this study, a qualitative approach was undertaken to determine the readiness of organizations to respond to unexpected security events. The study assessed the comprehensiveness of the programs and activities designed to improve readiness and the outcomes based on stakeholder participation and feedback. This approach showed some results but did not necessarily measure readiness of the organization or provide continuous and adequate situation awareness.

As discussed in Section 4.9, the concept of a *responsive* (or *readiness*) *index* has also been suggested. This index (as a quantitative indicator) should be assessed against a risk forecast based on indicators from public information sources and relevant threats. The index should examine the readiness status of individuals, groups, and IT infrastructures and systems to determine their understanding of the roles in a range of security scenarios based on developing threat trends and risk forecasts.

Many methods of quantitative measurement have been developed and standardized. A practical metric warrants a separate study to ensure its reliability, efficacy, fairness, and meaningfulness from the four windows systemic perspective. I propose this as a topic for future research and development.[4] Since completion of this study, more publications and discourses on security metrics and measurements (Jaquith 2007, ISO/IEC 2009b) have appeared and may serve as useful references for developing suitable metrics and responsive indices.

The lack of a responsive index is not, however, a significant issue in a responsive strategy. From the perspective of responsive learning (Section 4.10) in which an action research-based cyclical process is implemented as part of a responsive strategy, the action strategies that affect an organization's readiness are evaluated against its information risk management plan and outcomes determined from genuine incidents and scenario testing and drills. This process incorporates single- and double-loop learning and allows performance evaluation without a quantitative responsive index. It presents the advantage of avoiding the negative effects of a quantitative performance indicator (the responsive index) that causes individuals to focus on quantitative measures (like colors on a scorecard) instead of the underlying issues when outcomes and plans are mismatched.

From a learning perspective, integrated responsive learning within a responsive strategy provides more value for improving subsequent plans and action strategies. Responsive learning provides direct accountability for an information risk manager's responsiveness and readiness action strategies and eliminates the dilemmas of incident counting and compliance measurement noted in the earlier action research cycles (Section 3.2.1.6). It also addresses the problems underlying research question 3.

In summary, the study identified a suitable metaphor for assessing and improving organizational behavior relating to information risk and led to the development of a new substantive theory for information risk management. The study also developed tools and tactics that collectively help implement responsive strategy of managing information security risk based on the piezoelectric theory.

The piezoelectric theory remains substantive at this point because its implementation is limited to the scope and coverage of the study and available resources. Nevertheless, it provides a basis for a new perspective and understanding of information security risk management and contributes to the knowledge domain. Use of the responsive strategy by more organizations will lead to more new tools and tactics to support improved implementation of the strategy in the near future.

The piezoelectric approach and the responsive strategy suggest five implications for theory and five for policies and practices in information risk management and related fields and industries.

5.3   Implications for Theory

The first implication for theory relates to the objectives of information security. The development and successful application of the piezoelectric theory in the research study confirmed the first proposition synthesized in the literature review in Section 2.8. The outcome of this study suggests responsiveness as one of the objectives of information security, i.e., improving the responsiveness of an organization to a changing risk environment in addition to the five common objectives compiled from the literature reviewed in Section 2.2. This extension is supported by the piezoelectric theory that utilizes piezoelectric behavior as a metaphor for information security by focusing on change events, situation awareness, and criticality alignment to facilitate progress beyond the current methods.

The second implication for theory relates to responsiveness as an information security principle. As highlighted in the earlier sections, the piezoelectric theory resolves the problem of circularity inherent in existing principles when they are evaluated as parts of a system. Responsiveness introduces a new perspective on the principles of information security (Section 2.3). As part of the strategy, responsiveness addresses both the weakest links and no-perfect-security concerns. It leverages risk management, technology, and defense in depth principles to improve situation awareness and readiness for critical alignment.

The third implication for theory relates to the strategic thinking and approaches applicable to information risk management. The piezoelectric theory suggests a responsive strategy as an addition to the traditional protect–detect–react and detect–react–protect methods discussed in Section 2.4. The responsive strategy resolves the weaknesses of former strategies (Sections 2.4.1 and 2.4.2) and addresses the requirements for more strategic thinking covered in Section 2.4.3.

The fourth implication for theory relates to the IRM system reference model (Figure 4.7) discussed in Chapter 4 that exhibits both single- and double-loop learning. Single-loop learning is used to respond to changes, mostly at the micro level during the execution of action strategies to make real-time or near-real-time changes as required. Double-loop learning in such situations would stall the response and execution. When designing and revising action strategies after an incident or a scenario-based test when governing variables must be evaluated carefully, double-loop learning based on internal and external macro changes arising from individuals, groups, systems behaviors, threats, technology trends, and business directions will ensure that the governing variables are tested and up to date. Improvements in designing and executing action strategies will improve the readiness and responsiveness for dealing with internal and external changes and increase sensitivity to ongoing changes.

A combination of single- and double-loop learning in an organization's information risk management system is important for responsiveness. The combination is called responsive learning and emerged from Argyris and Schon's work. I named this emergent property "responsive learning," which suggests a relationship to Argyris and Schon's theory (1991) of single- and double-loop learning applied to a responsive strategy in a changing risk environment.

The final implication for theory relates to the use of action research methodology in information risk management research studies. Our outcome affirmed the applicability of action research as a method suitable for different disciplines and a meta-methodology that enables methodological pluralism to achieve desired outcomes. The outcome of the study adds to the body of knowledge about action research and provides rich descriptions of the conduct of action research for students and other researchers interested in the theoretical rigor of action research and adopting it as a method of research in the context of their studies.

5.4   Implications for Policy and Practice

The rapid changes in the information risk landscape and regulators' increased scrutiny for compliance purposes elevated the cost of information security and instill a compliance-focused and control-oriented information risk management system that is less flexible and adaptable to change. Information risk managers are expected to resolve these dilemmas and enable businesses to respond to change with agility while remaining compliant with policies and regulations. The outcome of this study was a responsive information security management system based on the piezoelectric theory. Based on the findings of our studies, a measurement of responsiveness provides a direct link to security status without the need for an organization to face a genuine security incident. The theory, and its supporting strategy and tools, can be incorporated into existing policies and practices.

The first implication for policy relates to opportunities for policy makers in the public and private sectors to use responsiveness as a new motivation and yardstick for improving information risk management. This means establishing a policy to encourage the organization to validate its information security status by demonstrating its ability to handle change events, situation awareness, and criticality alignment. Such a policy does not diminish the value of existing practices (risk identification, assessment, and treatment) that address known risk issues. Responsiveness activities add to the efficacy of an information risk management system by allowing it to handle known risks and discover new and emerging risks early enough to minimize damages and losses. Responsiveness provides a new way to address known risk issues by improving the readiness of an organization to deal with a changing risk environment.

The ability of an organization to respond to a changing risk environment provides a direct assurance to regulators and policy and decision makers about potential outcomes when an anticipated risk materializes or an unknown risk surfaces. This is better than having a conditional assurance that a risk is under control based on policy and an assessment of known risks when in reality unanticipated events and failures will cause unknown and potentially serious impacts.

Second, as discussed at an IT auditors' conference (Kang 2005b), the changing information risk landscape and the development of the piezoelectric theory suggest new practices. Auditors and security assurance professionals should revise their scopes of action to ensure the responsiveness of their information risk management systems. The existing methods of compliance testing to determine the integrity and reliability of controls remain important for addressing known risks. A technique known as scenario testing (Chapter 4) can determine an organization's responsiveness to change events. Situation awareness and critical alignment can be leveraged to ensure responsiveness.

Third, the development of piezoelectric theory, fueled by observations during the SARS epidemic when IT infrastructure systems were unable to respond to the changing risk situations, suggests that new strategies and thinking on IT infrastructure planning and design should focus on responsiveness. One response is an infrastructure addition such as a Sinkhole network to handle sudden attacks like the Antinny incidents (Chapter 4). Other measures are vulnerability management of software updates and flexible designs that leverage the distributed nature of the Internet to improve responsiveness to security and catastrophic events, for example, by introducing policies and designing infrastructures that incorporate security into broadband Internet use and computers used in employees' homes. The aim is to improve situation awareness and critical alignment among end users and ultimately reduce an organization's reliance on corporate computers and networks. It is important to note that although many existing technologies support such strategy requirements, their development was not motivated by the piezoelectric theory. Therefore, technological innovations must be aligned with an organization's responsive strategy.

The fourth implication relates to the structure and composition of information risk management and related units in an organization. As analyzed in Chapter 4, BCP, DRP, and emergency response (or crisis management) focus on recovery of business operations or IT functions after an incident. The choice of which measure to use depends on the nature and impact of an incident. In practice, the processes and systems supporting these functions often overlap, leading to increased costs and duplication of effort.

The piezoelectric theory fills a gap between control and recovery in existing systems. It uses responsiveness to detect emerging events (through situation awareness), reduce damage, and enable a business to continue to operate (through criticality alignment) and avoiding failure as much as possible. Again, responsiveness does not impact the relevance of BCP, DRP, and emergency response (ER). Responsiveness does not eliminate failure; it suggests advancement of these functions to a new level that leverages continuity, recovery, and response by organizing into readiness functions that focus on improving responsiveness.

Criticality alignment may also be expanded to include recovery as one of the components for aligning critical business functions with a changed situation. This measure was discussed at the fifth and sixth RAISE meetings and by the ISO/IEC JTC1 SC27 working group. The discussions led to the initiation of a study in the ISO/IEC standards arena in late 2006 and the development and publication of ISO/IEC 27031 in 2011 (ISO/IEC 2011a).

The final implication relates to the practices of information risk managers. For new practitioners, the piezoelectric theory and the concepts of responsiveness and responsive strategy are useful starting points for understanding how information risk may be managed in a changing risk environment. The piezoelectric theory will provide a balanced perspective and strategy for addressing both known and emerging or unknown risks simultaneously. It will help new practitioners address the issues and dilemmas of previous approaches when faced with changing risks in the business and IT environments.

The piezoelectric theory and responsive strategy provide a fresh perspective and approach for experienced practitioners to address recurring issues and dilemmas arising from a changing risk environment. The responsive strategy does not diminish existing approaches. Thus, an experienced risk manager will be able to leverage the piezoelectric theory to refocus his or her management strategy on responsiveness.

For both novice and experienced information risk managers, the SS-493 framework for information risk management (FIRM) governing variables, the FLAM, the SECD4 process, the DMSI, and the IRM system reference model collectively provide the required tools, processes, and models for establishing a responsive information risk management system in an organization.

In an organization that already has an information risk management system, the manager, whether novice or experienced, can use the adapted framework to master the existing system and incorporate the social–technical process to assess stakeholders' interactions before suggesting actions for improvement. The FLAM and IRM system reference model can be used to determine gaps in an existing system and the strategies required for implementing a responsive information risk management system.

To achieve these undertakings and implement a responsive strategy, education and training will be necessary. Training should cover methods of inquiry such as action research and dialectic modeling. Learning of, and competence in these methods will further enable information risk practitioners to conduct inquiries and improve their practices at the same time.

5.5 Suggestions for Further Research

The piezoelectric theory is a recent development in information risk management. The research study described in this book has contributed valuable insights and aided our ability to resolve the issues and dilemmas of managing information risk in a changing environment. Several topics for additional research will advance the use, understanding, and formalization of the theory:

1. The piezoelectric theory is applicable to the substantive areas of inquiry, that is, the financial industries and large multinational enterprises in the Asia Pacific region—Australia, China, Indonesia, Japan, Malaysia, The Philippines, Singapore, South Korea, and Thailand. Although it has been tested in a different geographical area from where it was developed, the substantive nature of the theory cannot be generalized beyond the current area of inquiry. Substantive theories can, however, act as building blocks for a formal theory that will be applicable to a wider scope. One opportunity

that was suggested shows potential for expansion of the piezoelectric theory into other vertical disciplines that exhibit similar issues and dilemmas, for example, in business continuity, disaster recovery, and emergency response, or *organization readiness* areas. Conduct of research on the implementation of the responsive strategy in more organizations in various industries and geographic settings is another thread of development suitable for formalization of the theory. Although the expansion may extend the usability of the theory, certain caveats must be noted because every exploration will likely discover new issues when context and scope are broadened. Further exploration may also give rise to new discoveries or developments that will contribute more knowledge and enrich the field. Further research focusing on expansion of the theory is therefore worthwhile and encouraged.

2. In addition to generalization, other benefits may accrue from further empirical research on the implementation and operation of the responsive strategy based on the piezoelectric theory to evaluate the consequences of such an approach over a longer time period. This will expose the strategy to more varieties of change events and lead to the development of new techniques for improving situation awareness and critical alignment and improve understanding of piezoelectric (responsive) behavior changes over time. More exposure to change events may encourage further study to understand whether more specific patterns of relationships exist between responsiveness and impact severity in relation to the tactics adopted or actions taken to determine change events, improve situation awareness, and increase readiness for critical alignment.

3. Finally, while this study addressed the issues and dilemmas of IRM performance in relation to security status, the tools, methods, and processes developed by the study are still limited. The study did not implement a specific method for continuous measurement and reporting of responsiveness status. Determining status may require a quantitative, qualitative, or hybrid measurement scheme covering an organization's understanding of changing risk environments and ability to execute required actions for critical alignment. Further work to identify and develop the required tools, methods, and measurements for a responsiveness matrix will enhance understanding of an organization's readiness status, and actions required to improve its responsiveness.

Endnotes

1. Weak links (or security vulnerabilities) may be residual in a system due to inadequacies of the risk assessment methods or emergent behavior resulting from the complexity of a defense in depth implementation. Adversaries exploit weak links to further their objectives of inflicting security threats on an organization.
2. Note that in empirical research such as this study, we can only affirm from observations made that the validity of the theory has not been disconfirmed in the study, but not claim that the theory is valid just because we did not find disconfirming evidence. This is a problem of inference as pointed out by Popper, also known as the Black Swan problem.
3. Another approach adopted by some information risk managers was estimating the savings resulting from incidents that did not produce significant impacts. This approach is also subjective because it does not correlate information risk management with the absence of an impact. Such estimates are questionable as methods for measuring IRM performance.
4. Two major limitations in the development and implementation of such a measurement system are time and accessibility to resources. Allocations of time and resources justify a separate project. We therefore propose allocations as a subproject of further research on the piezoelectric theory of information security risk management.

Appendix A: Action Research Cycles

This appendix provides an overview of the action research cycles and subcycles undertaken during the research study to understand the field of information security risk management from the practices in the two organizations, ALPHA and BETA.

Figure A.1 summarizes information risk management framework as part of this study. It shows a data analysis (DA) step at the end of each of six major cycles. The dotted lines at the DA steps indicate the scope of coverage of the steps that encompassed the interpretations and reflections of the data collected in that cycle as well as the output of data analysis from all previously completed cycles.

From a meta-methodology perspective, the six cycles are divided into four main action research cycles. The action research cycles involve four major activities (P, A, O, and R) as shown in Figure A.2:

1. Understanding the system in which the research focus was on knowing the organization and related systems and people. This was executed through two subcycles. In the "learning the rope" cycle, Kemmis and McTaggart's (1988) Action Research Planner was used to identify the key attributes of the environment, internal systems, and people in the organization.
2. Model A approach. The initial cycle was followed by a "do something different" cycle, whereby a system change was designed and introduced to the organization. The objectives of this cycle were to gain further understanding of the information risk management systems involved and begin the process of developing an information risk management model (Model A) for the questions relating to this study. Based on the understanding of the organizational and information risk management systems provided through the earlier subcycles, several key problems were identified. From a management perspective, these problems needed solutions. The next cycle—"solve the problem"—thus focused on improving the plan and using action research to apply it to the problem areas. Improvements were made to the model based on the learning gained. The outcome of these

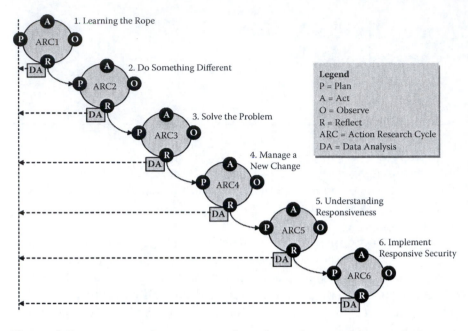

Figure A.1 Summary of action research cycles and scope of data analysis.

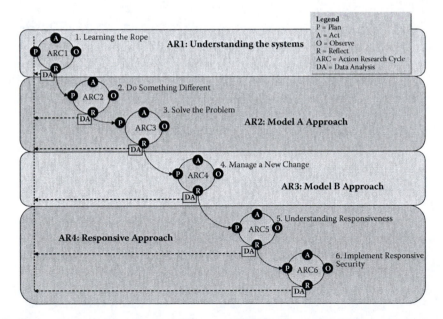

Figure A.2 Meta-methodology perspective depicting four main research cycles encompassing six subcycles.

subcycles was analyzed as part of the data analysis process to provide further understanding for the research objectives.

3. Model B approach. While Model A was stabilizing in the Asia Pacific region (where the research was conducted), senior management decided to reorganize the information risk management function globally. The reorganization introduced several changes to the regional organizational structure, reporting lines, and roles and responsibilities. The changes required Model A to evolve. A new action research cycle was therefore invoked to implement and manage the changes, focusing on implementing the evolved model (named Model B).

4. Responsive approach. Through analysis and interpretation of the outcomes of the previous cycles, the piezoelectric concept emerged as a plausible metaphor for approaching information risk management issues with a new perspective. The research was therefore directed toward gaining deeper understanding of this perspective. This resulted in discovering the concepts of criticality, criticality effects, and finally responsiveness that were studied and discoursed in the "understanding responsiveness" research cycle. From the new understanding, an evolved framework and methodology were developed and tested in the "implement responsive security" cycle. The detailed analysis and interpretation of this action research cycle are described in Chapter 4.

Appendix B: Dialectic Model of Systems Inquiry (DMSI)

The dialectic model of systems inquiry (DMSI) is based on Dick's (2002b) variation of the soft systems methodology and Tay and Lim's (2004, 2007) implementation. The list below provides a high-level illustration of the implementation of the dialectic model and the framework for information risk management (FIRM; see Appendix C) performed at GAMMA. It consists of four main dialectic processes as shown in Figure B.1:

1. The objective of this dialectic is to understand the problem situation and clarify the responsive and critical alignment requirements of the business and related resources (people, time, and competence), limitations, and constraints (regulatory compliance and physical characteristics of building or location) in the organization. The first dialectic involved the following steps:
   a. Plan. I listed the objectives of the project, its desired outcomes, and processes involved and presented to the CIO and CSO for agreement and feedback. I then developed the project plan with the help of the CSO to determine the stakeholders and the roles of the individuals in the project and the study. A list of questions was developed using the information security framework to prepare for the interviews in the next step.
   b. Act. I conducted the interviews with participants, i.e., six staff members and the CSO who described the organization's environment including its structure, IT infrastructure, applications, customers, and information in accordance with the components of the information risk management framework. This allowed me to ask questions interactively, and delve as deeply as possible into the organization to understand its businesses and priorities. Through the dialectic process, the essence of the organization system was determined. The IT systems required to support the primary priority were examined in further detail, identifying relevant risks and limitations in their existing state and including their criticality alignment requirements.

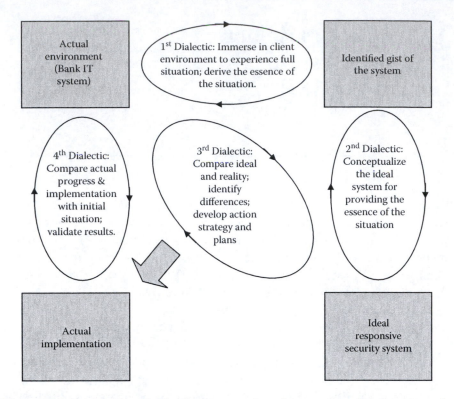

Figure B.1 Dialectic model for implementation of responsive security approach. (Adapted from Dick, Bob. 2002b; Tay, Boon-Hou and Bobby Kee-Pong Lim. 2004. A scenario-based training system for a railway service provider in Singapore. Paper read at SETE, Adelaide.)

    c. Observe. I listened to the verbal statements and observed the nonverbal feedback of the participants during the interviews to understand the situation. I also reviewed the available documentation to identify critical incidents while learning about the existing system practices and the business requirements relevant to information security planning.

    d. Reflect. I performed critical reflection on the information gathered and established key risk issues and concerns, responsive and business-critical alignment requirements, and looked for contrary evidence. I also reflected on the outcome against the plan and the execution of the actions to determine possible improvement for subsequent actions.

2. The purpose of the second dialectic was to conceptualize the ideal information security system for providing the critical functions required by GAMMA by determining and reviewing the components of the information risk management framework, assuming availability of required resources. The steps of the second dialectic were:

a. Plan. The CSO agreed that the routine function was out of scope for the initial implementation. The CIO identified a suitable IT provider to design and implement new IT systems (to be developed) and scheduled the second dialectic. I prepared the documents based on the essence of the organization systems developed from the first dialectic and distributed to all participants for review.

b. Act. Two sets of participants, one from GAMMA as in the first dialectic, and the other from the IT systems design team of an external IT company engaged by the CIO to design the new infrastructure gathered for the dialectic session. I facilitated the dialectic session by reviewing the set of prepared questions and shared knowledge on the information security framework and the responsive approach with the participants. The provider learned the new model and approach, and in turn contributed by sharing ideas about solutions and approaches for the problems identified in the first dialectic, in line with the responsive and criticality alignment requirements. Most of the ideal system requirements were dependent on GAMMA's new IT infrastructure project. The ideal security systems included all key components of a responsive system supported by comprehensive security training and education programs customized for different staff groups to improve their security competency and readiness. After the dialectic session, the IT provider proceeded to design the ideal solution in line with the requirements of the responsive approach and criticality alignment needs of the business. The CSO and I reviewed the recommendations before the solution was used as the ideal model. As the CSO wanted the security systems to be certifiable under the ISO/IEC 27001 standard, the information security management system was designed based on the guidelines in the standard.

c. Observe. I observed the proceedings of the dialectic session, including the participants' comments and understanding of the responsive approach, and how they will support the responsive approach requirements with the available IT solutions. I then reviewed the ideal solution documentation and clarified with the IT provider the specific technical details to ensure its satisfaction of the business criticality alignment requirements (identified in dialectic 1) and the responsive security requirements.

d. Reflect. I reviewed and performed critical reflection on the outcomes of the above steps and the final documentation from the dialectic session for possible improvement in the subsequent dialectic cycle. The critical reflection involved seeking of evidence against the completeness of the ideal solution to ensure its practicality in meeting the responsive and business critical alignment requirements.

3. In the third dialectic process, the ideal responsive security system was compared with the existing environment and the CIO's IT infrastructure plan to derive a rationalized system that meets the critical alignment and responsive requirements within the limitation of available resources identified in the first dialectic. The action research cycle involved the following:

a. Plan. I collated all the documentation derived from the output of the first and second dialectics, established with the CSO the objectives of the third dialectic session, provided required knowledge sharing with the CSO on the process for this dialectic, and scheduled the session. The CSO informed the relevant stakeholders (CSO team members and IT provider) and prepared them for the session.

b. Act. The stakeholders met and the ideal responsive security system was rationalized against available resources and recognized limitations of the business environment. The final agreed system included a vulnerability management system that provided for swift updating of anti-malicious software programs and patching of IT systems that were critical to support the new policies requirements. The IT plan included a small number of desktop and network systems for the bank's senior executives supported by the core customer database system and a management infrastructure. A system for improving the redundancy and availability of the core database system was also proposed, since the existing system was still on a legacy platform, and would be upgraded to a new platform only when the new IT infrastructure was implemented, likely in two years. An incident readiness and response process was also identified through the dialectic session as essential and will be supported by a training program for relevant stakeholders and staff members of GAMMA. The implementation plan included the selection and assignment of a third party security consulting service provider to conduct an external security penetration test to verify the security of the system against known risks upon completion. The output of the dialectic was documented and circulated to stakeholders for confirmation before implementation. The CSO was responsible for obtaining the internal budget approval from his senior management for the implementation.

c. Observe. I observed the actions of the stakeholders to determine their understanding of the process, the responsive approach, and the design of the final IT systems to support the responsive needs and business-critical alignment requirements, and the proceedings of the dialectic session. I took written notes of the participants' comments, concerns, issues, and assumptions. I then reviewed the documentation of the rationalized solution and clarified with the IT provider the technical details to ensure its satisfaction of the critical alignment requirements (identified in the previous dialectic sessions) and the responsive security requirements.

d. Reflect. I reviewed and performed critical reflection on the outcomes of the above steps and the final documentation from the dialectic session for possible improvement in the subsequent dialectic cycle. The critical reflection involved seeking of evidence against the completeness of the rationalized solution to ensure its practicality in meeting the responsive and business-critical alignment requirements.

4. The fourth and final dialectic was conducted after completion of implementation of the final IT system. Follow-up interviews were held with the CSO and related stakeholders to determine the actual status of implementation of the plan devised from the previous dialectics, again using the information risk management framework to ensure completeness. The objective of this dialectic was to determine whether the implementation of the rationalized systems achieved the desired outcomes identified at the completion of the first dialectic. This involved the following action research steps:

a. Plan. I collated all the documentation derived from the outputs of the earlier three dialectics, established with the CSO the objectives of the four dialectic sessions, shared knowledge with the CSO about the process for this dialectic, and scheduled the session. The CSO informed the relevant stakeholders (CSO team members and the IT provider) and prepared them for the session.

b. Act. The CSO gathered the stakeholders and I facilitated the review of the implementation of the rationalized system with the IT provider as the main contributor sharing information on the status and outstanding issues to be resolved, including action plans. The security penetration testing provider's test plan and report were also reviewed. I reviewed the information against the requirements established in the first dialectic and the rationalized systems agreed through the third dialectic to determine contrary evidence against the claimed status of implementation by the providers.

c. Observe. I observed the session and the comments and feedback of the stakeholders. At the completion of this dialectic, a new vulnerability management system was implemented and the IT systems used by senior executives and supporting staff for critical policies implementation requirements were refreshed with the most up-to-date platform and security capability. A security awareness program has also been implemented and included training all 2,000 employees, starting with the senior executives. An external security consultant was engaged to perform security testing on the new systems and showed that the implementation has been effective against known security attacks and the vulnerability management system was ready for implementing newer security updates when available.

d. Reflect. I reviewed the outcomes of the actions and performed critical reflection on the observations and analysis to seek contrary evidence to determine whether the results of the security testing performed by the external consultant and the state of implementation of the improved systems were as claimed and presented and improved the security readiness of the organization.

Appendix C: Framework for Information Risk Management

The framework for information risk management (Figure C.1) is based on the IT Security Standards Framework (SPRING Singapore 2001) that I co-developed in 2001 as a structure supporting or containing the key areas that required identification and assessment as part of the security requirements definitions before designing the security plan (Princeton University 2003).

In accordance with the definition of *framework* provided in the *American Heritage Dictionary*, an information security framework in essence encapsulates "a set of assumptions, concepts, values, and practices that constitutes a way of viewing reality" in relation to the information security of an organization. Our framework incorporates the learning and understanding gained from the research study, in particular, in the design of an information security risk management program for ALPHA.

The framework consists of seven components or primary governing variables that influence the information risk management action strategy and plans. It is also called the "framework for identifying information risk management governing variables."

Each component has four parameters: "input," "output," "outcome," and "measure by" to aid its identification, description, design, and implementation. A set of document templates was also designed for developing and documenting key deliverables of each component of the framework.

The framework should be applied from the top down, beginning with the identification of relevant laws, regulations, and policies to determine the boundaries and constraints of the business, information security, and related compliance requirements. The identification framework should determine (1) the governing internal and external rules and regulations that influence the business, security programs, and organization strategy and (2) the required policies of the overall security strategy based on an assessment of the related business and information risks to be addressed.

Besides the business rules, and related laws and regulations, the assessment should also consider external and internal risk factors (i.e., the threat environment), existing corporate business policies, new security policies that may need to be added or existing security policies that may be changed/deleted

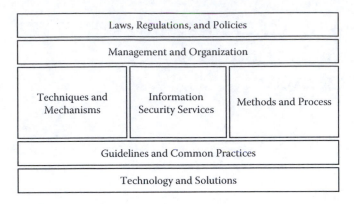

Figure C.1 Information risk management framework.

Table C.1   Laws, Regulations, and Policy Parameters

Input	Output	Outcome	Measure By
Relevant laws and regulations Threat assessment Business and information risk	Threat model Corporate information security policy	Understanding what is at risk Clarity of boundaries of protection and risk management	Extent of compliance required Required verification frequency Types of validation or compliance certification

based on continuous risk assessment, changes in laws and regulations, and business environment (Table C.1).

The next component is the current management and organization structure along with plans for changes in the near future (Table C.2). The objectives are to (1) identify and define the desired management commitment, vision, and mission objectives of a security initiative/program and organization structure to support implementation and (2) clarify roles and responsibilities

Table C.2   Management and Organization Parameters

Input	Output	Outcome	Measure By
Business vision and mission Business and IT management organizations and structures	Security vision and mission Security organization structure Security financial model Security program strategy Security roles and responsibilities	Clarity of desired outcomes, roles and responsibilities, financial commitments, and structures	Completeness of output documents based on assessment templates User awareness

and develop a financial model for security organization and program implementation. In assessing this component based on the data analysis, the following questions were developed for consideration:

1. How is security managed? Will it be managed entirely internally, outsourced, or consist of a hybrid of internal and external activities?
2. Who owns security responsibilities? Does the organization have a security and/or privacy controller or chief information risk officer? What are his or her roles and responsibilities?
3. What is the organization reporting structure? To whom does the security function report? Is the security function based on a distributed, centralized, or hybrid model?
4. How is the security function supported financially? How will information security solutions be funded? Do business units, the corporate division, or a combination fund security?
5. What is the process for determining and procuring the financial and other resources required for information security? Do any laws, regulations, or corporate policies govern this aspect of security?
6. What are the current practices in relation to the above questions?

After listing the outputs produced and the desired outcomes identified in the tables for the two components above, the next step is to develop the security requirements specifications that constitute the security services component of the framework.

The key component of the framework is information security services to which all the other components are linked or support. The set of services required should be based on business requirements including short and long term plans. Table C.3 outlines the four parameters to be determined for the information security services component.

Table C.3 Security Services Parameters

Input	Output	Outcome	Measure By
Business functions and application requirements IT infrastructure system blueprint Service level and assurance requirements	Security requirements specifications List of required security services based on business function, application, and IT infrastructure Security acceptance criteria	Determination of what must be protected and how to gain assurance	Level of protection accorded, level of assurance attained, and/or timeliness of services specific to each service

Table C.4   Methods and Processes Parameters

Input	Output	Outcome	Measure By
Security requirements specifications Security acceptance criteria	Security management blueprint List of processes and methods for meeting security services requirements	System to manage and monitor security of business and IT System should identify and respond to emerging security issues and breaches and address known risks	Security management reports Readiness indicators such as timeliness of security updates; incident and alert readiness and responsiveness

Common information security services include identification and authentication, access control (or authorization), information confidentiality protection, information integrity protection, nonrepudiation, accountability, and availability of systems, information, and people.

Depending on organization and country, personal data privacy protection may be an important requirement for a program. In such cases, privacy services may need to be identified and supported along with other information security services. Privacy services may include clear notices, choices, data collection limitations, and data use controls as suggested by local privacy regulations or accepted international or regional frameworks such as the APEC privacy framework (APEC-TEL 2004b).

After the identification of information security services requirements, the next component to evaluate covers methods and processes (Table C.4) used by an organization along with those required to support the implementation and operation of the services. Examples of common methods and processes are:

Threat modeling and risk identification to provide input for identification and prioritization of information security services
Validation and assurance of completion of solutions and processes
Risk monitoring, metrics, and indicators
Secure baseline engineering and build process
Application security development assurance process
Incident response and handling
Security update and change management
Business continuity and disaster recovery planning and management
Emergency communication and management
Continuous awareness and education programs

Table C.5   Techniques and Mechanisms Parameters

Input	Output	Outcome	Measure By
Security requirement specifications Security acceptance criteria	Security architecture blueprint	System to provide services to support technical and management security requirements that will ensure compliance with policy and provide capability for ongoing security management	Completeness Preventing gaps in requirement specifications Residual risk indicators

The ISO/IEC 27002 Code of Practices for Information Security Management (2000, 2005f) was adopted as a reference for this component. The methods and processes component may be evaluated in parallel, before, or after the techniques and mechanisms component (Table C.5), which is based on the same set of input documents.

These two components should be integrated to ensure adequate processes and methodologies to support the implementation and operation of the technical measures. Wherever possible, technology should be used to enable automation to reduce human errors and improve efficiency and effectiveness of the information security systems.

In general, the technical and mechanisms component may be categorized into (1) infrastructure security systems and (2) resource security systems. Infrastructure security systems are technical mechanisms that provide a foundation for implementing and achieving information security:

Authentication systems
Authorization systems
Audit and accounting systems
Network security systems
Perimeter isolation
Network isolation
Host isolation
Public key infrastructure (PKI) systems such as certificate authority and directory services
Cryptographic systems (libraries, security modules, etc.)

Resource security systems implement specific controls of the resources (including infrastructures such as networks) to achieve the desired security properties:

Table C.6   Guidelines and Common Practices

Input	Output	Outcome	Measure By
Security management and architecture blueprints	List of required and helpful guidance and best practices	Clarity of detailed resources, procedures, and configurations for implementation	Awareness indicators Practice and efficacy measurement Readiness indicators

> Network access authorization and protection system
> Information access authorization and protection services
> Database access and security services
> Business applications access and security services

Based on the outputs of the five components above, the next step is to assess common practices and available guidance (Table C.6) to identify suitable standards and guidelines for a comparison of existing and desired practices. The organization can now identify suitable practices for implementation before devising specific technical mechanisms required for action strategies. These steps are intended to determine what other common practices and standards are available to meet the organization's needs in order to achieve:

> Better interoperability
> Common baseline
> Error reduction
> Assurance improvement

The ISO/IEC 27001 standard (2005e) and others provide useful references for this component. The final component covers technology and solutions for implementing the mechanisms and processes devised in the earlier steps (Table C.7).

The existing and desired technology blueprints are reviewed and refined. The impacts of policies and implementation on resources, compliance, and

Table C.7   Technology and Solutions Parameters

Input	Output	Outcome	Measure By
Security management and architecture blueprints	Physical security management and architecture design specification	Clarity of physical infrastructure and system, including details of resources required for implementation, maintenance, and operations.	Cost efficacy Extent and status of implementation Readiness indicators

timeliness are assessed because technology choices may be affected by policies and regulations. Policies may also need revision to meet the challenges presented by the new technology chosen.

References

Abrams, Marshall D., Edward G. Amoroso, Leonard J. LaPadula et al. 1993. Report of an integrity research study group. *Computers & Security* 12, 679–689.

Ackoff, Russell L. 1999. *Ackoff's Best: His Classic Writings on Management*. New York: John Wiley & Sons.

Adams, John. 1995. *Risk*. New York: Routledge.

Adams, John. 1999. Cars, cholera, and cows: The management of risk and uncertainty. *Policy Analysis* (March 4) 335.

Adams, Nan B. 2013. *Andragogy: Adult Learning Theory*. Hammond: Southeastern Louisiana University. http://www2.selu.edu/Academics/Faculty/nadams/etec630&665/Knowles.html

Alberts, Christopher and Audrey Dorofee. 2002. *Managing Information Security Risks: The OCTAVE Approach*. Reading, MA: Addison Wesley.

Allen, Paul. 2002. Security still hung up on technology. VNU Network, Incisive Media Investments Ltd.

American Heritage Dictionary of the English Language, 4th ed. 2000. New York: Houghton Mifflin.

Amoroso, Edward. 1999. *Intrusion Detection: An Introduction to Internet Surveillance, Correlation, Trace Back, Traps, and Response*. New York: AT&T.

Anderson, Ross. 2001a. *Security Engineering: A Guide to Building Dependable Distributed Systems*. New York: John Wiley & Sons.

Anderson, Ross. 2001b. *Why Information Security is Hard—An Economic Perspective*. Cambridge: University of Cambridge Computer Laboratory.

Anderson, Ross. 2006. Economics and Security Resource Page. Cambrdge: University of Cambridge Computer Laboratory. http://www.cl.cam.ac.uk/~rja14/econsec.html.

Anderson, Ross and Tyler Moore. 2006. The economics of information security. *Science* 314 (5799), 610–613.

Anderson, Ross and Tyler Moore. 2007. The Economics of information security: survey and open questions. Fourth Biannual Conference on Economics of the Software and Internet Industries. Toulouse, France.

APCERT. 2010. APCERT knocks down cyber crimes with financial incentives in drill exercise. http://www.apcert.org/documents/pdf/Drill2010_PressRelease.pdf

APCERT. 2011. APCERT protects critical infrastructure against cyber attacks in drill exercise. http://www.apcert.org/documents/pdf/Drill2011_PressRelease.pdf

APCERT. 2012. APCERT embarks on global coordination to mitigate advanced persistent threats. http://www.apcert.org/documents/pdf/APCERTDrill2012PressRelease_AP.pdf

APCERT. 2013. APCERT embarks on global coordination to mitigate large scale denial of services attacks. http://www.apcert.org/documents/pdf/APCERTDrill2013PressRelease_AP.pdf

APEC-TEL. 2004a. APEC Cybersecurity Strategy. Recommendation by APEC Telecommunications and Information Working Group (TEL) to APEC Senior Officials (SOM). Asia Pacific Economic Cooperation.

APEC-TEL. 2004b. APEC Privacy Framework V. 1.0. Asia Pacific Economic Cooperation.

Argyris, Chris. 2004. *Reasons and Rationalizations: The Limits to Organizational Knowledge*. Oxford: Oxford University Press.

Argyris, Chris and Donald A. Schon. 1991. *Theory in Practice: Increasing Professional Effectiveness*. San Francisco: Jossey-Bass.

Arora, Ashish, Ramayya Krishnan, Anand Nandkumar et al. 2004. *Impact of Vulnerability Disclosure and Patch Availability: An Empirical Analysis*. Pittsburgh: Carnegie Mellon University.

AusCERT. 2002. Australian Computer Crime and Security Survey. Australia Computer Emergency Response Team (CERT), University of Queensland.

AusCERT. 2003. Australian Computer Crime and Security Survey. Australia Computer Emergency Response Team (CERT), University of Queensland.

AusCERT. 2004. Australian Computer Crime and Security Survey. Australia Computer Emergency Response Team (CERT), University of Queensland.

AusCERT. 2005. Australian Computer Crime and Security Survey. Australia Computer Emergency Response Team (CERT), University of Queensland.

Avison, David, Francis Lau, Michael Myers, and Peter Axel Niesen. 1999. Action research. *Communications of ACM* 42 (1).

Bace, Rebecca and Peter Mell. 2001. *Intrusion Detection Systems*. Washington: National Institute of Standards and Technology.

Bailey, Michael, Evan Cooke, Farnam Jahanian et al. 2004. *The Internet Motion Sensor: A Distributed Blackhole Monitoring System*. Ann Arbor: University of Michigan.

Bailey, Michael, Evan Cooke, Farnam Jahanian et al. 2005. Reduction for scalable automated analysis of distributed Darknet traffic. Internet Measurement Conference, Berkeley, CA.

Bank of Thailand. 2003. *Practicing Guidelines for IT Outsourcing*. Bangkok. http://www.bot.or.th/Thai/PressAndSpeeches/Press/News2546/n1446e.pdf

Barton, Thomas L., William G. Shenkir, and Paul L. Walker. 2002. *Making Enterprise Risk Management Pay Off: How Leading Companies Implement Risk Management*. New York: Prentice Hall.

Baskerville, Richard L. 1991. Risk analysis as a source of professional knowledge. *Computer & Security*, no. 10 (8):749–764.

Baskerville, Richard L. 1993. Information systems security design methods: Implications for information system development. *ACM Computing Survey* 25, 375–414.

Bazerman, Max H. and Michael D. Watkins. 2004. The collapse of Enron and the failure of auditor independence. In *Predictable Surprises*. Cambridge: Harvard Business School Press, pp. 43–67.

BBC Online. 1999. How Leeson Broke the Bank. http://news.bbc.co.uk/2/hi/business/375259.stm

BBC Online. 2005. *Award for tsunami warning pupil*. British Broadcasting Corporation (BBC) News, September 9 2005 [cited September 22, 2006. Available from http://news.bbc.co.uk/1/hi/uk/4229392.stm.

Bell, David E. and Leonard LaPadula. 1976. Secure Computer System: Unified Exposition and MULTICS Interpretation. Bedford, MA: Hanscom Air Force Base.

Berghel, Hal. 2005. The two sides of ROI: return on investment versus risk of incarceration. *Communications of ACM* 48, 15–20.

Berti, John, Susan Hansche, and Chris Hare. 2003. *Official (ISC)² Guide to the CISSP Exam*. New York: Auerbach.

Bhagyavati and Glenn Hicks. 2003. A basic security plan for a generic organization. CCSC Rocky Mountain Conference. http://ftp.cleary.edu/BCS/450/BCS_450_Basic_Security_Plan.pdf

Birkland, Thomas A. 1997. *After Disaster: Agenda Setting, Public Policy, and Focusing Events*. Washington: Georgetown University Press.

Bjorck, Fredrik J. 2005. *Discovering Information Security Management*. Stockholm: Stockholm University and Royal Institute of Technology.

Blakley, Bob, Ellen McDermott, and Dan Geer. 2001. Less is more: information security is information risk management. Workshop on New Security Paradigms, Cloudcroft, NM.

Blank, Dennis. 2001. *Hacker Hit Men for Hire*. Bloomberg. http://www.businessweek.com/stories/2001-05-02/hacker-hit-men-for-hire

Bogolea, Bradley and Kay Wijekumar. 2004. Information security curriculum creation: a case study. Information Security Curriculum Development Conference, Kennesaw, GA.

Borge, Dan. 2001. *The Book of Risk*. New York: John Wiley & Sons.

Boyne, Roy. 2003. *Risk, Concepts in the Social Sciences*. Philadelphia: Open University Press.

Brotby, W. Krag, Jennifer Bayuk, Curtis Coleman et al. 2006. *Information Security Governance: Guidance for Boards of Directors and Executive Management*, 2nd ed. Washington: IT Governance Institute.

Browne, Peter S. 1976. Computer security: A survey. A FIPS National Computer Conference 1976: 53–63.

BSI. 1999a. *BS 7799-1 Part 1: Code of Practice for Information Security Management*, 2nd ed. London: Bristish Standards Instituion.

BSI. 1999b. *BS 7799-2 Part 2: Information Security Management Systems*, 2nd ed. London: British Standards Institution.

Burger, Edward B. and Michael Starbird. 2005. *Coincidences, Chaos, and All That Math Jazz: Making Light of Weighty Ideas*. New York: W.W. Norton.

Burrell, Gibson and Gareth Morgan. 1979. *Sociological Paradigms and Organizational Analysis: Elements of the Sociology of Corporate Life*. London: Heinemann.

Byrum, Scott. 2003. The impact of the Sarbanes–Oxley Act on IT security. SANS Institute. http://www.sans.org/rr/whitepapers/casestudies/1344.php

Caritas India. 2005. Caritas Tsunami Relief: One Year Report. Tranzmedia Netvision Pvt. Ltd. http://www.caritasindia.org/MiscelImg/tsunami-1year-rpt.pdf

Carlson, Robert. 1989. Malcolm Knowles: apostle of andragogy. *Vitae Scholasticae* 8, 1.

Cavusoglu, Huseyin, Birendra Mishra, and Srinivasan Raghunathan. 2004. A model for evaluating IT security investments. *Communications of ACM* 47, 87–92.

CBC. 2005. Hurricane Katrina timeline. September 4. http://www.cbc.ca/news/background/katrina/katrina_timeline.html

CERT/CC. 2001a. CA-2001-11: Sadmind/IIS worm. Carnegie Mellon Software Engineering Institute, May 10. http://www.cert.org/advisories/CA-2001-11.html

CERT/CC. 2001b. CA-2001-26: Nimda worm. Carnegie Mellon Software Engineering Institute, September 25. http://www.cert.org/advisories/CA-2001-26.html

CERT/CC. 2001c. Incident Note IN-2001-09. Code Red II: Another worm exploiting buffer overflow in IIS indexing service DLL. Carnegie Mellon Software Engineering Institute, August 6. http://www.cert.org/incident_notes/IN-2001-09.html

CERT/CC. 2002. CA-2002-03: Multiple vulnerabilities in many implementations of the Simple Network Management Protocol (SNMP). Carnegie Mellon Software Engineering Institute, May 24. http://www.cert.org/advisories/CA-2002-03.html

CERT/CC. 2003a. CA-2003-04 MS-SQL: Server worm. Carnegie Mellon University, January 27. http://www.cert.org/advisories/CA-2003-04.html

CERT/CC. 2003b. CA-2003-20 W32: Blaster worm. Carnegie Mellon University, August 14. http://www.cert.org/advisories/CA-2003-20.html

CERT/CC. 2004a. Incident Note IN-2004-01: W32/Novarg.A virus. Carnegie Mellon Software Engineering Institute, January 30. http://www.cert.org/incident_notes/IN-2004-01.html

CERT/CC. 2004b. Incident Note IN-2004-02: W32/Netsky.B virus. Carnegie Mellon Software Engineering Institute, February 18. http://www.cert.org/incident_notes/IN-2004-02.html

Chapple, Mike. 2007. Network isolation as a PCI data security standard compliance strategy. *Information Security Magazine.* http://searchsecurity.techtarget.com/tip/Network-isolation-as-a-PCI-Data-Security-Standard-compliance-strategy

Charette, Robert N. 1991. The risks with risk analysis. *Communications of ACM 34,* 106.

Charter-2000-Aliran. 2004. Earthquake-tsunami catches local media napping. In *Malaysia Media Monitors' Diary.*

Checkland, Peter. 1981. *Systems Thinking, Systems Practice.* New York: John Wiley & Sons.

Checkland, Peter and Sue Holwell. 1998. *Information, Systems, and Information Systems: Making Sense of the Field.* New York: John Wiley & Sons.

Checkland, Peter and Jim Scholes. 1990. *Soft Systems Methodology in Action.* Toronto: John Wiley & Sons.

Chew, Elizabeth, Alicia Clay, Joan Hash et al. 2006. *Guide for Developing Performance Metrics for Information Security.* NIST Special Publication. Washington: US Department of Commerce.

Chin, Saik Yoon. 2004. Phone call saved scores of Indian villagers from tsunami. International Development Research Center. http://www.mail-archive.com/gkd@phoenix.edc.org/msg02013.html

Clark, D. and D.A. Wilson. 1987. A comparison of commercial and military computer security policies. IEEE Symposium on Security and Privacy.

Clark, David Leon. 2003. *Enterprise Security: The Manager's Defense Guide.* Information Technology Series. Reading, MA: Addison Wesley.

Clark, Steve, David Coombes, Charles Denny et al. 2006. *Server and Domain Isolation Using IPsec and Group Policy.* Redmond, WA: Microsoft Press.

Clarke, Steve and Paul Drake. 2003. A social perspective on information security: theoretically grounding the domain. In *Social–Technical and Human Cognition Elements of Information Systems*. Hershey, PA: Idea Group Publishing.

CNN. 1998a. Tsunamis threaten world's coastlines. August 25. http://www.cnn.com/TECH/science/9808/25/tsunamis.yoto/index.html?eref=sitesearch

CNN. 1998b. USGS studies tsunamis in the Atlantic. http://www.cnn.com/TECH/science/9806/16/tsunami.yoto/index.html?eref=sitesearch

CNN. 2002. Deadly bird flu sweeps across Hong Kong. http://archives.cnn.com/2002/WORLD/asiapcf/east/02/05/hk.flu/index.html

CNN. 2005a. Getting word out a challenge in tsunami warnings: system for Indian Ocean would require reaching remote areas. February 4. http://www.cnn.com/2005/TECH/science/01/06/tsunami.science/index.html

CNN. 2005b. Hurricane Katrina: voices from the Gulf Coast. August 29. http://www.cnn.com/SPECIALS/2005/katrina/

CNN. 2006. Tsunami: a timeline. http://www.cnn.com/interactive/world/0412/time-line.tsunami/frameset.exclude.html

Cohen, Fred. 1998. Time-based security. Fred Cohen & Associates. http://all.net/Analyst/netsec/1998-10.html

Colebatch, H.K. 2002. *Policy Concepts in Social Science*, 2nd ed. Philadelphia: Open University Press.

Colombo, Jesse. 2005. Nick Leeson and the collapse of Barings Bank. The Bubble Bubble. http://www.thebubblebubble.com/barings-collapse/

Computing Research Association. 2003. CRA Conference on Grand Research Challenges in Information Security and Assurance.

Control Data Systems. 1999. *Why Security Policies Fail*. Arden Hills: Control Data Systems.

Costello, Patrick J. 2003. *Action Research*. Continuum Research Methods Series. London: Continuum.

CSA. 2012. Cloud Controls Matrix (CCM) 1.3. Cloud Security Alliance. https://cloudsecurityalliance.org/research/ccm/

Daniels, Ronald J., Donald F. Kettl, and Howard Kunreuther. 2006. *On Risk and Disaster: Lessons from Hurricane Katrina*. Philadelphia: University of Pennyslvania Press.

Davis, L. and Stewart Hase. 1999. Developing capable employees: the work activity briefing. *Journal of Workplace Learning* 8, 35–42.

Degraeve, Zeger. 2004. *Risk: How to Make Decisions in an Uncertain World*. London: Format Publishing.

Dempsey, Kelley, Nirali Shah Chawla, Arnold Johnson et al. 2011. Information Security Continuous Monitoring (ISCM) for Federal Information Systems and Organizations.Washington: National Institute of Standards and Technology.

Denning, Dorothy E. 1982. *Cryptography and Data Security*. Reading, MA: Addison Wesley.

Denning, Dorothy E. 1999. *Information Warfare and Security*. Reading, MA: Addison Wesley.

Denning, Dorothy E. and Peter J. Denning. 1979. Data security. *Computing Survey* 11, 227–249.

Denning, Peter J. 2002. Career redux: How can one design a career when career as an institution is dead? Entrepreneur has an answer. *Communications of ACM* 45, 21–26.

Denning, Peter J. 2003. Accomplishment: Language-action philosophy uncovers the truth about effective coordination and accomplishment. *Communications of ACM* 46, 19–23.

Dhillon, Gurpreet and James Backhouse. 2000. Information system security management in the new millennium. *Communications of ACM*. 43, 125–129.

Dhillon, Gurpreet and James Backhouse. 2001. Current directions in IS security research: toward socio-organizational perspectives. *Information Systems Journal* 11, 127–153.

Dick, Bob. 1993. You want to do an action research thesis? How to conduct and report *action research*. Graduate School of Management, Southern Cross University. http://www.scu.edu.au/schools/gcm/ar/arthesis.html

Dick, Bob. 1997a. Dialectic processes. Graduate School of Management, Southern Cross University. http://www.scu.edu.au/schools/gcm/ar/arp/dialectic.html

Dick, Bob. 1997b. Rigour and relevance in action research. Graduate School of Management, Southern Cross University. http://www.scu.edu.au/schools/gcm/ar/arp/rigour.html

Dick, Bob. 2000. Data-driven action research. Graduate School of Management, Southern Cross University. http://www.scu.edu.au/schools/gcm/ar/arp/datadriv.html

Dick, Bob. 2001. Action research: action and research. In *Effective Change Management Using Action Learning and Action Research—Concepts, Frameworks, Processes, Applications.* Southern Cross University Press, pp. 21–28.

Dick, Bob. 2002a. Entry and contracting. Session 3 of AREOL. Graduate School of Management, Southern Cross University. http://www.scu.edu.au/schools/gcm/ar/areol/areol-session03.html

Dick, Bob. 2002b. Soft systems methodology. Graduate School of Management, Southern Cross University. http://www.scu.edu.au/schools/gcm/ar/areol/areol-session13.html

Dick, Bob, Ron Passfield, Shankar Sankaran et al. 2001. *Effective Change Management Using Action Learning and Action Research: Concepts, Frameworks, Processes and Applications.* New South Wales, Australia: Southern Cross University Press.

Dodge, Robert. 2006. *The Strategist: The Life and Times of Thomas Schelling.* Hollis, NH: Hollis Publishing.

Doll, Mark W., Sajay Rai, and Jose Granado. 2003. *Defending the Digital Frontier: A Security Agenda.* Ernst & Young LLP.

Dorey, Paul. 1994. Security management and policy. In *Information Security Handbook.* New York: Stockton Press.

Drucker, Peter F. 1973. *Management: Tasks, Responsibilities, Practices.* New York: Harper & Row.

Drucker, Peter F. 1990. *Managing the Non-Profit Organization: Principles and Practices.* New York: HarperCollins.

Economist. 2003. Stopping SPAM April 26, p. 56.

eEye Digital Security. 2004. Windows local security authority service remote buffer overflow, April 13. http://research.eeye.com/html/advisories/published/AD20040413C.html

Egan, Mark and Tim Mather. 2005. *The Executive Guide to Information Security: Threats, Challenges, and Solutions.* Symantec Press.

Electronic Banking Group of the Basel Committee on Banking Supervision. 2003. Risk Management Principles for Electronic Banking.

Emery, Merrelyn and Tom Devane. 1999. Search conference. In *The Change Handbook: Group Methods for Shaping the Future.* Berrett-Koehler Publishers.

Ernst & Young. 2004. Global Information Security Survey. Technology and Security Risk Services.

Ernst & Young. 2005. Global Information Security Survey. Report on the Widening Gap.

Ernst & Young. 2006. Global Information Security Survey. Achieving Success in a Globalized World.

Ernst & Young. 2008. Global Information Security Survey. Moving beyond Compliance.

Ernst & Young. 2012a. Cybersecurity: an emerging risk for global banks and the financial system. ViewPoints.

Ernst & Young. 2012b. Global Information Security Survey. Fighting to Close the Gap.

Evernote. 2013. *Security Notice: Service-Wide Password Reset.* http://evernote.com/corp/news/password_reset.php

Fadlovich, Erik. 2007. Performing failure mode and effect analysis. http://www.embeddedtechmag.com/component/content/article/6134

Ferris, J.M. 1994. Using standards as a security policy tool. *Standard View* 2, 72–77.

Finlay, Ian A. and Damon G. Morda. 2003. Vulnerability Note 568148: Microsoft Windows RPC vulnerable to buffer overflow. US Computer Emergency Readiness Team (CERT). http://www.kb.cert.org/vuls/id/568148

Flood, Robert Louis. 1999. *Rethinking the Fifth Discipline: Learning within the Unknowable.* New York: Routledge.

Frahim, Jazib. 2005. Intrusion detection and prevention technologies. In *Cisco ASA: All-in-One Firewall, IPS, and VPN Adaptive Security Appliance.* Indianapolis, IN: Cisco Press.

Fukuyama, Francis. 1995. *Trust: The Social Virtues and the Creation of Prosperity.* New York: Simon & Schuster.

Furnell, Steven. 2002. *Cybercrime: Vandalizing the Information Society.* London: Addison Wesley.

Gagliardi, Gary. 2004. *The Warrior Class: 306 Lessons in Strategy*, Vol. 3. Seattle, WA: Clearbridge Publishing.

Garfinkel, Simson and Gene Spafford. 1997. *Web Security and Commerce.* Sebastopol: O'Reilly.

Gigerenzer, Gred. 2002. *Reckoning with Risk: Learning to Live with Uncertainty.* London: Penguin Books.

Gladwell, Malcolm. 2005. *Blink—The Power of Thinking without Thinking.* New York; Boston: Back Bay Books.

Goh, Moh-Heng. 1999. *Business Continuity Planning for Banks in Asia: A Case Study in Standard Chartered Bank.* University of South Australia, Australia.

Goh, Moh-Heng. 2003. The severe acute respiratory syndrome (SARS) epidemic in Asia: Business continuity planning considerations. Discussion paper. Singapore: DRI Asia.

Gordon, Lawrence A. and Martin P. Loeb. 2002. The economics of information security investment. *ACM Transactions on Information and System Security* 5, 438–457.

Gordon, Lawrence A., Martin P. Loeb, and Tashfeen Sohail. 2003. A framework for using insurance for cyber risk management. *Communications of ACM* 46, 81–85.

Graham, Robert. 1998. FAQ: network intrusion detection systems. http://www.windowsecurity.com/whitepapers/intrusion_detection/FAQ_Network_Intrusion_Detection_Systems_.html

Grance, Tim, Joan Hash, and Marc Stevens. 2004. *Security Considerations in the Information System Development Life Cycle.* Washington: National Institute of Standards and Technology.

Grance, Tim, Joan Hash, Marc Stevens et al. 2003. *Guide to Information Technology Security Services.* Washington: National Institute of Standards and Technology, US Dept. of Commerce. Special Publication 800-35.

Greenberg, Eric. 2003. *Mission-Critical Security Planner: When Hackers Don't Take No for an Answer.* Indianapolis, IN: Wiley.

Greenspan, Alan. 2007. *The Age of Turbulence: Adventures in a New World.* New York: Penguin Books.

Griffey, Jason. 2012. The rise of the tablet. *Library Technology Reports* 48, 7.

Grow, Brian, Steve Hamm, Jay Greene et al. 2005. From black market to free market. *Bloomberg Businessweek*, August 21. http://www.businessweek.com/stories/2005-08-21/from-black-market-to-free-market

Gupta, Mukul, Alok R. Chaturvedi, Shailendra Mehta et al. 2002. The experimental analysis of information security management issues for online financial services. 21st International Conference on Information Systems.

Hall, Robert E. 2001. *Digital Dealing: How e-Markets are Transforming the Economy.* London: Texere Publishing.

Handwerk, Brian. 2005. Education is key to tsunami safety, experts say. *National Geographic.* http://news.nationalgeographic.com/news/2005/01/0124_050124_tsunami_warn.html

Handy, Charles. 2002. *The Elephant and the Flea: Reflections of a Reluctant Capitalist.* Cambridge, MA: Harvard Business School Press.

Hanford, Phil. 2003. Developing director and executive competencies in strategic thinking. In *Developing Strategic Thought: A Collection of the Best Thinking on Business Strategy.* London: Profile Books, pp. 191–226.

Hase, Stewart and Boon-Hou Tay. 2004. Capability for complex systems: beyond competence. Systems Engineering Test and Evaluation (SETE) Conference, Adelaide.

Heijden, Kees van der. 1996. *Scenarios: The Art of Strategic Conversation.* London: John Wiley & Sons.

Hellen, Ian and Stirling Goetz. 2004. Securing wireless LANs with certificate services. Microsoft TechNet, November 24. http://technet.microsoft.com/library/cc527055

Hinson, Gary. 2005. The true value of information security awareness. September 9. *Noticebored.* http://www.noticebored.com/html/why_awareness_.html

Holton, A. Glyn. 2006a. Barings debacle. riskglossary.com. http://www.riskglossary.com/link/barings_debacle.htm

Holton, A. Glyn. 2006b. Enron debacle. riskglossary.com. http://www.riskglossary.com/link/enron.htm

Honeynet Project. 2002. *Know Your Enemy: Revealing the Security Tools, Tactics, and Motives of the Blackhat Community*. Reading, MA: Addison Wesley.

Hoo, Kevin J. Soo. 2000. How Much Is Enough? A Risk-Management Approach to Computer Security. Consortium for Research on Information Security Policy (CRISP).

Howard, Michael and David LeBlanc. 2003. *Writing Secure Code: Practical Strategies and Techniques for Secure Application Coding in a Networked World*, 2nd ed. Redmond, WA: Microsoft Press.

Howard, Michael and Steve Lipner. 2005. *The Trustworthy Computing Security Development Lifecycle*. MSDN Library.

Humphrey, Ted. 2002. Information security management. BS7799 Goes Global: First International Summit on Information Security Management Standards and Practice, Singapore.

ISO/IEC. 1999. TR 13335-4: Guidelines for the management of IT security. Part 4: selection of safeguards. In Information Technology Security Techniques.

ISO/IEC. 2000. IS 17799: Code of practice for information security management. In Information Technology Security Techniques.

ISO. 2001. ISO Guide 73: Risk management vocabulary guidelines for use in standards.

ISO/IEC. 2004. IS 13335: Management of information and communications technology security. Part 1: concepts and models for information and communications technology security management. In Information Technology Security Techniques.

ISO/IEC. 2005a. CD 13335: Management of information and communications technology security. Part 2: information security risk management. In *Information Technology Security Techniques*.

ISO/IEC. 2005b. IS 15408-1: Evaluation criteria for IT security. Part 1: introduction and general model. In Information Technology Security Techniques.

ISO/IEC. 2005c. IS 15408-2: Evaluation criteria for IT security. Part 2: security functional requirements. In Information Technology Security Techniques.

ISO/IEC. 2005d. IS 15408-3: Evaluation criteria for IT security. Part 3: security assurance requirements. In Information Technology Security Techniques.

ISO/IEC. 2005e. IS 27001: Information security management system requirements. In Information Technology Security Techniques.

ISO/IEC. 2005f. IS 27002: Code of practice for information security management. In Information Technology Security Techniques.

ISO/IEC. 2006a. IS 18043: Information technology security techniques. Selection, deployment, and operations of intrusion detection system. In *Information Technology Security Techniques*.

ISO/IEC. 2006b. Selection, deployment and operations of intrusion detection systems. In *Information Technology Security Techniques*.

ISO/IEC. 2008. IS 27005: Information security risk management. In *Information Technology Security Techniques*.

ISO/IEC. 2009a. IS 27000: Information security management system: overview and vocabulary. In *Information Technology Security Techniques*.

ISO/IEC. 2009b. IS 27004: Information security management system measurement. In *Information Technology Security Techniques*.

ISO/IEC. 2011a. IS 27031: Guidelines for information and communication technology readiness for business continuity. In *Information Technology—Security Techniques*: ISO/IEC.

ISO/IEC. 2011b. IS 27035: Information security incident management. In *Information Technology Security Techniques*.

ISO/IEC JTC1 SC27. 2004. CD 13335: Information technology security techniques. Part 1: concepts and models for information and communications technology security management.

ISO/IEC JTC1 SC27. 2005. CD 13335: Information technology security techniques. Part 2: information security risk management.

Jackson, K.M., J. Hruska, and Donn B. Parker. 1994. Computer Security Reference Book: London: Butterworth Heinemann.

Jackson, Michael C. 2003. *Systems Thinking: Creative Holism for Managers*. New York: John Wiley & Sons.

Jaquith, Andrew. 2007. *Security Metrics: Replacing Fear, Uncertainty, and Doubt*. Reading, MA: Addison Wesley Pearson.

Jones, Jack A. 2005. Introduction to factor analysis of information risk (FAIR). *Journal of Information Assurance* 2, 67.

Jones, Jack. 2006. Comparing your security budget or the lemming approach to management risk analysis. *Risk Analysis: A Weblog for Risk Geeks* (June 26, 2006). http://riskmanagementinsight.com/riskanalysis/?p=221

Kabay, M. E. 1993. Social psychology and INFOSEC: psycho-social factors in the implementation of information security policy. 16th National Computer Security Conference, Baltimore.

Kabay, M.E. 2002. Using social psychology to implement security policies. In *Computer Security Handbook*. New York: John Wiley & Sons, pp. 35-1–35-22.

Kahn, David. 1996. *The Codebreakers: The Comprehensive History of Secret Communication from Ancient Times to the Internet*. New York: Scribners.

Kang, Meng-Chow. 1996. Network Security—Have you installed a firewall or fireplace? Paper read at IT Security in Banking Conference, December 5, 1996, at Singapore.

Kang, Meng-Chow. 2004. A social perspective on information security. Review of Clarke, 2003, 48. *Computing Reviews*.

Kang, Meng-Chow. 2005a. Information security: A systemic view. *PISA Journal* 2, 14–18.

Kang, Meng-Chow. 2005b. IT Auditing in the face of the changing IT risk environment. It's not just about compliance. Internal Audit Asia Conference, Singapore.

Kang, Meng-Chow. 2007. Project discussions. Sixth RAISE Forum meeting, Singapore.

Kean, Thomas H., Lee H. Hamilton, Richard Ben-Veniste et al. 2004. *The 9/11 Commission: Final Report of the National Commission on Terrorist Attacks upon the United States*: New York: Norton.

Kelley, Michael. 2013. Newest cyber attacks on US banks are destroying data rather than stealing it. BusinessInsider.com. http://www.businessinsider.com/cyberattacks-erase-data-of-us-banks-2013-3

Kemmis, Stephen and Robin McTaggart. 1988. *The Action Research Reader*, 3rd ed. Australia: Deakin University Press.

Kerravala, Zeus. 2011. Making sense of Cisco's borderless networks architecture.

Kienzle, Darren M. and Mathew C. Elder. 2003. Recent worms: survey and trends. WORM Conference, Washington.

Kittler, Friedrich. 1998. On the history of the theory of information warfare. ARS Electronica Festival Symposium.

Klevinsky, T. J., Scott Laliberte, and Ajay Gupta. 2002. *Hack IT: Security through Penetration Testing.* Reading, MA: Addison Wesley.

Kluepfel, Henry M. 1994. Securing a global village and its resources. *IEEE Communications Magazine*, September, 82-89.

Knowles, John. 2005. Digital security risk management: basing security protection on business risk. FIRST Corporate Executives Program, Singapore.

Kohl, Ulrich. 1995. From social requirements to technical solutions: bridging the gap with user-oriented data security. Eleventh International Conference on Information Security, Capetown.

Koskosas, Ioannis V. and Ray J. Paul. 2004. The interrelationship and effect of culture and risk communication in setting Internet banking security goals. Sixth International Conference on Electronic Commerce. March, pp. 341–350.

Kovacich, Gerald L. 2003. *The Information Systems Security Officer's Guide,* 2nd ed. Amsterdam: Elsevier.

Kowalski, Stewart. 1995. A day in the life of a Swedish IT security officer. Eleventh International Conference on Information Security, Capetown.

Krebs, Brian. 2003. Internet worm hits airline, banks. *Washington Post.* http://archive.cert.uni-stuttgart.de/isn/2003/01/msg00133.html

Kwok, Richard. 2001. An action learning experience in an engineering organization. In *Effective Change Management Using Action Learning and Action Research: Concepts, Frameworks, Processes, Applications.* Southern Cross University Press, pp. 247–257.

La Monica, Paul R. 2003. Bounty hunter: the world's #1 software company announces a $5M reward program to help catch virus authors. CNN Money. http://money.cnn.com/2003/11/05/technology/microsoftbounty/index.htm?cnn=yes

Lanza, Jeffrey P. 2002. *Vulnerability Note VU#484891: Microsoft SQL Server 2000 contains stack buffer overflow in SQL Server Resolution Service.* United States Computer Emergency Readiness Team (US-CERT), August 5, 2002 [cited Sep 5 2006]. Available from http://www.kb.cert.org/vuls/id/484891.

Lawson, Hilary. 2004. Philosophy as saying the unsayable. In *What Philosophy Is.* New York: Continuum, pp. 274–291.

Leeson, Nick. 1996. *Rogue Trader.* New York: Little, Brown.

Legon, Jeordan. 2004. Tricky MyDoom e-mail worm spreading quickly. Worm launches attack on site for Unix-owner SCO Group. Cable News Network. http://www.cnn.com/2004/TECH/internet/01/26/mydoom.worm/index.html

Lemos, Robert. 2004. Microsoft shrugs off MyDoom attack. CNET News. February 3. http://news.com.com/Microsoft+shrugs+off+MyDoom+attack/2100-7349_3-5152702.html

LeVegue, Vincent. 2006. *Information Security: A Strategic Approach:* New York: John Wiley & Sons.

Levinson, Horace C. 1963. *Chance, Luck, and Statistics.* Toronto: Dover Publications.

Lubon, Lydia. 2006. Making heroes out of children with a new emergency preparedness programme. UNICEF, September 1. http://www.unicef.org/infobycountry/malaysia_35589.html

Lupton, Deborah. 1999. Risk. In *Key Ideas*. New York: Routledge.

Lynley, Matthew. 2011. PBS hackers: we cracked Sony Pictures, compromised 1M accounts. VentureBeat. http://venturebeat.com/2011/06/02/lulzsec-hacks-sony/

Madrick, Jeff. 2002. Economic scene; effective victory in the war against terror hinges on cutting off resources. *New York Times*, March 21, p. 2.

Magretta, Joan. 2002. *What Management Is*. New York: Free Press.

Mahtani, Anil. 2004. False sense of security in the enterprise. Microsoft Asia Trustworthy Computing Council, Singapore.

Maiwald, Eric. 2004. *Fundamentals of Network Security Technology Education*. New York: McGraw Hill.

Maiwald, Eric and William Sieglein. 2002. *Security Planning and Disaster Recovery*. New York: McGraw Hill/Osborne.

Mandia, Kevin, Chris Prosise, and Matt Pepe. 2001. *Incident Response: Investigating Computer Crime*. New York: McGraw Hill/Osborne.

Manser, Martin H. and Nigel D. Turton. 1987. *The Pengiun Wordmaster Dictionary*. New York: Pengiun Books.

March, J. G. and H. A. Simon. 1958. *Organizations*. New York: John Wiley & Sons.

Marin, A. 1992. Cost and benefits of risk reduction. In *Risk: Analysis, Perception and Management*. London, UK: Royal Society.

Masnick, Mike. 2006. Virus writers looking to slow things down. Techdirt.com. http://techdirt.com/articles/20060925/170612.shtml

Matsushima, Masayuki. 2001. Opening remarks. Bank of Japan. http://www.boj.or.jp/en/research/wps_rev/wps_2001/iwp01e01.htm/

Mayengbam, Sophia. 2006. Research exposes business risk blind spot. SDA Asia Conference on Software Development & IT Architecture.

McDougall, Paul. 2002a. Bank outsourcing for big savings. Deutsche Bank and Washington Mutual want to cut costs but stay cutting edge. *Information Week*, December 25. http://www.informationweek.com/bank-on-outsourcing-for-big-savings/6504588

McDougall, Paul. 2002b. Unisys wins outsourcing deal with Seattle bank. *Information Week*, December 19.

McGee, Kenneth G. 2004. *Heads Up: How to Anticipate Business Surprises and Seize Opportunities First*. Cambridge, MA: Harvard Business School Press.

McKeown, Kathleen, Lori Clarke, and John Stankovic. 2003. CRA Workshop on Research Related to National Security: Report and Recommendations. *Computing Research News* 15, 5.

Meier, J.D., Alex Mackman, Michael Dunner et al. 2003. Building secure ASP. NET pages and controls. In *Improving Web Application Security: Threats and Countermeasures*. Redmond, WA: Microsoft Press, p. 919.

Mello Jr., John P. 2013. Ransomware gang nabbed by European cops. CXO Media. http://m.csoonline.com/article/728915/ransomware-gang-nabbed-by-european-cops?source=CSONLE_nlt_update_2013-02-19

Mercuri, Rebecca T. 2003. Analyzing security costs. *Communications of ACM* 46, 15–18.

Merriam-Webster Dictionary. 2006. http://www.merriam-webster.com/dictionary/habituating

Microsoft Corporation. 2002. *Microsoft Security Bulletin MS02-039: Buffer Overruns in SQL Server 2000 Resolution Service Could Enable Code Execution (Q323875)*, 2002 [cited Jan 2003]. Available from http://www.microsoft.com/technet/security/bulletin/ms02-039.mspx.

Microsoft Corporation. 2003a. Security Bulletin MS02-039: Buffer Overruns in SQL Server 2000 Resolution Service Could Enable Code Execution (Q323875). http://technet.microsoft.com/en-us/security/bulletin/ms02-039

Microsoft Corporation. 2003b. Microsoft Security Bulletin MS03-026: Buffer Overrun In RPC Interface Could Allow Code Execution (823980). http://technet.microsoft.com/en-us/security/bulletin/ms03-026

Microsoft Corporation. 2004a. Security Bulletin MS04-011: Security Update for Microsoft Windows (835732). http://technet.microsoft.com/en-us/security/bulletin/ms04-011

Microsoft Corporation. 2004b. PSS Security Response Team Alert: Sasser Worm and Variants. TechNet Security Virus Alert. Microsoft.com.

Microsoft Corporation. 2005. Win32/Antinny. http://www.microsoft.com/security/portal/threat/encyclopedia/entry.aspx?name=Win32%2fAntinny.

Microsoft Corporation. 2006a. *Learning Paths for Security*. Redmond, WA: Microsoft Press.

Microsoft Corporation. 2006b. *The Security Risk Management Guide: Microsoft Solutions for Security Compliance*. Redmond, WA: Microsoft Press.

MicroWorld. 2006. Winny Virus Wreaks Data Havoc in Japan. MicroWorld, March 22. http://www.mwti.net/Microworld_press/Winny_Virus_Wrecks_Data_Havoc_in_Japan.asp

Ministry of Health of Singapore. 2003. Advice on SARS for Singaporeans and Residents Travelling Overseas. Health Advisory.

Mirkovic, Jelena, Sven Dietrich, David Dittrich et al. 2005. *Internet Denial of Service: Attack and Defense Mechanisms*. New York: Prentice Hall.

Mitnick, Kevin and William L. Simon. 2005. *The Art of Intrusion: Real Stories behind the Exploits of Hackers, Intruders, and Deceivers*. New York: John Wiley & Sons.

Mitnick, Kevin, William L. Simon, and Steve Wozniak. 2002. *The Art of Deception: Controlling the Human Element of Security*. New York: John Wiley & Sons.

Moeller, Robert R. 2004. *Sarbanes–Oxley and the New Internal Auditing Rules*. Hoboken: John Wiley & Sons.

Moniz, Dave. 2003. Monthly costs of Iraq, Afghan wars approach that of Vietnam. *USA Today*, September 7.

Moses, Robin. 1994. Risk analysis and management. In *Computer Security Reference Book*. London: Butterworth Heinemann, pp. 227–263.

Nakao, Koji. 2004. Information security technologies in Japan. Inaugural Regional Asia Information Security Standards Forum Meeting, Tokyo.

Nakao, Koji. 2005. Introduction and updates on information security technologies and activities in Japan. Second Regional Asia Information Security Standards Forum Meeting, Singapore.

Nakao, Koji. 2006. Collaboration of security operation: Telecom-ISAC Japan. ISO/IEC JTC 1/SC 27 Cybersecurity Seminar, Singapore.

NASA. 1966. Failure modes, effects, and criticality analysis (FMECA), JPL PD–AD–1307. http://ntrs.nasa.gov/archive/nasa/casi.ntrs.nasa.gov/19700076494_1970076494.pdf

National Bureau of Standards. 1975. Guidelines for automatic data processing risk analysis. In Federal Information Processing Standard. FIP Publication 65. Washington: National Bureau of Standards.

National Geographic. 2004a. The deadliest tsunami in history? January 14. http://news.nationalgeographic.com/news/2004/12/1227_041226_tsunami.html.

National Geographic. 2004b. Tsunamis: facts about killer waves. January 14. http://news.nationalgeographic.com/news/2004/12/1228_041228_tsunami.html

NIST. 2000. Federal Information Technology Security Assessment Framework. Washington: US General Accounting Office.

NOAA. 2004. NOAA and the Indian Ocean tsunami. US Department of Commerce, http://www.noaanews.noaa.gov/stories2004/s2358.htm

Northcutt, Stephen. 1999. *Network Intrusion Detection: An Analyst's Handbook.* New Riders Publishing.

Norton, Michael. 2001. Basics of network segmentation: switching and bridging. O'Reilly Network, http://www.oreillynet.com/pub/a/network/2001/03/16/net_2nd_lang.html

OECD. 1992. Guidelines for the security of information systems. In *Recommendation of the Information, Computer and Communications Policy (ICPP) Committee.* Paris: OECD.

O'Kelley, Nan. 2013. Three ways technology works to improve security. Redwre Blog, http://info.redwireus.com/blog/bid/221513/Three-Ways-Technology-Works-to-Improve-Security

Ormerod, Paul. 2005. *Why Most Things Fail... And How to Avoid It.* London: Faber & Faber.

Owano, Nancy. 2012. *Daedalus catches cyber attacks in real time.* Phys.Org. http://phys.org/news/2012-06-daedalus-cyber-attacks-realtime.html

Parker, Donn B. 1998. *Fighting Computer Crime: A New Framework for Protecting Information,* 2nd ed. New York: John Wiley & Sons.

PCB Piezotronics Inc. 2002. *General Piezoelectric Theory,* [cited Oct 9 2002]. Available from http://www.pcb.com/techsupport/tech_gen.php.

Pelline, Jeff. 2004. MyDoom downs SCO site. CNET News.com, February 2. http://news.com.com/MyDoom+downs+SCO+site/2100-7349_3-5151572.html

Perrow, Charles. 1999. *Normal Accidents: Living with High-Risk Technologies.* Princeton: Princeton University Press.

Perry, William E. 1985. *Management Strategies for Computer Security.* Boston: Butterworth.

Pethia, Richard D. 2001. *Information Technology: Essential but Vulnerable. How Prepared Are We for Attacks?* Computer Emergency Response Team (CERT).

Pfleeger, Charles P. 1997. *Security in Computing,* 2nd ed. New York: Prentice Hall.

Piper, Fred. 2006. Planning a global strategy for the future of information security. International Symposium on the Future of Security and Privacy, Seoul.

Popper, Karl Raimund. 1992. *The Logic of Scientific Discovery.* London: Routledge.

Posner, Richard A. 2004. *Catastrophe: Risk and Response.* Oxford: Oxford University Press.

Potter, Bruce and Bob Fleck. 2003. *802.11 Security, Securing Wireless Networks.* Sebastopol, CA: O'Reilly Media.

PricewaterhouseCoopers. 2003. Information Security: A Strategic Guide for Business. In *A Technology Forecast.* PricewaterhouseCoopers Global Technology Centre.

PricewaterhouseCoopers. 2011. The consumerization of IT: the next-generation CIO: PwC. http://www.pwc.com/us/en/technology-innovation-center/consumerization-information-technology-transforming-cio-role.jhtml

PricewaterhouseCoopers and DTI. 2002. Information Security Breaches Survey. London: Department of Trade and Industry.

PricewaterhouseCoopers and DTI. 2004. Information Security Breaches Survey. London: Department of Trade and Industry.

Princeton University. 2003. *WordNet 2.0.* http://wordnetweb.princeton.edu/

Prystay, Cris. 2003. SARS squeezes travel industry in Asia. *Asian Wall Street Journal,* May 16, p. 8.

Ptacek, Thomas H. and Timothy N. Newsham. 1998. Insertion, evasion, and denial of service: eluding network intrusion detection. http://cs.unc.edu/~fabian/course_papers/PtacekNewsham98.pdf

Pugh, David S. and David J. Hickson. 1996. *Writers on Organizations,* 5th ed. New York: Penguin Books.

Rafail, Jason A. 2004. Vulnerability Note 753212: Microsoft LSA Service contains buffer overflow in DsRolepInitializeLog() function. United States Computer Emergency Readiness Team (CERT), April 13. http://www.kb.cert.org/vuls/id/753212

Raymond, Eric Steven, and Rob W. Landley. 2004. "Habituation, Expertise, and Undo Operations." In *The Art of Unix Usability,* E.S. Raymond (ed.). Pearson Education.

Rees, Jackie, Subhajyoti Bandyopadnyay, and Eugene H. Spafford. 2003. PFIRES: A Policy Framework for Information Security. *Communications of the ACM,* no. 46(7):101-196.

Revans, Reginald. 1980. *Action Learning: New Techniques for Management.* London: Blond & Briggs.

Revans, Reginald. 1982. *The Origins and Growth of Action Learning.* Bromley: Chartwell-Bratt.

Revans, Reginald. 1998. *ABCs of Action Learning: Empowering Managers to Act to Learn from Action,* 3rd ed. London: Leomos and Crane.

Richmond, Riva. 2011. The RSA hack: how they did it. *New York Times,* April 2.

Ringland, Gill. 1998. *Scenario Planning: Managing for the Future.* New York: John Wiley & Sons.

Ringland, Gill. 2002. *Scenarios in Business.* New York: John Wiley & Sons.

Roach, John. 2003. Supercities vulnerable to killer quakes, expert warns. *National Geographic,* May 2. http://news.nationalgeographic.com/news/2003/05/0502_030502_killerquakes.html

Rodewald, Gus. 2005. Aligning information security investments with a firm's risk tolerance. Information Security Curriculum Development (InfosecCD) Conference, Kennesaw, GA.

Sankaran, Shankar, Boon-Hou Tay, and You-Sum Cheah. 2004. Application of dialectical model of soft systems methodology to conduct action research. *Action Learning and Action Research Journal* 9, 93–104.

Schelling, Thomas C. 1960. *The Strategy of Conflicts.* Cambridge: Harvard University Press.

Schneier, Bruce. 1997. Cryptography, security and the future. *Communications of ACM* 40, 138.

Schneier, Bruce. 2001. *Secrets and Lies*. New York: John Wiley & Sons.

Schneier, Bruce. 2002. How to think about security. Counterpane Systems, April 15. http://www.schneier.com/crypto-gram-0204.html-1

Schneier, Bruce. 2003. *Beyond Fear: Thinking Sensibly about Security in an Uncertain World*. Gottingen, Germany: Copernicus Books.

Schwartau, Winn. 2001. *Time Based Security: Measuring Security and Defensive Strategies in a Networked Environment*. Interpact Press.

Schwartz, Peter. 1996. *The Art of the Long View*. New York: Doubleday.

Senge, Peter M. 1990. *The Fifth Discipline—The Art and Practice of The Learning Organization*. New York: Random House.

Senge, Peter M. 2006. *The Fifth Discipline: The Art and Practice of the Learning Organization*, Revised Edition. New York: Currency Doubleday.

Shain, Michael. 1994. An overview of security. In *Information Security Handbook*. New York: Stockton Press, pp. 1–26.

Singh, Simon. 1999. *The Code Book: The Science of Secrecy from Ancient Egypt to Quantum Cryptography*. London: Fourth Estate Limited.

Siponen, Mikko T. 2000a. A conceptual foundation for organizational information security awareness. *Information Management and Computer Security* 8, 31–41.

Siponen, Mikko T. 2000b. Critical analysis of different approaches to minimizing user-related faults in information systems security: implications for research and practice. *Information Management and Computer Security* 8, 197–209.

Skoudis, Ed and Lenny Zeltser. 2004. *Malware: Fighting Malicious Code*. New York: Prentice Hall.

Smith, Marina. 1998. *Virtual LANs: Construction, Operation, Utilization, Computer Communications*. New York: McGraw Hill.

Song, Kimberly. 2003. Finance firm risk officers say outbreak will reduce earnings. *Asian Wall Street Journal*, May 14, p. 8.

Sophos Plc. 2006. W32/Antinny-R. Sophos. http://www.sophos.com/virusinfo/analyses/w32antinnyr.html

SPRING Singapore. 2001. Singapore Standard 493: Specification for IT Security Standards Framework, Part 1.

Stacey, Ralph D. 1992. *Managing the Unknowable: Strategic Boundaries between Order and Chaos in Organizations*. New York: John Wiley & Sons.

Stoneburner, Gary, Alice Goguen, and Alexis Feringa. 2002. Risk management guide for information technology systems. In *NIST Special Publication 800-30*. Washington: National Institute of Standards and Technology.

Styles, Elizabeth A. 2005. *Attention, Perception and Memory: An Integrated Introduction*. New York: Psychology Press.

Sullivan, Laurie. 2006. Compliance, not malware, drives IT budgets: survey. Techweb.com, April 6. http://www.informationweek.com/compliance-not-malware-drives-it-budgets/184429550

Summers, Rita C. 1997. *Secure Computing: Threats and Safeguards*. New York: McGraw Hill.

Swanson, Marianne, Nadya Bartol, John Sabato et al. 2003. Security metrics guide for information technology systems. In *NIST Special Publication*. Washington: National Institute of Standards and Technology.

Swanson, Marianne and Barbara Guttman. 1996. *Generally Accepted Principles and Practices for Securing Information Technology Systems*. Washington: National Institute of Standards and Technology.

Symantec. 2004a. W32.HLLW.Antinny/G. http://www.symantec.com/security_response/writeup.jsp?docid=2004-031917-3952-99

Symantec. 2004b. W32.Sasser.worm. http://www.symantec.com/security_response/writeup.jsp?docid=2004-050116-1831-99

Takakura, Hiroki. 2006. Design and deployment of self-configurable Honeypot systems to detect unknown malicious code. In *Joint Information Security Workshop on Internet Monitor and Analysis*. Tokyo: National Institute of Information Communication Technology.

Taleb, Nassim Nicholas. 2004. *Fooled by Randomness: The hidden role of chance in life and in the markets*. Second ed: New York: TEXERE.

Taleb, Nassim Nicholas. 2007. *The Black Swan*. New York: Random House.

Tay, Boon-Hou. 2003. Using Action Research to develop a Social Technical Diagnostic Expert Systems for an Industrial Environment. Southern Cross University.

Tay, Boon-Hou and Stewart Hase. 2004. Role of action research in workplace PhD research. *Action Learning and Action Research Journal* 9, 81–97.

Tay, Boon-Hou and Bobby Kee-Pong Lim. 2004. A scenario-based training system for a railway service provider in Singapore. SETE Conference, Adelaide.

Tay, Boon-Hou and Bobby Kee-Pong Lim. 2007. Using Dialectic Soft Systems Methodology as an Ongoing Self-evaluation Process for a Singapore Railway Service Provider. American Evaluation Association.

Telegraph. 2005. Girl, 10, used geography lesson to save lives. Telegraph Group Limited. http://www.telegraph.co.uk/news/1480192/Girl-10-used-geography-lesson-to-save-lives.html

Tiller, James S. 2003. The Ethical Hack: A Framework for Business Value Penetration Testing. New York: Auerbach.

Timm, Kevin. 2010. Intrusion detection FAQs. How does an attacker evade IDS with session splicing? SANS, May 19. http://www.sans.org/security-resources/idfaq/sess_splicing.php

UNESCAP. 2006. Disaster Management and Prevention. United Nations Economic and Social Commission for Asia and the Pacific, http://www.unescap.org/icstd/dmp.aspx

US DoD. 1983. Trusted Computer System Evaluation Criteria. Washington: Department of Defense Computer Security Center.

US DoD. 1985. Trusted Computer System Evaluation Criteria. Washington: US Department of Defense Computer Security Center.

Venables, Phil. 2004. Information security and complexity: challenges and approaches. Burton Group Conference on Identity Management.

Viega, John. 2005. Security problem solved? Solutions to many of our security problems already exist, so why are we still so vulnerable? *Queue*, June, 41–50.

Vijayan, Jaikumar. 2005. Focus on compliance could weaken info security. Execs warn IT needs a broader strategy. IDG Network. http://www.computerworld.com/printthis/2005/0,4814,106370,00.html

Volonino, Linda and Stephen R. Robinson. 2004. *Principles and Practices of Information Security*. New York: Prentice Hall Pearson.

Wang, George. 2005. Strategy and Influence for Security Success. IDG SecurityWorld Conference, Singapore.

Wang, Yi-Min, Doug Beck, Xuxian Jiang, et al. 2005. *Automated Web Patrol with Strider HoneyMonkeys: Finding Web Sites That Exploit Browser Vulnerabilities.* Redmond, WA: Microsoft Press.

Weick, Karl E. and Kathleen M. Sutcliffe. 2001. *Managing the Unexpected: Assuring High Performance in an Age of Complexity.* San Francisco: Jossey Bass.

Whitman, Michael E. 2003. Enemy at the gate: threats to information security. *Communications of ACM* 46, 91–95.

Whittaker, Zack. 2012. A year in cybersecurity and cybercrime: 2012 review. CBS Interactive. http://www.zdnet.com/a-year-in-cybersecurity-and-cybercrime-2012-review-7000007521/-photo

Wilson, Mark and Joan Hash. 2003. *Building an Information Technology Security Awareness Program.* Special Publication. Washington: National Institute of Standards and Technology.

Wood, Cresson C. 1995. Writing InfoSec Policies. *Computers & Security* 14.

Yakcop, Mohamed. 2000. BNM/ABM Circular. Outsourcing of Banking Operations. Bank Negara Malaysia.

Yngstrom, Louise. 1995. A holistic approach to IT security. Eleventh International Conference on Information Security, Capetown.

Yourdon, Edward. 2002. *Byte Wars: The Impact of September 11 on Information Technology.* New York: Prentice Hall.

Index

Note: Page numbers ending in "f" refer to figures. Page numbers ending in "t" refer to tables.

A

Action
- five-level action map, 104–105, 104f, 185
- research cycles, 9, 67, 74, 75f, 81, 92–94, 93t, 133, 172, 189, 195–197, 196f
- response as, 135–136
- strategies for, 169–171
- theory of, 72–76, 94–101, 124

Adams, John, 34–35, 86

Annual loss expectancy (ALE), 28–31

Antinny worm case, 156–160, 182

Art of Socratic Questioning, The, 181

Art of War, The, 43

Attacks. *See also* Risk management
- response readiness for, 136–142, 171–172
- responsive security for, 137–143
- visibility of, 136, 145–148, 147f
- worm attacks, 90, 117–120, 137–138, 156–160, 182

Audit issues
- audit interventions, 95–97, 96f
- compliance issues and, 6, 75–77, 75f, 93t
- management commitments and, 40, 68–77, 75f
- pre-audit reviews, 71–75, 75f, 95–99, 95f, 96f, 97f, 110
- risk management and, 68–77, 75f

B

Baseline security, 22–25, 33

Biba Integrity Model, 16

Blaster worm incident, 119–122, 137, 139

Bounty programs, 42, 64n27

Business continuity
- disaster recovery and, 51, 88, 123–124, 123f, 161, 191, 193

effects on, 17, 184

importance of, 17, 161, 177n10

Business continuity management (BCM), 88, 122–123, 161

Business investment, 90–92, 91f

Business risk management framework, 29–30, 63n15

Business value (BV), 90–92, 91f

C

Causal analysis
- of information security systems, 88–92, 89f
- risk analysis and, 88–92, 89f

Change, response to, 55–61, 134–136, 173–175, 174f, 184–185, 190–191

Chaotic responses, 134–135

Circularity problems, 38, 38f, 59, 181–183, 183f. *See also* Information security

Competency
- information risk management and, 19, 74–76, 89–90, 89f, 109
- of information risk manager, 186, 201
- trust and, 101–104

Compliance issues
- audit issues and, 6, 75–77, 75f, 93t
- information risk management and, 71–72, 75–76, 75f, 189–190

Computer Research Association (CRA), 24, 26, 31

Control self-assessment (CSA), 73–77, 75f, 95–99, 95f, 96f, 97f, 98f, 116–117, 126n7

Crisis management, 122, 191

Criticality alignment
- piezoelectric behavior and, 152, 182–185, 188–191
- for responsive security, 151–155, 163, 164f, 168–175, 170f, 174f, 177n9, 188
- risk forecasting and, 160–164, 162f, 164f

Cryptography, 15, 20, 25–26, 209